Functional-Light JavaScript

Balanced, Pragmatic FP in JavaScript

Kyle Simpson

Functional-Light JavaScript

Balanced, Pragmatic FP in JavaScript

Kyle Simpson

ISBN 978-1-98167-234-9

Published by GetiPub (http://getipub.com), a division of Getify Solutions, Inc., and produced by Leanpub (https://leanpub.com/fljs).

Editors: Brian MacDonald and Brian Lonsdorf

Copyeditor: Jasmine Kwityn

November 2017: First Edition

Revision History for the First Edition

2017-11-27: First Release

2017-12-05, 2017-12-14, 2018-01-29: Reformat For Print, Errata Updates

While the publisher and the author have used good faith efforts to ensure that the information and instructions contained in this work are accurate, the publisher and the author disclaim all responsibility for errors or omissions, including without limitation responsibility for damages resulting from the use of or reliance on this work. Use of the information and instructions contained in this work is at your own risk. If any code samples or other technology this work contains or describes is subject to open source licenses or the intellectual property rights of others, it is your responsibility to ensure that your use thereof complies with such licenses and/or rights.

© 2016 - 2018 Getify Solutions, Inc.

I owe gratitude to dozens of folks in the JS and FP communities whose work has helped me on my multiple-year journey to try to learn what FP is all about. I'm also grateful to all 738 backers of my crowd-funding campaign (listed at the very end of the book), who helped make this happen.

But I especially want to give a deep and profound thank you to Brian Lonsdorf for allowing me to pester him endlessly with FP questions, and for being so patient and attentive in his assistance. He even tech-edited this book, and wrote the Foreword. You're my FP hero, man!

Contents

Foreword i

Preface iii
    Mission iv

Chapter 1: Why Functional Programming? 1
    At a Glance 2
    Confidence 4
    Communication 5
    Readability 7
    Perspective 9
    How to Find Balance 10
    Resources 11
    Summary 13

Chapter 2: The Nature Of Functions 15
    What Is a Function? 15
    Function Input 17
    Named Arguments 26
    Function Output 28
    Functions of Functions 34
    Syntax 40
    What's This? 48
    Summary 51

Chapter 3: Managing Function Inputs 53
    All for One 53

CONTENTS

    Adapting Arguments to Parameters 58
    Some Now, Some Later 61
    One at a Time 70
    Order Matters 81
    No Points 86
    Summary 92

Chapter 4: Composing Functions **93**
    Output to Input 93
    General Composition 100
    Reordered Composition 108
    Abstraction 110
    Revisiting Points 117
    Summary 122

Chapter 5: Reducing Side Effects **123**
    Effects on the Side, Please 123
    Once Is Enough, Thanks 133
    Pure Bliss 138
    There or Not 145
    Purifying 151
    Summary 160

Chapter 6: Value Immutability **161**
    Primitive Immutability 161
    Value to Value 163
    Reassignment 166
    Performance 172
    Treatment 175
    Summary 178

Chapter 7: Closure vs. Object **181**
    The Same Page 182
    Look Alike 183
    Two Roads Diverged in a Wood.... 194
    Summary 205

Chapter 8: Recursion — 207
- Definition — 208
- Declarative Recursion — 215
- Stack — 218
- Rearranging Recursion — 224
- Summary — 233

Chapter 9: List Operations — 235
- Non-FP List Processing — 236
- Map — 236
- Filter — 243
- Reduce — 247
- Advanced List Operations — 255
- Method vs. Standalone — 263
- Looking for Lists — 270
- Fusion — 273
- Beyond Lists — 276
- Summary — 286

Chapter 10: Functional Async — 287
- Time as State — 287
- Eager vs. Lazy — 290
- Reactive FP — 291
- Summary — 299

Chapter 11: Putting It All Together — 301
- Setup — 301
- Stock Events — 303
- Stock Ticker UI — 306
- Summary — 318

Appendix A: Transducing — 321
- Why, First — 321
- How, Next — 324
- What, Finally — 338
- Summary — 341

CONTENTS

Appendix B: The Humble Monad **343**
    Type 344
    Loose Interface 344
    Just a Monad 345
    Maybe 350
    Humble 353
    Summary 357

Appendix C: FP Libraries **359**
    Stuff to Investigate 359
    Ramda (0.23.0) 360
    Lodash/fp (4.17.4) 362
    Mori (0.3.2) 363
    Bonus: FPO 364
    Bonus #2: fasy 366
    Summary 370

Foreword

It's no secret that I am a Functional Programming nut. I evangelize functional ideas and languages wherever I can, try to read the latest academic papers, study abstract algebra in my spare time...the works. Even in JavaScript, I refuse to write an impure statement, which is what led to writing *Professor Frisby's Mostly Adequate Guide to Functional Programming*. Yep, full on, dogmatic zealot.

I was not always this way... I was once obsessed with objects. I loved modeling the "real world". I was the inventor of synthetic automatons, tinkering through the night with masterful precision. The creator of sentient puppets, fingers dancing on the keyboard to give them life – a real 1337 h4x0r Geppetto. Yet, after 5 *solid* years of writing object-oriented code, I was never quite satisfied with the outcome. It just never worked out well for me. I felt like a lousy programmer. I even lost faith that a simple, flexible codebase of decent scale was possible.

I figured I'd try something different: Functional Programming. I began to dabble with functional ideas in my everyday codebase, and much to my coworkers' dismay, hadn't the slightest clue what I was doing. The code I wrote in those days was awful. Atrocious. Digital sewage. The reason was a lack of clear vision or goal on what I was even trying to accomplish. My Jiminy-Coding-Cricket, if you like, was not there to guide me. It took a long time and a lot of garbage programs to figure out how to FP.

Now, after all that messy exploration, I feel that pure Functional Programming has delivered on its promise. Readable programs do exist! Reuse does exist! I no longer invent, but rather discover my model. I've become a rogue detective uncovering a vast conspiracy, cork board pinned full of mathematical evidence. A digital-age Cousteau logging the characteristics of this bizarre land in the name of science! It's not perfect and I still have a lot to learn, but I've never been more satisfied in my work and pleased with the outcome.

Had this book existed when I was starting out, my transition into the world of Functional Programming would have been much easier and less destructive. This book is two-fold (right and left): it will not only teach you how to use various constructs from FP effectively in your daily code, but more importantly, provide you with an aim; guiding principles that will keep you on track.

You will learn Functional-Light: A paradigm that Kyle has pioneered to enable declarative, Functional Programming while providing balance and interop with the rest of the JavaScript world. You will understand the foundation which pure FP is built upon without having to subscribe to the paradigm in its entirety. You will gain the skills to practice and explore FP without having to rewrite existing code for it to work well together. You can take a step forward in your software career without backtracking and wandering aimlessly as I did years ago. Coworkers and colleagues rejoice!

Kyle is a great teacher known for his relentless pursuit of the whole picture, leaving no nook or cranny unexplored, yet he maintains an empathy for the learner's plight. His style has resonated with the industry, leveling us all up as a whole. His work has a solid place in JavaScript's history and most people's bookmarks bar. You are in good hands.

Functional Programming has many different definitions. A Lisp programmer's definition is vastly different from a Haskell perspective. OCaml's FP bears little resemblance to the paradigm seen in Erlang. You will even find several competing definitions in JavaScript. Yet there is a tie that binds – some blurry know-it-when-I-see-it definition, much like obscenity (indeed, some do find FP obscene!) and this book certainly captures it. The end result might not be considered idiomatic in certain circles, but the knowledge acquired here directly applies to any flavor of FP.

This book is a terrific place to begin your FP journey. Take it away, Kyle...

-Brian Lonsdorf (@drboolean)

Preface

A monad is just a monoid in the category of endofunctors.

Did I just lose you? Don't worry, I'd be lost, too! All those terms that only mean something to the already-initiated in Functional Programming™ (FP) are just jumbled nonsense to many of the rest of us.

This book is not going to teach you what those words mean. If that's what you're looking for, keep looking. In fact, there are already plenty of great books that teach FP the *right way*, from the top-down. Those words have important meanings and if you formally study FP in-depth, you'll absolutely want to get familiar with them.

But this book is going to approach the topic quite differently. I'm going to present fundamental FP concepts from the ground-up, with fewer special or non-intuitive terms than most approaches to FP. We'll try to take a practical approach to each principle rather than a purely academic angle. **There will be terms,** no doubt. But we'll be careful and deliberate about introducing them and explaining why they're important.

Sadly, I am not a card-carrying member of the FP Cool Kids Club. I've never been formally taught anything about FP. And though I have a CS academic background and I am decent at math, mathematical notation is not how my brain understands programming. I have never written a line of Scheme, Clojure, or Haskell. I'm not an old-school Lisp'r.

I *have* attended countless conference talks about FP, each one with the desperate clinging hope that finally, *this time* would be the time I understood what this whole functional programming mysticism is all about. And each time, I came away frustrated and reminded that those terms got all mixed up in my head and I had no idea if or what I learned. Maybe I learned things. But I couldn't figure out what those things were for the longest time.

Little by little, across those various exposures, I teased out bits and pieces of important concepts that seem to just come all too naturally to the formal FPer.

I learned them slowly and I learned them pragmatically and experientially, not academically with appropriate terminology. Have you ever known a thing for a long time, and only later found out it had a specific name you never knew!?

Maybe you're like me; I heard terms such as "map-reduce" around industry segments like "big data" for years with no real idea what they were. Eventually I learned what the `map(..)` function did – all long before I had any idea that list operations were a cornerstone of the FPer path and what makes them so important. I knew what *map* was long before I ever knew it was called `map(..)`.

Eventually I began to gather all these tidbits of understanding into what I now call "Functional-Light Programming" (FLP).

Mission

But why is it so important for you to learn functional programming, even the light form?

I've come to believe something very deeply in recent years, so much so you could *almost* call it a religious belief. I believe that programming is fundamentally about humans, not about code. I believe that code is first and foremost a means of human communication, and only as a *side effect* (hear my self-referential chuckle) does it instruct the computer.

The way I see it, functional programming is at its heart about using patterns in your code that are well-known, understandable, *and* proven to keep away the mistakes that make code harder to understand. In that view, FP – or, ahem, FLP! – might be one of the most important collections of tools any developer could acquire.

> The curse of the monad is that... once you understand... you lose the ability to explain it to anyone else.

Douglas Crockford 2012 "Monads and Gonads"

https://www.youtube.com/watch?v=dkZFtimgAcM

I hope this book "Maybe" breaks the spirit of that curse, even though we won't talk about "monads" until the very end in the appendices.

The formal FPer will often assert that the *real value* of FP is in using it essentially 100%: it's an all-or-nothing proposition. The belief is that if you use FP in one part of your program but not in another, the whole program is polluted by the non-FP stuff and therefore suffers enough that the FP was probably not worth it.

I'll say unequivocally: **I think that absolutism is bogus**. That's as silly to me as suggesting that this book is only good if I use perfect grammar and active voice throughout; if I make any mistakes, it degrades the entire book's quality. Nonsense.

The better I am at writing in a clear, consistent voice, the better your reading experience will be. But I'm not a 100% perfect author. Some parts will be better written than others. The parts where I can still improve are not going to invalidate the other parts of this book which are useful.

And so it goes with our code. The more you can apply these principles to more parts of your code, the better your code will be. Use them well 25% of the time, and you'll get some good benefit. Use them 80% of the time, and you'll see even more benefit.

With perhaps a few exceptions, I don't think you'll find many absolutes in this text. We'll instead talk about aspirations, goals, principles to strive for. We'll talk about balance and pragmatism and trade-offs.

Welcome to this journey into the most useful and practical foundations of FP. We both have plenty to learn!

Chapter 1: Why Functional Programming?

> Functional programmer: (noun) One who names variables "x", names functions "f", and names code patterns "zygohistomorphic prepromorphism"
>
> James Iry @jamesiry 5/13/2015
>
> https://twitter.com/jamesiry/status/598547781515485184

Functional Programming (FP) is not a new concept by any means. It's been around almost the entire history of programming. However, and I'm not sure it's fair to say, but... it sure hasn't seemed like as mainstream of a concept in the overall developer world until perhaps the last few years. I think FP has more been the realm of academics.

That's all changing, though. A groundswell of interest is growing around FP, not just at the languages level but even in libraries and frameworks. You very well might be reading this text because you've finally realized FP is something you can't ignore any longer. Or maybe you're like me and you've tried to learn FP many times before but struggled to wade through all the terms or mathematical notation.

This first chapter's purpose is to answer questions like "Why should I use FP style with my code?" and "How does Functional-Light JavaScript compare to what others say about FP?" After we've laid that groundwork, throughout the rest of the book we'll uncover, piece by piece, the techniques and patterns for writing JS in Functional-Light style.

At a Glance

Let's briefly illustrate the notion of "Functional-Light JavaScript" with a before-and-after snapshot of code. Consider:

```
var numbers = [4,10,0,27,42,17,15,-6,58];
var faves = [];
var magicNumber = 0;

pickFavoriteNumbers();
calculateMagicNumber();
outputMsg();                  // The magic number is: 42

// **************

function calculateMagicNumber() {
    for (let fave of faves) {
        magicNumber = magicNumber + fave;
    }
}

function pickFavoriteNumbers() {
    for (let num of numbers) {
        if (num >= 10 && num <= 20) {
            faves.push( num );
        }
    }
}

function outputMsg() {
    var msg = `The magic number is: ${magicNumber}`;
    console.log( msg );
}
```

Now consider a very different style that accomplishes exactly the same outcome:

```
var sumOnlyFavorites = FP.compose( [
    FP.filterReducer( FP.gte( 10 ) ),
    FP.filterReducer( FP.lte( 20 ) )
] )( sum );

var printMagicNumber = FP.pipe( [
    FP.reduce( sumOnlyFavorites, 0 ),
    constructMsg,
    console.log
] );

var numbers = [4,10,0,27,42,17,15,-6,58];

printMagicNumber( numbers );          // The magic number is: 42

// ***************

function sum(x,y) { return x + y; }
function constructMsg(v) { return `The magic number is: ${v}`; }
```

Once you understand FP and Functional-Light, this is likely how you'd *read* and mentally process that second snippet:

> We're first creating a function called sumOnlyFavorites(..) that's a combination of three other functions. We combine two filters, one checking if a value is greater-than-or-equal to 10 and one for less-than-or-equal to 20. Then we include the sum(..) reducer in the transducer composition. The resulting sumOnlyFavorites(..) function is a reducer that checks if a value passes both filters, and if so, adds the value to an accumulator value.
>
> Then we make another function called printMagicNumber(..) which first reduces a list of numbers using that sumOnlyFavorites(..) reducer we just defined, resulting in a sum of only numbers that passed the *favorite* checks. Then printMagicNumber(..) pipes that final sum into constructMsg(..), which creates a string value that finally goes into console.log(..).

All those moving pieces *speak* to an FP developer in ways that likely seem highly unfamiliar to you right now. This book will help you *speak* that same kind of reasoning so that it's as readable to you as any other code, if not more so!

A few other quick remarks about this code comparison:

- It's likely that for many readers, the former snippet feels closer to comfortable/readable/maintainable than the latter snippet. It's entirely OK if that's the case. You're in exactly the right spot. I'm confident that if you stick it out through the whole book, and practice everything we talk about, that second snippet will eventually become a lot more natural, maybe even preferable!
- You might have done the task significantly or entirely different from either snippet presented. That's OK, too. This book won't be prescriptive in dictating that you should do something a specific way. The goal is to illustrate the pros/cons of various patterns and enable you to make those decisions. By the end of this book, how you would approach the task may fall a little closer to the second snippet than it does right now.
- It's also possible that you're already a seasoned FP developer who's scanning through the start of this book to see if it has anything useful for you to read. That second snippet certainly has some bits that are quite familiar. But I'm also betting that you thought, "Hmmm, I wouldn't have done it *that* way..." a couple of times. That's OK, and entirely reasonable.

    This is not a traditional, canonical FP book. We'll at times seem quite heretical in our approaches. We're seeking to strike a pragmatic balance between the clear undeniable benefits of FP, and the need to ship workable, maintainable JS without having to tackle a daunting mountain of math/notation/terminology. This is not *your* FP, it's "Functional-Light JavaScript".

Whatever your reasons for reading this book, welcome!

Confidence

I have a very simple premise that sort of underlies everything I do as a teacher of software development (in JavaScript): code that you cannot trust is code that you do not understand. The reverse is true also: code that you don't understand is code you can't trust. Furthermore, if you cannot trust or understand your code, then you can't have any confidence whatsoever that the code you write is suitable to the task. You run the program and basically just cross your fingers.

What do I mean by trust? I mean that you can verify, by reading and reasoning, not just executing, that you understand what a piece of code *will* do; you aren't just relying on what it *should* do. More often than is perhaps prudent, we tend to rely on running test suites to verify our programs' correctness. I don't mean to suggest tests are bad. But I do think we should aspire to be able to understand our code well enough that we know the test suite will pass before it runs.

The techniques that form the foundation of FP are designed from the mindset of having far more confidence over our programs just by reading them. Someone who understands FP, and who's disciplined enough to diligently use it throughout their programs, will write code that they **and others** can read and verify that the program will do what they want.

Confidence is also increased when we use techniques that avoid or minimize likely sources of bugs. That's perhaps one of the biggest selling points of FP: FP programs often have fewer bugs, and the bugs that do exist are usually in more obvious places, so they're easier to find and fix. FP code tends to be more bug-resistant – certainly not bug-proof, though.

As you journey through this book, you will begin to develop more confidence in the code you write, because you will use patterns and practices that are already well proven; and you'll avoid the most common causes of program bugs!

Communication

Why is Functional Programming important? To answer that, we need to take a bigger step back and talk about why programming itself is important.

It may surprise you to hear this, but I don't believe that code is primarily a set of instructions for the computer. Actually, I think the fact that code instructs the computer is almost a happy accident.

I believe very deeply that the vastly more important role of code is as a means of communication with other human beings.

You probably know by experience that an awful lot of your time spent "coding" is actually spent reading existing code. Very few of us are so privileged as to spend all or most of our time simply banging out all new code and never dealing with code that others (or our past selves) wrote.

It's widely estimated that developers spend 70% of code maintenance time on reading to understand it. That is eye-opening. 70%. No wonder the global average for a programmer's lines of code written per day is about 10. We spend up to 7 hours of our day just reading the code to figure out where those 10 lines should go!

We need to focus a lot more on the readability of our code. And by the way, readability is not just about fewer characters. Readability is actually most impacted by familiarity.[1]

If we are going to spend our time concerned with making code that will be more readable and understandable, FP is central in that effort. The principles of FP are well established, deeply studied and vetted, and provably verifiable. Taking the time to learn and employ these FP principles will ultimately lead to more readily and recognizably familiar code for you and others. The increase in code familiarity, and the expediency of that recognition, will improve code readability.

For example, once you learn what map(..) does, you'll be able to almost instantly spot and understand it when you see it in any program. But every time you see a for loop, you're going to have to read the whole loop to understand it. The syntax of the for loop may be familiar, but the substance of what it's doing is not; that has to be *read*, every time.

By having more code that's recognizable at a glance, and thus spending less time figuring out what the code is doing, our focus is freed up to think about the higher levels of program logic; this is the important stuff that most needs our attention anyway.

FP (at least, without all the terminology weighing it down) is one of the most effective tools for crafting readable code. *That* is why it's so important.

---

[1] Buse, Raymond P. L., and Westley R. Weimer. "Learning a Metric for Code Readability." IEEE Transactions on Software Engineering, IEEE Press, July 2010, dl.acm.org/citation.cfm?id=1850615.

Readability

Readability is not a binary characteristic. It's a largely subjective human factor describing our relationship to code. And it will naturally vary over time as our skills and understanding evolve. I have experienced effects similar to the following figure, and anecdotally many others I've talked to have as well.

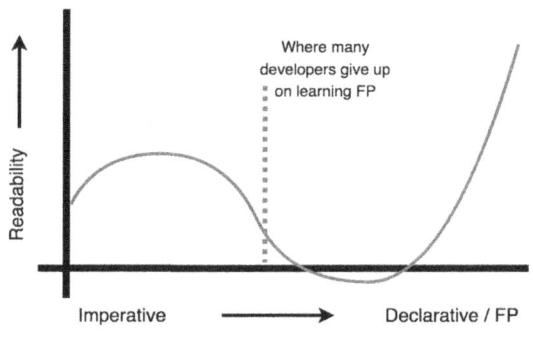

Readability of Declarative FP

You may just find yourself experiencing similar effects as you work through the book. But take heart; if you stick this out, the curve comes back up!

Imperative describes the code most of us probably already write naturally; it's focused on precisely instructing the computer *how* to do something. Declarative code – the kind we'll be learning to write, which adheres to FP principles – is code that's more focused on describing the *what* outcome.

Let's revisit the two code snippets presented earlier in this chapter.

The first snippet is imperative, focused almost entirely on *how* to do the tasks; it's littered with `if` statements, `for` loops, temporary variables, reassignments, value mutations, function calls with side effects, and implicit data flow between functions. You certainly *can* trace through its logic to see how the numbers flow and change to the end state, but it's not at all clear or straightforward.

The second snippet is more declarative; it does away with most of those aforementioned imperative techniques. Notice there's no explicit conditionals, loops, side effects, reassignments, or mutations; instead, it employs well-known (to the FP world, anyway!) and trustable patterns like filtering, reduction, transducing, and composition. The focus shifts from low-level *how* to higher level *what* outcomes.

Instead of messing with an `if` statement to test a number, we delegate that to a well-known FP utility like `gte(..)` (greater-than-or-equal-to), and then focus on the more important task of combining that filter with another filter and a summation function.

Moreover, the flow of data through the second program is explicit:

1. A list of numbers goes into `printMagicNumber(..)`.
2. One at a time those numbers are processed by `sumOnlyFavorites(..)`, resulting in a single number total of only our favorite kinds of numbers.
3. That total is converted to a message string with `constructMsg(..)`.
4. The message string is printed to the console with `console.log(..)`.

You may still feel this approach is convoluted, and that the imperative snippet was easier to understand. You're much more accustomed to it; familiarity has a profound influence on our judgments of readability. By the end of this book, though, you will have internalized the benefits of the second snippet's declarative approach, and that familiarity will spring its readability to life.

I know asking you to believe that at this point is a leap of faith.

It takes a lot more effort, and sometimes more code, to improve its readability as I'm suggesting, and to minimize or eliminate many of the mistakes that lead to bugs. Quite honestly, when I started writing this book, I could never have written (or even fully understood!) that second snippet. As I'm now further along on my journey of learning, it's more natural and comfortable.

If you're hoping that FP refactoring, like a magic silver bullet, will quickly transform your code to be more graceful, elegant, clever, resilient, and concise – that it will come easy in the short term – unfortunately that's just not a realistic expectation.

FP is a very different way of thinking about how code should be structured, to make the flow of data much more obvious and to help your reader follow your thinking. It will take time. This effort is eminently worthwhile, but it can be an arduous journey.

It still often takes me multiple attempts at refactoring a snippet of imperative code into more declarative FP, before I end up with something that's clear enough for me to understand later. I've found converting to FP is a slow iterative process rather than a quick binary flip from one paradigm to another.

I also apply the "teach it later" test to every piece of code I write. After I've written a piece of code, I leave it alone for a few hours or days, then come back and try to read it with fresh eyes, and pretend as if I need to teach or explain it to someone else. Usually, it's jumbled and confusing the first few passes, so I tweak it and repeat!

I'm not trying to dampen your spirits. I really want you to hack through these weeds. I am glad I did it. I can finally start to see the curve bending upward toward improved readability. The effort has been worth it. It will be for you, too.

Perspective

Most other FP texts seem to take a top-down approach, but we're going to go the opposite direction: working from the ground up, we'll uncover the basic foundational principles that I believe formal FPers would admit are the scaffolding for everything they do. But for the most part we'll stay arm's length away from most of the intimidating terminology or mathematical notation that can so easily frustrate learners.

I believe it's less important what you call something and more important that you understand what it is and how it works. That's not to say there's no importance to shared terminology – it undoubtedly eases communication among seasoned professionals. But for the learner, I've found it can be distracting.

So this book will try to focus more on the base concepts and less on the fancy fluff. That's not to say there won't be terminology; there definitely will be. But don't get too wrapped up in the sophisticated words. Wherever necessary, look beyond them to the ideas.

I call the less formal practice herein "Functional-Light Programming" because I think where the formalism of true FP suffers is that it can be quite overwhelming if you're not already accustomed to formal thought. I'm not just guessing; this is my own personal story. Even after teaching FP and writing this book, I can still say that the formalism of terms and notation in FP is very, very difficult for me to process. I've tried, and tried, and I can't seem to get through much of it.

I know many FPers who believe that the formalism itself helps learning. But I think there's clearly a cliff where that only becomes true once you reach a certain comfort with the formalism. If you happen to already have a math background or even some flavors of CS experience, this may come more naturally to you. But some of us don't, and no matter how hard we try, the formalism keeps getting in the way.

So this book introduces the concepts that I believe FP is built on, but comes at it by giving you a boost from below to climb up the cliff wall, rather than condescendingly shouting down at you from the top, prodding you to just figure out how to climb as you go.

How to Find Balance

If you've been around programming for very long, chances are you've heard the phrase "YAGNI" before: "You Ain't Gonna Need It". This principle primarily comes from extreme programming, and stresses the high risk and cost of building a feature before it's needed.

Sometimes we guess we'll need a feature in the future, build it now believing it'll be easier to do as we build other stuff, then realize we guessed wrong and the feature wasn't needed, or needed to be quite different. Other times we guess right, but build a feature too early, and suck up time from the features that are genuinely needed now; we incur an opportunity cost in diluting our energy.

YAGNI challenges us to remember: even if it's counterintuitive in a situation, we often should postpone building something until it's presently needed. We tend to exaggerate our mental estimates of the future refactoring cost of adding it later when it is needed. Odds are, it won't be as hard to do later as we might assume.

As it applies to functional programming, I would offer this admonition: there will be plenty of interesting and compelling patterns discussed in this text, but just because you find some pattern exciting to apply, it may not necessarily be appropriate to do so in a given part of your code.

This is where I will differ from many formal FPers: just because you *can* apply FP to something doesn't mean you *should* apply FP to it. Moreover, there are many ways to slice a problem, and even though you may have learned a more sophisticated approach that is more "future-proof" to maintenance and extensibility, a simpler FP pattern might be more than sufficient in that spot.

Generally, I'd recommend seeking balance in what you code, and to be conservative in your application of FP concepts as you get the hang of things. Default to the YAGNI principle in deciding if a certain pattern or abstraction will help that part of the code be more readable or if it's just introducing clever sophistication that isn't (yet) warranted.

> Reminder, any extensibility point that's never used isn't just wasted effort, it's likely to also get in your way as well
>
> ---
>
> Jeremy D. Miller @jeremydmiller 2/20/15
>
> https://twitter.com/jeremydmiller/status/568797862441586688

Remember, every single line of code you write has a reader cost associated with it. That reader may be another team member, or even your future self. Neither of those readers will be impressed with overly clever, unnecessary sophistication just to show off your FP prowess.

The best code is the code that is most readable in the future because it strikes exactly the right balance between what it can/should be (idealism) and what it must be (pragmatism).

Resources

I have drawn on a great many different resources to be able to compose this text. I believe you, too, may benefit from them, so I wanted to take a moment to point them out.

Books

Some FP/JavaScript books that you should definitely read:

- Professor Frisby's Mostly Adequate Guide to Functional Programming[2] by Brian Lonsdorf[3]
- JavaScript Allongé[4] by Reg Braithwaite[5]
- Functional JavaScript[6] by Michael Fogus[7]

Blogs/sites

Some other authors and content you should check out:

- Fun Fun Function Videos[8] by Mattias P Johansson[9]
- Awesome FP JS[10]
- Kris Jenkins[11]
- Eric Elliott[12]
- James A Forbes[13]
- James Longster[14]
- André Staltz[15]
- Functional Programming Jargon[16]
- Functional Programming Exercises[17]

---

[2] https://drboolean.gitbooks.io/mostly-adequate-guide/content/ch1.html
[3] https://twitter.com/drboolean
[4] https://leanpub.com/javascriptallongesix
[5] https://twitter.com/raganwald
[6] http://shop.oreilly.com/product/0636920028857.do
[7] https://twitter.com/fogus
[8] https://www.youtube.com/watch?v=BMUiFMZr7vk
[9] https://twitter.com/mpjme
[10] https://github.com/stoeffel/awesome-fp-js
[11] http://blog.jenkster.com/2015/12/what-is-functional-programming.html
[12] https://medium.com/@_ericelliott
[13] https://james-forbes.com/
[14] https://github.com/jlongster
[15] http://staltz.com/
[16] https://github.com/hemanth/functional-programming-jargon#functional-programming-jargon
[17] https://github.com/InceptionCode/Functional-Programming-Exercises

Libraries

The code snippets in this book largely do not rely on libraries. Each operation that we discover, we'll derive how to implement it in standalone, plain ol' JavaScript. However, as you begin to build more of your real code with FP, you'll soon want a library to provide optimized and highly reliable versions of these commonly accepted utilities.

By the way, you need to check the documentation for the library functions you use to ensure you know how they work. There will be a lot of similarities in many of them to the code we build on in this text, but there will undoubtedly be some differences, even between popular libraries.

Here are a few popular FP libraries for JavaScript that are a great place to start your exploration with:

- Ramda[18]
- lodash/fp[19]
- functional.js[20]
- Immutable.js[21]

Appendix C takes a deeper look at these libraries and others.

Summary

You may have a variety of reasons for starting to read this book, and different expectations of what you'll get out of it. This chapter has explained why I want you to read the book and what I want you to get out of the journey. It also helps you articulate to others (like your fellow developers) why they should come on the journey with you!

---

[18] http://ramdajs.com
[19] https://github.com/lodash/lodash/wiki/FP-Guide
[20] http://functionaljs.com/
[21] https://github.com/facebook/immutable-js

Functional programming is about writing code that is based on proven principles so we can gain a level of confidence and trust over the code we write and read. We shouldn't be content to write code that we anxiously *hope* works, and then abruptly breathe a sigh of relief when the test suite passes. We should *know* what it will do before we run it, and we should be absolutely confident that we've communicated all these ideas in our code for the benefit of other readers (including our future selves).

This is the heart of Functional-Light JavaScript. The goal is to learn to effectively communicate with our code but not have to suffocate under mountains of notation or terminology to get there.

The journey to learning functional programming starts with deeply understanding the nature of what a function is. That's what we tackle in the next chapter.

Chapter 2: The Nature Of Functions

Functional Programming is **not just programming with the `function` keyword.** Oh, if only it was that easy – I could end the book right here! Nevertheless, functions really *are* at the center of FP. And it's how we use functions that makes our code *functional*.

But how sure are you that you know what *function* really means?

In this chapter, we're going to lay the groundwork for the rest of the book by exploring all the foundational aspects of functions. Actually, this is a review of all the things even a non-FP programmer should know about functions. But certainly if we want to get the most out of FP concepts, it's essential we *know* functions inside and out.

Brace yourself, because there's a lot more to the function than you may have realized.

What Is a Function?

The question "What is a function?" superficially seems to have an obvious answer: a function is a collection of code that can be executed one or more times.

While this definition is reasonable, it's missing some very important essence that is the core of a *function* as it applies to FP. So let's dig below the surface to understand functions more completely.

Brief Math Review

I know I've promised we'd stay away from math as much as possible, but bear with me for a moment as we quickly observe some fundamental things about functions and graphs from algebra before we proceed.

Do you remember learning anything about f(x) back in school? What about the equation y = f(x)?

Let's say an equation is defined like this: $f(x) = 2x^2 + 3$. What does that mean? What does it mean to graph that equation? Here's the graph:

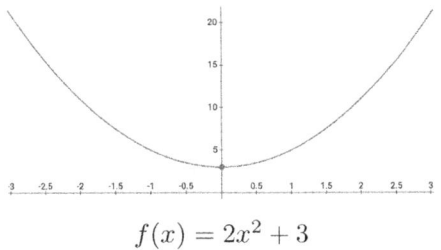

$$f(x) = 2x^2 + 3$$

What you can notice is that for any value of x, say 2, if you plug it into the equation, you get 11. What is 11, though? It's the *return value* of the f(x) function, which earlier we said represents a y value.

In other words, we can choose to interpret the input and output values as a point at (2,11) on that curve in the graph. And for every value of x we plug in, we get another y value that pairs with it as a coordinate for a point. Another is (0,3), and another is (-1,5). Put all those points together, and you have the graph of that parabolic curve as shown here.

So what's any of this got to do with FP?

In math, a function always takes input(s), and always gives an output. A term you'll often hear around FP is "morphism"; this is a fancy way of describing a set of values that maps to another set of values, like the inputs of a function related to the outputs of that function.

In algebraic math, those inputs and outputs are often interpreted as components of coordinates to be graphed. In our programs, however, we can define functions with all sorts of input(s) and output(s), even though they'll rarely be interpreted as a visually plotted curve on a graph.

Function vs Procedure

So why all the talk of math and graphs? Because essentially Functional Programming is about embracing using functions as *functions* in this mathematical sense.

You may be more accustomed to thinking of functions as procedures. What's the difference? A procedure is an arbitrary collection of functionality. It may have inputs, it may not. It may have an output (`return` value), it may not.

A function takes input(s) and definitely always has a `return` value.

If you plan to do Functional Programming, **you should be using functions as much as possible**, and trying to avoid procedures wherever possible. All your `functions` should take input(s) and return output(s).

Why? The answer to that will have many levels of meaning that we'll uncover throughout this book.

Function Input

So far, we can conclude that functions must expect input. But let's dig into how function inputs work.

You sometimes hear people refer to these inputs as "arguments" and sometimes as "parameters". So what's that all about?

Arguments are the values you pass in, and *parameters* are the named variables inside the function that receive those passed-in values. Example:

```
function foo(x,y) {
    // ..
}

var a = 3;

foo( a, a * 2 );
```

a and a * 2 (actually, the result of a * 2, which is 6) are the *arguments* to the `foo(..)` call. x and y are the *parameters* that receive the argument values (3 and 6, respectively).

Note

In JavaScript, there's no requirement that the number of *arguments* matches the number of *parameters*. If you pass more *arguments* than you have declared *parameters* to receive them, the values pass in just fine untouched. These values can be accessed in a few different ways, including the old-school `arguments` object you may have heard of before. If you pass fewer *arguments* than the declared *parameters*, each unmatched parameter is treated as an "undefined" variable, meaning it's present and available in the scope of the function, but just starts out with the empty `undefined` value.

Defaulting Parameters

As of ES6, parameters can declare *default values*. In the case where the argument for that parameter is not passed, or it's passed the value `undefined`, the default assignment expression is substituted.

Consider:

```
function foo(x = 3) {
    console.log( x );
}

foo();                   // 3
foo( undefined );        // 3
foo( null );             // null
foo( 0 );                // 0
```

It's always a good practice to think about any default cases that can aid the usability of your functions. However, defaulting parameters can lead to more complexity in terms of reading and understanding the variations of how a function is called. Be judicious in how much you rely on this feature.

Counting Inputs

The number of arguments a function "expects" – how many arguments you'll likely want to pass to it – is determined by the number of parameters that are declared:

```
function foo(x,y,z) {
    // ..
}
```

`foo(..)` *expects* three arguments, because it has three declared parameters. This count has a special term: arity. Arity is the number of parameters in a function declaration. The arity of `foo(..)` is 3.

Furthermore, a function with arity 1 is also called "unary", a function with arity 2 is also called "binary", and a function with arity 3 or higher is called "n-ary".

You may wish to inspect a function reference during the runtime of a program to determine its arity. This can be done with the `length` property of that function reference:

```
function foo(x,y,z) {
    // ..
}

foo.length;             // 3
```

One reason for determining the arity during execution would be if a piece of code received a function reference from multiple sources, and sent different values depending on the arity of each.

For example, imagine a case where an `fn` function reference could expect one, two, or three arguments, but you always want to just pass a variable x in the last position:

```
// `fn` is set to some function reference
// `x` exists with some value

if (fn.length == 1) {
    fn( x );
}
else if (fn.length == 2) {
    fn( undefined, x );
}
```

Functional-Light JavaScript

```
else if (fn.length == 3) {
    fn( undefined, undefined, x );
}
```

 Tip

The `length` property of a function is read-only and it's determined at the time you declare the function. It should be thought of as essentially a piece of metadata that describes something about the intended usage of the function.

One gotcha to be aware of is that certain kinds of parameter list variations can make the `length` property of the function report something different than you might expect:

```
function foo(x,y = 2) {
    // ..
}

function bar(x,...args) {
    // ..
}

function baz( {a,b} ) {
    // ..
}

foo.length;             // 1
bar.length;             // 1
baz.length;             // 1
```

What about counting the number of arguments the current function call received? This was once trivial, but now the situation is slightly more complicated. Each function has an `arguments` object (array-like) available that holds a reference to each of the arguments passed in. You can then inspect the `length` property of `arguments` to figure out how many were actually passed:

```
function foo(x,y,z) {
    console.log( arguments.length );
}

foo( 3, 4 );      // 2
```

As of ES5 (and strict mode, specifically), `arguments` is considered by some to be sort of deprecated; many avoid using it if possible. In JS, we "never" break backward compatibility no matter how helpful that may be for future progress, so `arguments` will never be removed. But it's now commonly suggested that you avoid using it whenever possible.

However, I suggest that `arguments.length`, and only that, is OK to keep using for those cases where you need to care about the passed number of arguments. A future version of JS might possibly add a feature that offers the ability to determine the number of arguments passed without consulting `arguments.length`; if that happens, then we can fully drop usage of `arguments`!

Be careful: **never** access arguments positionally, like `arguments[1]`. Stick to `arguments.length` only, and only if you must.

Except, how will you access an argument that was passed in a position beyond the declared parameters? I'll answer that in a moment; but first, take a step back and ask yourself, "Why would I want to do that?" Seriously. Think about that closely for a minute.

It should be pretty rare that this occurs; it shouldn't be something you regularly expect or rely on when writing your functions. If you find yourself in such a scenario, spend an extra 20 minutes trying to design the interaction with that function in a different way. Name that extra argument even if it's exceptional.

A function signature that accepts an indeterminate amount of arguments is referred to as a variadic function. Some people prefer this style of function design, but I think you'll find that often the FPer wants to avoid these where possible.

OK, enough harping on that point.

Say you do need to access the arguments in a positional array-like way, possibly because you're accessing an argument that doesn't have a formal parameter at that position. How do we do it?

ES6 to the rescue! Let's declare our function with the ... operator – variously referred to as "spread", "rest", or (my preference) "gather":

```
function foo(x,y,z,...args) {
    // ..
}
```

See the ...args in the parameter list? That's an ES6 declarative form that tells the engine to collect (ahem, "gather") all remaining arguments (if any) not assigned to named parameters, and put them in a real array named args. args will always be an array, even if it's empty. But it **will not** include values that are assigned to the x, y, and z parameters, only anything else that's passed in beyond those first three values:

```
function foo(x,y,z,...args) {
    console.log( x, y, z, args );
}

foo();                  // undefined undefined undefined []
foo( 1, 2, 3 );         // 1 2 3 []
foo( 1, 2, 3, 4 );      // 1 2 3 [ 4 ]
foo( 1, 2, 3, 4, 5 );   // 1 2 3 [ 4, 5 ]
```

So, if you *really* want to design a function that can account for an arbitrary number of arguments to be passed in, use ...args (or whatever name you like) on the end. Now, you'll have a real, non-deprecated, non-yucky array to access those argument values from.

Just pay attention to the fact that the value 4 is at position 0 of that args, not position 3. And its length value won't include those three 1, 2, and 3 values. ...args gathers everything else, not including the x, y, and z.

You *can* use the ... operator in the parameter list even if there's no other formal parameters declared:

```
function foo(...args) {
    // ..
}
```

Now `args` will be the full array of arguments, whatever they are, and you can use `args.length` to know exactly how many arguments have been passed in. And you're safe to use `args[1]` or `args[317]` if you so choose. Please don't pass in 318 arguments, though.

Arrays of Arguments

What if you wanted to pass along an array of values as the arguments to a function call?

```
function foo(...args) {
    console.log( args[3] );
}

var arr = [ 1, 2, 3, 4, 5 ];

foo( ...arr );                          // 4
```

Our new friend `...` is used, but now not just in the parameter list; it's also used in the argument list at the call-site. It has the opposite behavior in this context. In a parameter list, we said it *gathered* arguments together. In an argument list, it *spreads* them out. So the contents of `arr` are actually spread out as individual arguments to the `foo(..)` call. Do you see how that's different from just passing in a reference to the whole `arr` array?

By the way, multiple values and `...` spreadings can be interleaved, as you see fit:

```
var arr = [ 2 ];

foo( 1, ...arr, 3, ...[4,5] );         // 4
```

Think of ... in this symmetric sense: in a value-list position, it *spreads*. In an assignment position – like a parameter list, because arguments get *assigned to* parameters – it *gathers*.

Whichever behavior you invoke, ... makes working with arrays of arguments much easier. Gone are the days of `slice(..)`, `concat(..)`, and `apply(..)` to wrangle our argument value arrays.

 Tip

Actually, these methods are not entirely useless. There will be a few places we rely on them throughout the code in this book. But certainly in most places, ... will be much more declaratively readable, and preferable as a result.

Parameter Destructuring

Consider the variadic `foo(..)` from the previous section:

```
function foo(...args) {
    // ..
}

foo( ...[1,2,3] );
```

What if we wanted to change that interaction so the caller of our function passes in an array of values instead of individual argument values? Just drop the two ... usages:

```
function foo(args) {
    // ..
}

foo( [1,2,3] );
```

Simple enough. But what if now we wanted to give a parameter name to each of the first two values in the passed-in array? We aren't declaring individual parameters anymore, so it seems we lost that ability.

Thankfully, ES6 destructuring is the answer. Destructuring is a way to declare a *pattern* for the kind of structure (object, array, etc.) that you expect to see, and how decomposition (assignment) of its individual parts should be processed.

Consider:

```
function foo( [x,y,...args] = [] ) {
    // ..
}

foo( [1,2,3] );
```

Do you spot the [..] brackets around the parameter list now? This is called array parameter destructuring.

In this example, destructuring tells the engine that an array is expected in this assignment position (aka parameter). The pattern says to take the first value of that array and assign to a local parameter variable called x, the second to y, and whatever is left is *gathered* into args.

The Importance of Declarative Style

Considering the destructured foo(..) we just looked at, we could instead have processed the parameters manually:

```
function foo(params) {
    var x = params[0];
    var y = params[1];
    var args = params.slice( 2 );

    // ..
}
```

But here we highlight a principle we only briefly introduced in Chapter 1: declarative code communicates more effectively than imperative code.

Declarative code (for example, the destructuring in the former `foo(..)` snippet, or the `...` operator usages) focuses on what the outcome of a piece of code should be.

Imperative code (such as the manual assignments in the latter snippet) focuses more on how to get the outcome. If you later read such imperative code, you have to mentally execute all of it to understand the desired outcome. The outcome is *coded* there, but it's not as clear because it's clouded by the details of *how* we get there.

The earlier `foo(..)` is regarded as more readable, because the destructuring hides the unnecessary details of *how* to manage the parameter inputs; the reader is free to focus only on *what* we will do with those parameters. That's clearly the most important concern, so it's what the reader should be focused on to understand the code most completely.

Wherever possible, and to whatever degrees our language and our libraries/frameworks will let us, **we should be striving for declarative, self-explanatory code.**

Named Arguments

Just as we can destructure array parameters, we can destructure object parameters:

```
function foo( {x,y} = {} ) {
    console.log( x, y );
}

foo( {
    y: 3
} );                        // undefined 3
```

We pass in an object as the single argument, and it's destructured into two separate parameter variables x and y, which are assigned the values of those corresponding property names from the object passed in. It didn't matter that the x property wasn't on the object; it just ended up as a variable with undefined like you'd expect.

But the part of parameter object destructuring I want you to pay attention to is the object being passed into foo(..).

With a normal call-site like foo(undefined,3), position is used to map from argument to parameter; we put the 3 in the second position to get it assigned to a y parameter. But at this new kind of call-site where parameter destructuring is involved, a simple object-property indicates which parameter (y) the argument value 3 should be assigned to.

We didn't have to account for x in *that* call-site because in effect we didn't care about x. We just omitted it, instead of having to do something distracting like passing undefined as a positional placeholder.

Some languages have an explicit feature for this: named arguments. In other words, at the call-site, labeling an input value to indicate which parameter it maps to. JavaScript doesn't have named arguments, but parameter object destructuring is the next best thing.

Another FP-related benefit of using an object destructuring to pass in potentially multiple arguments is that a function that only takes one parameter (the object) is much easier to compose with another function's single output. Much more on that in Chapter 4.

Unordered Parameters

Another key benefit is that named arguments, by virtue of being specified as object properties, are not fundamentally ordered. That means we can specify inputs in whatever order we want:

```
function foo( {x,y} = {} ) {
    console.log( x, y );
}

foo( {
    y: 3
} );                    // undefined 3
```

We're skipping the x parameter by simply omitting it. Or we could specify an x argument if we cared to, even if we listed it after y in the object literal. The call-site is no longer cluttered by ordered-placeholders like undefined to skip a parameter.

Named arguments are much more flexible, and attractive from a readability perspective, especially when the function in question can take three, four, or more inputs.

Tip

If this style of function arguments seems useful or interesting to you, check out coverage of the FPO library in Appendix C.

Function Output

Let's shift our attention from a function's inputs to its output.

In JavaScript, functions always return a value. These three functions all have identical return behavior:

```
function foo() {}

function bar() {
    return;
}

function baz() {
    return undefined;
}
```

The `undefined` value is implicitly `return`ed if you have no `return` or if you just have an empty `return;`.

But keeping as much with the spirit of FP function definition as possible – using functions and not procedures – our functions should always have outputs, which means they should explicitly `return` a value, and usually not `undefined`.

A `return` statement can only return a single value. So if your function needs to return multiple values, your only viable option is to collect them into a compound value like an array or an object:

```
function foo() {
    var retValue1 = 11;
    var retValue2 = 31;
    return [ retValue1, retValue2 ];
}
```

Then, we'll assign x and y from two respective items in the array that comes back from `foo()`:

```
var [ x, y ] = foo();
console.log( x + y );           // 42
```

Collecting multiple values into an array (or object) to return, and subsequently destructuring those values back into distinct assignments, is a way to transparently express multiple outputs for a function.

Tip

I'd be remiss if I didn't suggest you take a moment to consider if a function needing multiple outputs could be refactored to avoid that, perhaps separated into two or more smaller single-purpose functions? Sometimes that will be possible, sometimes not; but you should at least consider it.

Early Returns

The `return` statement doesn't just return a value from a function. It's also a flow control structure; it ends the execution of the function at that point. A function with multiple `return` statements thus has multiple possible exit points, meaning that it may be harder to read a function to understand its output behavior if there are many paths that could produce that output.

Consider:

```
function foo(x) {
    if (x > 10) return x + 1;

    var y = x / 2;

    if (y > 3) {
        if (x % 2 == 0) return x;
    }

    if (y > 1) return y;

    return x;
}
```

Pop quiz: without cheating and running this code in your browser, what does `foo(2)` return? What about `foo(4)`? And `foo(8)`? And `foo(12)`?

How confident are you in your answers? How much mental tax did you pay to get those answers? I got it wrong the first two times I tried to think it through, and I wrote it!

I think part of the readability problem here is that we're using `return` not just to return different values, but also as a flow control construct to quit a function's execution early in certain cases. There are obviously better ways to write that flow control (the `if` logic, etc.), but I also think there are ways to make the output paths more obvious.

Note

The answers to the pop quiz are 2, 2, 8, and 13.

Consider this version of the code:

```
function foo(x) {
    var retValue;

    if (retValue == undefined && x > 10) {
        retValue = x + 1;
    }

    var y = x / 2;

    if (y > 3) {
        if (retValue == undefined && x % 2 == 0) {
            retValue = x;
        }
    }

    if (retValue == undefined && y > 1) {
        retValue = y;
    }

    if (retValue == undefined) {
        retValue = x;
```

```
    }

    return retValue;
}
```

This version is unquestionably more verbose. But I would argue it's slightly simpler logic to follow, because every branch where `retValue` can get set is *guarded* by the condition that checks if it's already been set.

Rather than `return`ing from the function early, we used normal flow control (`if` logic) to determine the `retValue`'s assignment. At the end, we simply `return retValue`.

I'm not unconditionally saying that you should always have a single `return`, or that you should never do early `return`s, but I do think you should be careful about the flow control part of `return` creating more implicitness in your function definitions. Try to figure out the most explicit way to express the logic; that will often be the best way.

Unreturned Outputs

One technique that you've probably used in most code you've written, and maybe didn't even think about it much, is to have a function output some or all of its values by simply changing variables outside itself.

Remember our $f(x) = 2x^2 + 3$ function from earlier in the chapter? We could have defined it like this in JS:

```
var y;

function f(x) {
    y = (2 * Math.pow( x, 2 )) + 3;
}

f( 2 );

y;                      // 11
```

I know this is a silly example; we could just as easily have `returnd` the value instead of setting it into y from within the function:

```
function f(x) {
    return (2 * Math.pow( x, 2 )) + 3;
}

var y = f( 2 );

y;                      // 11
```

Both functions accomplish the same task, so is there any reason we should pick one version over the other? **Yes, absolutely.**

One way to explain the difference is that the `return` in the latter version signals an explicit output, whereas the y assignment in the former is an implicit output. You may already have some intuition that guides you in such cases; typically, developers prefer explicit patterns over implicit ones.

But changing a variable in an outer scope, as we did with the y assignment inside of `foo(..)`, is just one way of achieving an implicit output. A more subtle example is making changes to non-local values via reference.

Consider:

```
function sum(list) {
    var total = 0;
    for (let i = 0; i < list.length; i++) {
        if (!list[i]) list[i] = 0;

        total = total + list[i];
    }

    return total;
}

var nums = [ 1, 3, 9, 27, , 84 ];

sum( nums );                // 124
```

The most obvious output from this function is the sum 124, which we explicitly returned. But do you spot the other output? Try that code and then inspect the nums array. Now do you spot the difference?

Instead of an undefined empty slot value in position 4, now there's a 0. The harmless looking list[i] = 0 operation ended up affecting the array value on the outside, even though we operated on a local list parameter variable.

Why? Because list holds a reference-copy of the nums reference, not a value-copy of the [1,3,9,..] array value. JavaScript uses references and reference-copies for arrays, objects, and functions, so we may create an accidental output from our function all too easily.

This implicit function output has a special name in the FP world: side effects. And a function that has *no side effects* also has a special name: pure function. We'll talk a lot more about these in Chapter 5, but the punchline is that we'll want to prefer pure functions and avoid side effects wherever possible.

Functions of Functions

Functions can receive and return values of any type. A function that receives or returns one or more other function values has the special name: higher-order function.

Consider:

```
function forEach(list,fn) {
    for (let v of list) {
        fn( v );
    }
}

forEach( [1,2,3,4,5], function each(val){
    console.log( val );
} );
// 1 2 3 4 5
```

forEach(..) is a higher-order function because it receives a function as an argument.

A higher-order function can also output another function, like:

```
function foo() {
    return function inner(msg){
        return msg.toUpperCase();
    };
}

var f = foo();

f( "Hello!" );           // HELLO!
```

return is not the only way to "output" an inner function:

```
function foo() {
    return bar( function inner(msg){
        return msg.toUpperCase();
    } );
}

function bar(func) {
    return func( "Hello!" );
}

foo();                      // HELLO!
```

Functions that treat other functions as values are higher-order functions by definition. FPers write these all the time!

Keeping Scope

One of the most powerful things in all of programming, and especially in FP, is how a function behaves when it's inside another function's scope. When the inner function makes reference to a variable from the outer function, this is called closure.

Defined pragmatically:

> Closure is when a function remembers and accesses variables from outside of its own scope, even when that function is executed in a different scope.

Consider:

```
function foo(msg) {
    var fn = function inner(){
        return msg.toUpperCase();
    };

    return fn;
}

var helloFn = foo( "Hello!" );

helloFn();                  // HELLO!
```

The `msg` parameter variable in the scope of `foo(..)` is referenced inside the inner function. When `foo(..)` is executed and the inner function is created, it captures the access to the `msg` variable, and retains that access even after being `return`ed.

Once we have `helloFn`, a reference to the inner function, `foo(..)` has finished and it would seem as if its scope should have gone away, meaning the `msg` variable would no longer exist. But that doesn't happen, because the inner function has a closure over `msg` that keeps it alive. The closed over `msg` variable survives for as long as the inner function (now referenced by `helloFn` in a different scope) stays around.

Let's look at a few more examples of closure in action:

```
function person(name) {
    return function identify(){
        console.log( `I am ${name}` );
    };
}

var fred = person( "Fred" );
var susan = person( "Susan" );

fred();                 // I am Fred
susan();                // I am Susan
```

The inner function `identify()` has closure over the parameter name.

The access that closure enables is not restricted to merely reading the variable's original value – it's not just a snapshot but rather a live link. You can update the value, and that new current state remains remembered until the next access:

```
function runningCounter(start) {
    var val = start;

    return function current(increment = 1){
        val = val + increment;
        return val;
    };
}

var score = runningCounter( 0 );

score();                   // 1
score();                   // 2
score( 13 );               // 15
```

 Warning

For reasons that we'll explore in more depth later in the book, this example of using closure to remember a state that changes (val) is probably something you'll want to avoid where possible.

If you have an operation that needs two inputs, one of which you know now but the other will be specified later, you can use closure to remember the first input:

```
function makeAdder(x) {
    return function sum(y){
        return x + y;
    };
}

// we already know `10` and `37` as first inputs, respectively
var addTo10 = makeAdder( 10 );
var addTo37 = makeAdder( 37 );

// later, we specify the second inputs
addTo10( 3 );           // 13
addTo10( 90 );          // 100

addTo37( 13 );          // 50
```

Normally, a sum(..) function would take both an x and y input to add them together. But in this example we receive and remember (via closure) the x value(s) first, while the y value(s) are separately specified later.

Note

This technique of specifying inputs in successive function calls is very common in FP, and comes in two forms: partial application and currying. We'll dive into them more thoroughly in Chapter 3.

Of course, since functions are just values in JS, we can remember function values via closure:

```
function formatter(formatFn) {
    return function inner(str){
        return formatFn( str );
    };
}

var lower = formatter( function formatting(v){
    return v.toLowerCase();
} );

var upperFirst = formatter( function formatting(v){
    return v[0].toUpperCase() + v.substr( 1 ).toLowerCase();
} );

lower( "WOW" );                 // wow
upperFirst( "hello" );          // Hello
```

Instead of distributing/repeating the `toUpperCase()` and `toLowerCase()` logic all over our code, FP encourages us to create simple functions that encapsulate – a fancy way of saying wrapping up – that behavior.

Specifically, we create two simple unary functions `lower(..)` and `upperFirst(..)`, because those functions will be much easier to wire up to work with other functions in the rest of our program.

 Tip

Did you spot how `upperFirst(..)` could have used `lower(..)`?

We'll use closure heavily throughout the rest of the text. It may just be the most important foundational practice in all of FP, if not programming as a whole. Make sure you're really comfortable with it!

Syntax

Before we move on from this primer on functions, let's take a moment to discuss their syntax.

More than many other parts of this text, the discussions in this section are mostly opinion and preference, whether you agree with the views presented here or take opposite ones. These ideas are highly subjective, though many people seem to feel rather absolutely about them.

Ultimately, you get to decide.

What's in a Name?

Syntactically speaking, function declarations require the inclusion of a name:

```
function helloMyNameIs() {
    // ..
}
```

But function expressions can come in both named and anonymous forms:

```
foo( function namedFunctionExpr(){
    // ..
} );

bar( function(){     // <-- look, no name!
    // ..
} );
```

What exactly do we mean by anonymous, by the way? Specifically, functions have a `name` property that holds the string value of the name the function was given syntactically, such as `"helloMyNameIs"` or `"namedFunctionExpr"`. This `name` property is most notably used by the console/developer tools of your JS environment to list the function when it participates in a stack trace (usually from an exception).

Anonymous functions are generally displayed as `(anonymous function)`.

If you've ever had to debug a JS program from nothing but a stack trace of an exception, you probably have felt the pain of seeing `(anonymous function)` appear line after line. This listing doesn't give a developer any clue whatsoever as to the path the exception came from. It's not doing the developer any favors.

If you name your function expressions, the name is always used. So if you use a good name like `handleProfileClicks` instead of `foo`, you'll get much more helpful stack traces.

As of ES6, anonymous function expressions are in certain cases aided by *name inferencing*. Consider:

```
var x = function(){};

x.name;            // x
```

If the engine is able to guess what name you *probably* want the function to take, it will go ahead and do so.

But beware, not all syntactic forms benefit from name inferencing. Probably the most common place a function expression shows up is as an argument to a function call:

```
function foo(fn) {
    console.log( fn.name );
}

var x = function(){};

foo( x );                // x
foo( function(){} );     //
```

When the name can't be inferred from the immediate surrounding syntax, it remains an empty string. Such a function will be reported as `(anonymous function)` in a stack trace should one occur.

There are other benefits to a function being named besides the debugging question. First, the syntactic name (aka lexical name) is useful for internal self-reference. Self-reference is necessary for recursion (both sync and async) and also helpful with event handlers.

Consider these different scenarios:

```js
// sync recursion:
function findPropIn(propName,obj) {
    if (obj == undefined || typeof obj != "object") return;

    if (propName in obj) {
        return obj[propName];
    }
    else {
        for (let prop of Object.keys( obj )) {
            let ret = findPropIn( propName, obj[prop] );
            if (ret !== undefined) {
                return ret;
            }
        }
    }
}


// async recursion:
setTimeout( function waitForIt(){
    // does `it` exist yet?
    if (!o.it) {
        // try again later
        setTimeout( waitForIt, 100 );
    }
}, 100 );


// event handler unbinding
document.getElementById( "onceBtn" )
    .addEventListener( "click", function handleClick(evt){
        // unbind event
        evt.target.removeEventListener( "click", handleClick, false );

        // ..
    }, false );
```

In all these cases, the named function's lexical name was a useful and reliable self-reference from inside itself.

Moreover, even in simple cases with one-liner functions, naming them tends to make code more self-explanatory and thus easier to read for those who haven't read it before:

```
people.map( function getPreferredName(person){
    return person.nicknames[0] || person.firstName;
} )
// ..
```

The function name `getPreferredName(..)` tells the reader something about what the mapping operation is intending to do that is not entirely obvious from just its code. This name label helps the code be more readable.

Another place where anonymous function expressions are common is with immediately invoked function expressions (IIFEs):

```
(function(){

    // look, I'm an IIFE!

})();
```

You virtually never see IIFEs using names for their function expressions, but they should. Why? For all the same reasons we just went over: stack trace debugging, reliable self-reference, and readability. If you can't come up with any other name for your IIFE, at least use the word IIFE:

```
(function IIFE(){

    // You already knew I was an IIFE!

})();
```

What I'm getting at is there are multiple reasons why **named functions are always more preferable to anonymous functions**. As a matter of fact, I'd go so far as to say that there's basically never a case where an anonymous function is more preferable. They just don't really have any advantage over their named counterparts.

It's incredibly easy to write anonymous functions, because it's one less name we have to devote our mental attention to figuring out.

I'll be honest; I'm as guilty of this as anyone. I don't like to struggle with naming. The first few names I come up with for a function are usually bad. I have to revisit the naming over and over. I'd much rather just punt with a good ol' anonymous function expression.

But we're trading ease-of-writing for pain-of-reading. This is not a good trade-off. Being lazy or uncreative enough to not want to figure out names for your functions is an all too common, but poor, excuse for using anonymous functions.

Name every single function. And if you sit there stumped, unable to come up with a good name for some function you've written, I'd strongly suggest you don't fully understand that function's purpose yet – or it's just too broad or abstract. You need to go back and re-design the function until this is more clear. And by that point, a name will become more apparent.

In my practice, if I don't have a good name to use for a function, I name it `TODO` initially. I'm certain that I'll at least catch that later when I search for "TODO" comments before committing code.

I can testify from my own experience that in the struggle to name something well, I usually have come to understand it better, later, and often even refactor its design for improved readability and maintainability.

This time investment is well worth it.

Functions Without `function`

So far we've been using the full canonical syntax for functions. But you've no doubt also heard all the buzz around the ES6 => arrow function syntax.

Compare:

```
people.map( function getPreferredName(person){
    return person.nicknames[0] || person.firstName;
} );

// vs.

people.map( person => person.nicknames[0] || person.firstName );
```

Whoa.

The keyword `function` is gone, so is `return`, the parentheses (`( )`), the curly braces (`{ }`), and the innermost semicolon (`;`). In place of all that, we used a so-called fat arrow symbol (`=>`).

But there's another thing we omitted. Did you spot it? The `getPreferredName` function name.

That's right; `=>` arrow functions are lexically anonymous; there's no way to syntactically provide it a name. Their names can be inferred like regular functions, but again, the most common case of function expression values passed as arguments won't get any assistance in that way. Bummer.

If `person.nicknames` isn't defined for some reason, an exception will be thrown, meaning this `(anonymous function)` will be at the top of the stack trace. Ugh.

Honestly, the anonymity of `=>` arrow functions is a `=>` dagger to the heart, for me. I cannot abide by the loss of naming. It's harder to read, harder to debug, and impossible to self-reference.

But if that wasn't bad enough, the other slap in the face is that there's a whole bunch of subtle syntactic variations that you must wade through if you have different scenarios for your function definition. I'm not going to cover all of them in detail here, but briefly:

```
people.map( person => person.nicknames[0] || person.firstName );

// multiple parameters? need ( )
people.map( (person,idx) => person.nicknames[0] || person.firstName );

// parameter destructuring? need ( )
people.map( ({ person }) => person.nicknames[0] || person.firstName );

// parameter default? need ( )
people.map( (person = {}) => person.nicknames[0] || person.firstName );

// returning an object? need ( )
people.map( person =>
    ({ preferredName: person.nicknames[0] || person.firstName })
);
```

The case for excitement over => in the FP world is primarily that it follows almost exactly from the mathematical notation for functions, especially in FP languages like Haskell. The shape of => arrow function syntax communicates mathematically.

Digging even further, I'd suggest that the argument in favor of => is that by using much lighter-weight syntax, we reduce the visual boundaries between functions which lets us use simple function expressions much like we'd use lazy expressions – another favorite of the FPer.

I think most FPers are going to wave off the concerns I'm sharing. They love anonymous functions and they love saving on syntax. But like I said before: you decide.

Note

Though I do not prefer to use => in practice in my production code, they are useful in quick code explorations. Moreover, we will use arrow functions in many places throughout the rest of this book – especially when we present typical FP utilities – where conciseness is preferred to optimize for the limited physical space in code snippets. Make your own determinations whether this approach will make your own production-ready code more or less readable.

What's This?

If you're not familiar with the `this` binding rules in JavaScript, I recommend checking out my book *You Don't Know JS: this & Object Prototypes*. For the purposes of this section, I'll assume you know how `this` gets determined for a function call (one of the four rules). But even if you're still fuzzy on *this*, the good news is we're going to conclude that you shouldn't be using `this` if you're trying to do FP.

Note

We're tackling a topic that we'll ultimately conclude we shouldn't use. Why!? Because the topic of `this` has implications for other topics covered later in this book. For example, our notions of function purity are impacted by `this` being essentially an implicit input to a function (see Chapter 5). Additionally, our perspective on `this` affects whether we choose array methods (`arr.map(..)`) versus standalone utilities (`map(..,arr)`) (see Chapter 9). Understanding `this` is essential to understanding why `this` really should *not* be part of your FP!

JavaScript `functions` have a `this` keyword that's automatically bound per function call. The `this` keyword can be described in many different ways, but I prefer to say it provides an object context for the function to run against.

`this` is an implicit parameter input for your function.

Consider:

```
function sum() {
    return this.x + this.y;
}

var context = {
    x: 1,
    y: 2
};

sum.call( context );        // 3
```

```
context.sum = sum;
context.sum();              // 3

var s = sum.bind( context );
s();                        // 3
```

Of course, if `this` can be input into a function implicitly, the same object context could be sent in as an explicit argument:

```
function sum(ctx) {
    return ctx.x + ctx.y;
}

var context = {
    x: 1,
    y: 2
};

sum( context );
```

Simpler. And this kind of code will be a lot easier to deal with in FP. It's much easier to wire multiple functions together, or use any of the other input wrangling techniques we will get into in the next chapter, when inputs are always explicit. Doing them with implicit inputs like `this` ranges from awkward to nearly impossible depending on the scenario.

There are other tricks we can leverage in a `this`-based system, including prototype-delegation (also covered in detail in *You Don't Know JS: this & Object Prototypes*):

```js
var Auth = {
    authorize() {
        var credentials = `${this.username}:${this.password}`;
        this.send( credentials, resp => {
            if (resp.error) this.displayError( resp.error );
            else this.displaySuccess();
        } );
    },
    send(/* .. */) {
        // ..
    }
};

var Login = Object.assign( Object.create( Auth ), {
    doLogin(user,pw) {
        this.username = user;
        this.password = pw;
        this.authorize();
    },
    displayError(err) {
        // ..
    },
    displaySuccess() {
        // ..
    }
} );

Login.doLogin( "fred", "123456" );
```

Note

`Object.assign(..)` is an ES6+ utility for doing a shallow assignment copy of properties from one or more source objects to a single target object: `Object.assign( target, source1, ... )`.

In case you're having trouble parsing what this code does: we have two separate objects `Login` and `Auth`, where `Login` performs prototype-delegation to `Auth`.

Through delegation and the implicit `this` context sharing, these two objects virtually compose during the `this.authorize()` function call, so that properties/methods on `this` are dynamically shared with the `Auth.authorize(..)` function.

This code doesn't fit with various principles of FP for a variety of reasons, but one of the obvious hitches is the implicit `this` sharing. We could be more explicit about it and keep code closer to FP-friendly style:

```
// ..

authorize(ctx) {
    var credentials = `${ctx.username}:${ctx.password}`;
    Auth.send( credentials, function onResp(resp){
        if (resp.error) ctx.displayError( resp.error );
        else ctx.displaySuccess();
    } );
}

// ..

doLogin(user,pw) {
    Auth.authorize( {
        username: user,
        password: pw
    } );
}

// ..
```

From my perspective, the problem is not with using objects to organize behavior. It's that we're trying to use implicit input instead of being explicit about it. When I'm wearing my FP hat, I want to leave `this` stuff on the shelf.

Summary

Functions are powerful.

But let's be clear what a function is. It's not just a collection of statements/operations. Specifically, a function needs one or more inputs (ideally, just one!) and an output.

Functions inside of functions can have closure over outer variables and remember them for later. This is one of the most important concepts in all of programming, and a fundamental foundation of FP.

Be careful of anonymous functions, especially => arrow functions. They're convenient to write, but they shift the cost from author to reader. The whole reason we're studying FP here is to write more readable code, so don't be so quick to jump on that bandwagon.

Don't use `this`-aware functions. Just don't.

You should now be developing a clear and colorful perspective in your mind of what *function* means in Functional Programming. It's time to start wrangling functions to get them to interoperate, and the next chapter teaches you a variety of critical techniques you'll need along the way.

Chapter 3: Managing Function Inputs

Chapter 2 explored the core nature of JS `functions`, and laid the foundation for what makes a `function` an FP *function*. But to leverage the full power of FP, we also need patterns and practices for manipulating functions to shift and adjust their interactions – to bend them to our will.

Specifically, our attention for this chapter will be on the parameter inputs of functions. As you bring functions of all different shapes together in your programs, you'll quickly face incompatibilities in the number/order/type of inputs, as well as the need to specify some inputs at different times than others.

As a matter of fact, for stylistic purposes of readability, sometimes you'll want to define functions in a way that hides their inputs entirely!

These kinds of techniques are absolutely essential to making functions truly *functional*.

All for One

Imagine you're passing a function to a utility, where the utility will send multiple arguments to that function. But you may only want the function to receive a single argument.

We can design a simple helper that wraps a function call to ensure only one argument will pass through. Since this is effectively enforcing that a function is treated as unary, let's name it as such:

```
function unary(fn) {
    return function onlyOneArg(arg){
        return fn( arg );
    };
}
```

Many FPers tend to prefer the shorter => arrow function syntax for such code (see Chapter 2, "Functions without `function`"), such as:

```
var unary =
    fn =>
        arg =>
            fn( arg );
```

Note

No question this is more terse, sparse even. But I personally feel that whatever it may gain in symmetry with the mathematical notation, it loses more in overall readability with the functions all being anonymous, and by obscuring the scope boundaries, making deciphering closure a little more cryptic.

A commonly cited example for using `unary(..)` is with the `map(..)` utility (see Chapter 9, "Map") and `parseInt(..)`. `map(..)` calls a mapper function for each item in a list, and each time it invokes the mapper function, it passes in three arguments: `value`, `idx`, `arr`.

That's usually not a big deal, unless you're trying to use something as a mapper function that will behave incorrectly if it's passed too many arguments. Consider:

```
["1","2","3"].map( parseInt );
// [1,NaN,NaN]
```

For the signature `parseInt(str,radix)`, it's clear that when `map(..)` passes `index` in the second argument position, it's interpreted by `parseInt(..)` as the `radix`, which we don't want.

`unary(..)` creates a function that will ignore all but the first argument passed to it, meaning the passed-in `index` is never received by `parseInt(..)` and mistaken as the `radix`:

```
["1","2","3"].map( unary( parseInt ) );
// [1,2,3]
```

One on One

Speaking of functions with only one argument, another common base utility in the FP toolbelt is a function that takes one argument and does nothing but return the value untouched:

```
function identity(v) {
    return v;
}

// or the ES6 => arrow form
var identity =
    v =>
        v;
```

This utility looks so simple as to hardly be useful. But even simple functions can be helpful in the world of FP. Like they say in acting: there are no small parts, only small actors.

For example, imagine you'd like to split up a string using a regular expression, but the resulting array may have some empty values in it. To discard those, we can use JS's `filter(..)` array operation (see Chapter 9, "Filter") with `identity(..)` as the predicate:

```
var words = "   Now is the time for all...   ".split( /\s|\b/ );
words;
// ["","Now","is","the","time","for","all","...",""]

words.filter( identity );
// ["Now","is","the","time","for","all","..."]
```

Because `identity(..)` simply returns the value passed to it, JS coerces each value into either `true` or `false`, and that determines whether to keep or exclude each value in the final array.

 Tip

Another unary function that can be used as the predicate in the previous example is JS's built-in `Boolean(..)` function, which explicitly coerces a value to `true` or `false`.

Another example of using `identity(..)` is as a default function in place of a transformation:

```
function output(msg,formatFn = identity) {
    msg = formatFn( msg );
    console.log( msg );
}

function upper(txt) {
    return txt.toUpperCase();
}

output( "Hello World", upper );    // HELLO WORLD
output( "Hello World" );           // Hello World
```

You also may see `identity(..)` used as a default transformation function for `map(..)` calls or as the initial value in a `reduce(..)` of a list of functions; both of these utilities will be covered in Chapter 9.

Unchanging One

Certain APIs don't let you pass a value directly into a method, but require you to pass in a function, even if that function literally just returns the value. One such API is the then(..) method on JS Promises:

```
// doesn't work:
p1.then( foo ).then( p2 ).then( bar );

// instead:
p1.then( foo ).then( function(){ return p2; } ).then( bar );
```

Many claim that ES6 => arrow functions are the best "solution":

```
p1.then( foo ).then( () => p2 ).then( bar );
```

But there's an FP utility that's more well suited for the task:

```
function constant(v) {
    return function value(){
        return v;
    };
}

// or the ES6 => form
var constant =
    v =>
        () =>
            v;
```

With this tidy little FP utility, we can solve our then(..) annoyance properly:

```
p1.then( foo ).then( constant( p2 ) ).then( bar );
```

Warning

Although the `() => p2` arrow function version is shorter than `constant(p2)`, I would encourage you to resist the temptation to use it. The arrow function is returning a value from outside of itself, which is a bit worse from the FP perspective. We'll cover the pitfalls of such actions later in the book (see Chapter 5).

Adapting Arguments to Parameters

There are a variety of patterns and tricks we can use to adapt a function's signature to match the kinds of arguments we want to provide to it.

Recall this function signature from Chapter 2 which highlights using array parameter destructuring:

```
function foo( [x,y,...args] = [] ) {
```

This pattern is handy if an array will be passed in but you want to treat its contents as individual parameters. `foo(..)` is thus technically unary – when it's executed, only one argument (an array) will be passed to it. But inside the function, you get to address different inputs (x, y, etc) individually.

However, sometimes you won't have the ability to change the declaration of the function to use array parameter destructuring. For example, imagine these functions:

```
function foo(x,y) {
    console.log( x + y );
}

function bar(fn) {
    fn( [ 3, 9 ] );
}

bar( foo );          // fails
```

Do you spot why bar(foo) fails?

The array [3,9] is sent in as a single value to fn(..), but foo(..) expects x and y separately. If we could change the declaration of foo(..) to be function foo([x,y]) { .., we'd be fine. Or, if we could change the behavior of bar(..) to make the call as fn(...[3,9]), the values 3 and 9 would be passed in individually.

There will be occasions when you have two functions that are incompatible in this way, and you won't be able to change their declarations/definitions. So, how can you use them together?

We can define a helper to adapt a function so that it spreads out a single received array as its individual arguments:

```
function spreadArgs(fn) {
    return function spreadFn(argsArr){
        return fn( ...argsArr );
    };
}

// or the ES6 => arrow form
var spreadArgs =
    fn =>
        argsArr =>
            fn( ...argsArr );
```

Note

I called this helper spreadArgs(..), but in libraries like Ramda it's commonly called apply(..).

Now we can use `spreadArgs(..)` to adapt `foo(..)` to work as the proper input to `bar(..)`:

```
bar( spreadArgs( foo ) );          // 12
```

It won't seem clear yet why these occasions arise, but you will see them often. Essentially, `spreadArgs(..)` allows us to define functions that `return` multiple values via an array, but still have those multiple values treated independently as inputs to another function.

While we're talking about a `spreadArgs(..)` utility, let's also define a utility to handle the opposite action:

```
function gatherArgs(fn) {
    return function gatheredFn(...argsArr){
        return fn( argsArr );
    };
}

// or the ES6 => arrow form
var gatherArgs =
    fn =>
        (...argsArr) =>
            fn( argsArr );
```

Note

In Ramda, this utility is referred to as `unapply(..)`, being that it's the opposite of `apply(..)`. I think the "spread"/"gather" terminology is a little more descriptive for what's going on.

We can use this utility to gather individual arguments into a single array, perhaps because we want to adapt a function with array parameter destructuring to another utility that passes arguments separately. We will cover `reduce(..)` more fully in Chapter 9; in short, it repeatedly calls its reducer function with two individual parameters, which we can now *gather* together:

```
function combineFirstTwo([ v1, v2 ]) {
    return v1 + v2;
}

[1,2,3,4,5].reduce( gatherArgs( combineFirstTwo ) );
// 15
```

Some Now, Some Later

If a function takes multiple arguments, you may want to specify some of those up front and leave the rest to be specified later.

Consider this function:

```
function ajax(url,data,callback) {
    // ..
}
```

Let's imagine you'd like to set up several API calls where the URLs are known up front, but the data and the callback to handle the response won't be known until later.

Of course, you can just defer making the `ajax(..)` call until all the bits are known, and refer to some global constant for the URL at that time. But another way is to create a function reference that already has the `url` argument preset.

What we're going to do is make a new function that still calls `ajax(..)` under the covers, and it manually sets the first argument to the API URL you care about, while waiting to accept the other two arguments later:

```
function getPerson(data,cb) {
    ajax( "http://some.api/person", data, cb );
}

function getOrder(data,cb) {
    ajax( "http://some.api/order", data, cb );
}
```

Manually specifying these function call wrappers is certainly possible, but it may get quite tedious, especially if there will also be variations with different arguments preset, like:

```
function getCurrentUser(cb) {
    getPerson( { user: CURRENT_USER_ID }, cb );
}
```

One practice an FPer gets very used to is looking for patterns where we do the same sorts of things repeatedly, and trying to turn those actions into generic reusable utilities. As a matter of fact, I'm sure that's already the instinct for many of you readers, so that's not uniquely an FP thing. But it's unquestionably important for FP.

To conceive such a utility for argument presetting, let's examine conceptually what's going on, not just looking at the manual implementations shown here.

One way to articulate what's going on is that the getOrder(data,cb) function is a *partial application* of the ajax(url,data,cb) function. This terminology comes from the notion that arguments are *applied* to parameters at the function call-site. And as you can see, we're only applying some of the arguments up front – specifically, the argument for the url parameter – while leaving the rest to be applied later.

To be a tiny bit more formal about this pattern, partial application is strictly a reduction in a function's arity; remember, that's the number of expected parameter inputs. We reduced the original ajax(..) function's arity from 3 to 2 for the getOrder(..) function.

Let's define a partial(..) utility:

```
function partial(fn,...presetArgs) {
    return function partiallyApplied(...laterArgs){
        return fn( ...presetArgs, ...laterArgs );
    };
}

// or the ES6 => arrow form
var partial =
    (fn,...presetArgs) =>
        (...laterArgs) =>
            fn( ...presetArgs, ...laterArgs );
```

 Tip

Don't just take this snippet at face value. Pause for a few moments to digest what's going on with this utility. Make sure you really *get it*.

The `partial(..)` function takes an `fn` for which function we are partially applying. Then, any subsequent arguments passed in are gathered into the `presetArgs` array and saved for later.

A new inner function (called `partiallyApplied(..)` just for clarity) is created and `return`ed; the inner function's own arguments are gathered into an array called `laterArgs`.

Notice the references to `fn` and `presetArgs` inside this inner function? How does that work? After `partial(..)` finishes running, how does the inner function keep being able to access `fn` and `presetArgs`? If you answered **closure**, you're right on track! The inner function `partiallyApplied(..)` closes over both the `fn` and `presetArgs` variables so it can keep accessing them later, no matter where the function runs. This is why understanding closure is critical!

When the `partiallyApplied(..)` function is later executed somewhere else in your program, it uses the closed over `fn` to execute the original function, first providing any of the (closed over) `presetArgs` partial application arguments, then any further `laterArgs` arguments.

If any of that was confusing, stop and go re-read it. Trust me, you'll be glad you did as we get further into the text.

Let's now use the `partial(..)` utility to make those earlier partially applied functions:

```
var getPerson = partial( ajax, "http://some.api/person" );

var getOrder = partial( ajax, "http://some.api/order" );
```

Take a moment to consider the shape/internals of `getPerson(..)`. It will look sorta like this:

```
var getPerson = function partiallyApplied(...laterArgs) {
    return ajax( "http://some.api/person", ...laterArgs );
};
```

The same will be true of `getOrder(..)`. But what about `getCurrentUser(..)`?

```
// version 1
var getCurrentUser = partial(
    ajax,
    "http://some.api/person",
    { user: CURRENT_USER_ID }
);

// version 2
var getCurrentUser = partial( getPerson, { user: CURRENT_USER_ID } );
```

We can either define `getCurrentUser(..)` with both the `url` and `data` arguments specified directly (version 1), or define `getCurrentUser(..)` as a partial application of the `getPerson(..)` partial application, specifying only the additional `data` argument (version 2).

Version 2 is a little cleaner to express because it reuses something already defined. As such, I think it fits a little closer to the spirit of FP.

Just to make sure we understand how these two versions will work under the covers, they look respectively kinda like:

```
// version 1
var getCurrentUser = function partiallyApplied(...laterArgs) {
    return ajax(
        "http://some.api/person",
        { user: CURRENT_USER_ID },
        ...laterArgs
    );
};

// version 2
var getCurrentUser = function outerPartiallyApplied(...outerLaterArgs){
    var getPerson = function innerPartiallyApplied(...innerLaterArgs){
        return ajax( "http://some.api/person", ...innerLaterArgs );
    };

    return getPerson( { user: CURRENT_USER_ID }, ...outerLaterArgs );
}
```

Again, stop and re-read those code snippets to make sure you understand what's going on there.

Note

Version 2 has an extra layer of function wrapping involved. That may smell strange and unnecessary, but this is just one of those things in FP that you'll want to get really comfortable with. We'll be wrapping many layers of functions onto each other as we progress through the text. Remember, this is *function*al programming!

Let's take a look at another example of the usefulness of partial application. Consider an add(..) function which takes two arguments and adds them together:

```
function add(x,y) {
    return x + y;
}
```

Now imagine we'd like take a list of numbers and add a certain number to each of them. We'll use the map(..) utility (see Chapter 9, "Map") built into JS arrays:

```
[1,2,3,4,5].map( function adder(val){
    return add( 3, val );
} );
// [4,5,6,7,8]
```

The reason we can't pass `add(..)` directly to `map(..)` is because the signature of `add(..)` doesn't match the mapping function that `map(..)` expects. That's where partial application can help us: we can adapt the signature of `add(..)` to something that will match:

```
[1,2,3,4,5].map( partial( add, 3 ) );
// [4,5,6,7,8]
```

The `partial(add,3)` call produces a new unary function which is expecting only one more argument.

The `map(..)` utility will loop through the array (`[1,2,3,4,5]`) and repeatedly call this unary function, once for each of those values, respectively. So, the calls made will effectively be `add(3,1)`, `add(3,2)`, `add(3,3)`, `add(3,4)`, and `add(3,5)`. The array of those results is `[4,5,6,7,8]`.

bind(..)

JavaScript functions all have a built-in utility called `bind(..)`. It has two capabilities: presetting the `this` context and partially applying arguments.

I think it's incredibly misguided to conflate these two capabilities in one utility. Sometimes you'll want to hard-bind the `this` context and not partially apply arguments. Other times you'll want to partially apply arguments but not care about `this` binding at all. I have never needed both at the same time.

The latter scenario (partial application without setting `this` context) is awkward because you have to pass an ignorable placeholder for the `this`-binding argument (the first one), usually `null`.

Consider:

```
var getPerson = ajax.bind( null, "http://some.api/person" );
```

That `null` just bugs me to no end. Despite this *this* annoyance, it's mildly convenient that JS has a built-in utility for partial application. However, most FP programmers prefer using the dedicated `partial(..)` utility in their chosen FP library.

Reversing Arguments

Recall that the signature for our Ajax function is: `ajax( url, data, cb )`. What if we wanted to partially apply the `cb` but wait to specify `data` and `url` later? We could create a utility that wraps a function to reverse its argument order:

```
function reverseArgs(fn) {
    return function argsReversed(...args){
        return fn( ...args.reverse() );
    };
}

// or the ES6 => arrow form
var reverseArgs =
    fn =>
        (...args) =>
            fn( ...args.reverse() );
```

Now we can reverse the order of the `ajax(..)` arguments, so that we can then partially apply from the right rather than the left. To restore the expected order, we'll then reverse the subsequent partially applied function:

```
var cache = {};

var cacheResult = reverseArgs(
    partial( reverseArgs( ajax ), function onResult(obj){
        cache[obj.id] = obj;
    } )
);

// later:
cacheResult( "http://some.api/person", { user: CURRENT_USER_ID } );
```

Instead of manually using `reverseArgs(..)` (twice!) for this purpose, we can define a `partialRight(..)` which partially applies the rightmost arguments. Under the covers, it can use the same double-reverse trick:

```
function partialRight(fn,...presetArgs) {
    return reverseArgs(
        partial( reverseArgs( fn ), ...presetArgs.reverse() )
    );
}

var cacheResult = partialRight( ajax, function onResult(obj){
    cache[obj.id] = obj;
});

// later:
cacheResult( "http://some.api/person", { user: CURRENT_USER_ID } );
```

Another more straightforward (and certainly more performant) implementation of `partialRight(..)` that doesn't use the double-reverse trick:

```
function partialRight(fn,...presetArgs) {
    return function partiallyApplied(...laterArgs){
        return fn( ...laterArgs, ...presetArgs );
    };
}

// or the ES6 => arrow form
var partialRight =
    (fn,...presetArgs) =>
        (...laterArgs) =>
            fn( ...laterArgs, ...presetArgs );
```

None of these implementations of `partialRight(..)` guarantee that a specific parameter will receive a specific partially applied value; it only ensures that the partially applied value(s) appear as the rightmost (aka, last) argument(s) passed to the original function.

For example:

```
function foo(x,y,z,...rest) {
    console.log( x, y, z, rest );
}

var f = partialRight( foo, "z:last" );

f( 1, 2 );          // 1 2 "z:last" []

f( 1 );             // 1 "z:last" undefined []

f( 1, 2, 3 );       // 1 2 3 ["z:last"]

f( 1, 2, 3, 4 );    // 1 2 3 [4,"z:last"]
```

The value `"z:last"` is only applied to the z parameter in the case where `f(..)` is called with exactly two arguments (matching x and y parameters). In all other cases, the `"z:last"` will just be the rightmost argument, however many arguments precede it.

One at a Time

Let's examine a technique similar to partial application, where a function that expects multiple arguments is broken down into successive chained functions that each take a single argument (arity: 1) and return another function to accept the next argument.

This technique is called currying.

To first illustrate, let's imagine we had a curried version of `ajax(..)` already created. This is how we'd use it:

```
curriedAjax( "http://some.api/person" )
    ( { user: CURRENT_USER_ID } )
        ( function foundUser(user){ /* .. */ } );
```

The three sets of `(..)`s denote three chained function calls. But perhaps splitting out each of the three calls helps see what's going on better:

```
var personFetcher = curriedAjax( "http://some.api/person" );

var getCurrentUser = personFetcher( { user: CURRENT_USER_ID } );

getCurrentUser( function foundUser(user){ /* .. */ } );
```

Instead of taking all the arguments at once (like `ajax(..)`), or some of the arguments up front and the rest later (via `partial(..)`), this `curriedAjax(..)` function receives one argument at a time, each in a separate function call.

Currying is similar to partial application in that each successive curried call partially applies another argument to the original function, until all arguments have been passed.

The main difference is that `curriedAjax(..)` will return a function (we call it `personFetcher(..)`) that expects **only the next argument** data, not one that (like the earlier `getPerson(..)`) can receive all the rest of the arguments.

If an original function expected five arguments, the curried form of that function would take just the first argument, and return a function to accept the second. That one would take just the second argument, and return a function to accept the third. And so on.

So currying unwinds a single higher-arity function into a series of chained unary functions.

How might we define a utility to do this currying? Consider:

```
function curry(fn,arity = fn.length) {
    return (function nextCurried(prevArgs){
        return function curried(nextArg){
            var args = [ ...prevArgs, nextArg ];

            if (args.length >= arity) {
                return fn( ...args );
            }
            else {
                return nextCurried( args );
            }
        };
    })( [] );
}

// or the ES6 => arrow form
var curry =
    (fn,arity = fn.length,nextCurried) =>
        (nextCurried = prevArgs =>
            nextArg => {
                var args = [ ...prevArgs, nextArg ];

                if (args.length >= arity) {
                    return fn( ...args );
                }
                else {
                    return nextCurried( args );
                }
            }
        )( [] );
```

The approach here is to start a collection of arguments in `prevArgs` as an empty `[]` array, and add each received `nextArg` to that, calling the concatenation `args`. While `args.length` is less than `arity` (the number of declared/expected parameters of the original `fn(..)` function), make and return another `curried(..)` function to collect the next `nextArg` argument, passing the running `args` collection along as its `prevArgs`. Once we have enough `args`, execute the original `fn(..)` function with them.

By default, this implementation relies on being able to inspect the `length` property of the to-be-curried function to know how many iterations of currying we'll need before we've collected all its expected arguments.

Note

If you use this implementation of `curry(..)` with a function that doesn't have an accurate `length` property, you'll need to pass the `arity` (the second parameter of `curry(..)`) to ensure `curry(..)` works correctly. `length` will be inaccurate if the function's parameter signature includes default parameter values, parameter destructuring, or is variadic with `...args` (see Chapter 2).

Here's how we would use `curry(..)` for our earlier `ajax(..)` example:

```
var curriedAjax = curry( ajax );

var personFetcher = curriedAjax( "http://some.api/person" );

var getCurrentUser = personFetcher( { user: CURRENT_USER_ID } );

getCurrentUser( function foundUser(user){ /* .. */ } );
```

Each call partially applies one more argument to the original `ajax(..)` call, until all three have been provided and `ajax(..)` is actually invoked.

Remember our example from the discussion of partial application about adding 3 to each value in a list of numbers? As currying is similar to partial application, we could do that task with currying in almost the same way:

```
[1,2,3,4,5].map( curry( add )( 3 ) );
// [4,5,6,7,8]
```

The difference between the two? `partial(add,3)` vs `curry(add)(3)`.

Why might you choose `curry(..)` over `partial(..)`? It might be helpful in the case where you know ahead of time that `add(..)` is the function to be adapted, but the value 3 isn't known yet:

```
var adder = curry( add );

// later
[1,2,3,4,5].map( adder( 3 ) );
// [4,5,6,7,8]
```

Let's look at another numbers example, this time adding a list of them together:

```
function sum(...nums) {
    var total = 0;
    for (let num of nums) {
        total += num;
    }
    return total;
}

sum( 1, 2, 3, 4, 5 );                           // 15

// now with currying:
// (5 to indicate how many we should wait for)
var curriedSum = curry( sum, 5 );

curriedSum( 1 )( 2 )( 3 )( 4 )( 5 );            // 15
```

The advantage of currying here is that each call to pass in an argument produces another function that's more specialized, and we can capture and use *that* new function later in the program. Partial application specifies all the partially applied arguments up front, producing a function that's waiting for all the rest of the arguments **on the next call**.

If you wanted to use partial application to specify one parameter (or several!) at a time, you'd have to keep calling `partial(..)` again on each successive partially applied function. By contrast, curried functions do this automatically, making working with individual arguments one-at-a-time more ergonomic.

Both currying and partial application use closure to remember the arguments over time until all have been received, and then the original function can be invoked.

Visualizing Curried Functions

Let's examine more closely the `curriedSum(..)` from the previous section. Recall its usage: `curriedSum(1)(2)(3)(4)(5)`; five subsequent (chained) function calls.

What if we manually defined a `curriedSum(..)` instead of using `curry(..)`? How would that look?

```
function curriedSum(v1) {
    return function(v2){
        return function(v3){
            return function(v4){
                return function(v5){
                    return sum( v1, v2, v3, v4, v5 );
                };
            };
        };
    };
}
```

Definitely uglier, no question. But this is an important way to visualize what's going on with a curried function. Each nested function call is returning another function that's going to accept the next argument, and that continues until we've specified all the expected arguments.

When trying to decipher curried functions, I've found it helps me tremendously if I can unwrap them mentally as a series of nested functions.

In fact, to reinforce that point, let's consider the same code but written with ES6 arrow functions:

```
curriedSum =
    v1 =>
        v2 =>
            v3 =>
                v4 =>
                    v5 =>
                        sum( v1, v2, v3, v4, v5 );
```

And now, all on one line:

```
curriedSum = v1 => v2 => v3 => v4 => v5 => sum( v1, v2, v3, v4, v5 );
```

Depending on your perspective, that form of visualizing the curried function may be more or less helpful to you. For me, it's a fair bit more obscured.

But the reason I show it that way is that it happens to look almost identical to the mathematical notation (and Haskell syntax) for a curried function! That's one reason why those who like mathematical notation (and/or Haskell) like the ES6 arrow function form.

Why Currying and Partial Application?

With either style – currying (such as `sum(1)(2)(3)`) or partial application (such as `partial(sum,1,2)(3)`) – the call-site unquestionably looks stranger than a more common one like `sum(1,2,3)`. So **why would we ever go this direction** when adopting FP? There are multiple layers to answering that question.

The first and most obvious reason is that both currying and partial application allow you to separate in time/space (throughout your codebase) when and where separate arguments are specified, whereas traditional function calls require all the arguments to be present at the same time. If you have a place in your code where you'll know some of the arguments and another place where the other arguments are determined, currying or partial application are very useful.

Another layer to this answer, specifically for currying, is that composition of functions is much easier when there's only one argument. So a function that ultimately needs three arguments, if curried, becomes a function that needs just one, three times over. That kind of unary function will be a lot easier to work with when we start composing them. We'll tackle this topic later in Chapter 4.

But the most important layer is specialization of generalized functions, and how such abstraction improves readability of code.

Consider our running `ajax(..)` example:

```
ajax(
    "http://some.api/person",
    { user: CURRENT_USER_ID },
    function foundUser(user){ /* .. */ }
);
```

The call-site includes all the information necessary to pass to the most generalized version of the utility (`ajax(..)`). The potential readability downside is that it may be the case that the URL and the data are not relevant information at this point in the program, but yet that information is cluttering up the call-site nonetheless.

Now consider:

```
var getCurrentUser = partial(
    ajax,
    "http://some.api/person",
    { user: CURRENT_USER_ID }
);

// later

getCurrentUser( function foundUser(user){ /* .. */ } );
```

In this version, we define a `getCurrentUser(..)` function ahead of time that already has known information like URL and data preset. The call-site for `getCurrentUser(..)` then isn't cluttered by information that **at that point of the code** isn't relevant.

Moreover, the semantic name for the function `getCurrentUser(..)` more accurately depicts what is happening than just `ajax(..)` with a URL and data would.

That's what abstraction is all about: separating two sets of details – in this case, the *how* of getting a current user and the *what* we do with that user – and inserting a semantic boundary between them, which eases the reasoning of each part independently.

Whether you use currying or partial application, creating specialized functions from generalized ones is a powerful technique for semantic abstraction and improved readability.

Currying More Than One Argument?

The definition and implementation I've given of currying thus far is, I believe, as true to the spirit as we can likely get in JavaScript.

Specifically, if we look briefly at how currying works in Haskell, we can observe that multiple arguments always go in to a function one at a time, one per curried call – other than tuples (analogous to arrays for our purposes) that transport multiple values in a single argument.

For example, in Haskell:

```
foo 1 2 3
```

This calls the `foo` function, and has the result of passing in three values 1, 2, and 3. But functions are automatically curried in Haskell, which means each value goes in as a separate curried-call. The JS equivalent of that would look like `foo(1)(2)(3)`, which is the same style as the `curry(..)` I presented earlier.

Note

In Haskell, foo (1,2,3) is not passing in those three values at once as three separate arguments, but a tuple (kinda like a JS array) as a single argument. To work, foo would need to be altered to handle a tuple in that argument position. As far as I can tell, there's no way in Haskell to pass all three arguments separately with just one function call; each argument gets its own curried-call. Of course, the presence of multiple calls is transparent to the Haskell developer, but it's a lot more syntactically obvious to the JS developer.

For these reasons, I think the curry(..) that I demonstrated earlier is a faithful adaptation, or what I might call "strict currying". However, it's important to note that there's a looser definition used in most popular JavaScript FP libraries.

Specifically, JS currying utilities typically allow you to specify multiple arguments for each curried-call. Revisiting our sum(..) example from before, this would look like:

```
var curriedSum = looseCurry( sum, 5 );

curriedSum( 1 )( 2, 3 )( 4, 5 );          // 15
```

We see a slight syntax savings of fewer ( ), and an implied performance benefit of now having three function calls instead of five. But other than that, using looseCurry(..) is identical in end result to the narrower curry(..) definition from earlier. I would guess the convenience/performance factor is probably why frameworks allow multiple arguments. This seems mostly like a matter of taste.

We can adapt our previous currying implementation to this common looser definition:

```
function looseCurry(fn,arity = fn.length) {
    return (function nextCurried(prevArgs){
        return function curried(...nextArgs){
            var args = [ ...prevArgs, ...nextArgs ];

            if (args.length >= arity) {
                return fn( ...args );
            }
            else {
                return nextCurried( args );
            }
        };
    })( [] );
}
```

Now each curried-call accepts one or more arguments (as `nextArgs`). We'll leave it as an exercise for the interested reader to define the ES6 => version of `looseCurry(..)` similar to how we did it for `curry(..)` earlier.

No Curry for Me, Please

It may also be the case that you have a curried function that you'd like to essentially un-curry – basically, to turn a function like `f(1)(2)(3)` back into a function like `g(1,2,3)`.

The standard utility for this is (un)shockingly typically called `uncurry(..)`. Here's a simple naive implementation:

```
function uncurry(fn) {
    return function uncurried(...args){
        var ret = fn;

        for (let arg of args) {
            ret = ret( arg );
        }

        return ret;
    };
}

// or the ES6 => arrow form
var uncurry =
    fn =>
        (...args) => {
            var ret = fn;

            for (let arg of args) {
                ret = ret( arg );
            }

            return ret;
        };
```

Warning

Don't just assume that `uncurry(curry(f))` has the same behavior as `f`. In some libraries the uncurrying would result in a function like the original, but not all of them; certainly our example here does not. The uncurried function acts (mostly) the same as the original function if you pass as many arguments to it as the original function expected. However, if you pass fewer arguments, you still get back a partially curried function waiting for more arguments; this quirk is illustrated in the following snippet:

```
function sum(...nums) {
    var sum = 0;
    for (let num of nums) {
        sum += num;
    }
    return sum;
}

var curriedSum = curry( sum, 5 );
var uncurriedSum = uncurry( curriedSum );

curriedSum( 1 )( 2 )( 3 )( 4 )( 5 );        // 15

uncurriedSum( 1, 2, 3, 4, 5 );              // 15
uncurriedSum( 1, 2, 3 )( 4 )( 5 );          // 15
```

Probably the more common case of using `uncurry(..)` is not with a manually curried function as just shown, but with a function that comes out curried as a result of some other set of operations. We'll illustrate that scenario later in this chapter in the "No Points" discussion.

Order Matters

In Chapter 2, we explored the named arguments pattern. One primary advantage of named arguments is not needing to juggle argument ordering, thereby improving readability.

We've looked at the advantages of using currying/partial application to provide individual arguments to a function separately. But the downside is that these techniques are traditionally based on positional arguments; argument ordering is thus an inevitable headache.

Utilities like `reverseArgs(..)` (and others) are necessary to juggle arguments to get them into the right order. Sometimes we get lucky and define a function with parameters in the order that we later want to curry them, but other times that order is incompatible and we have to jump through hoops to reorder.

The frustration is not merely that we need to use some utility to juggle the properties, but the fact that the usage of the utility clutters up our code a bit with extra noise. These kinds of things are like little paper cuts; one here or there isn't a showstopper, but the pain can certainly add up.

Can we improve currying/partial application to free it from these ordering concerns? Let's apply the tricks from named arguments style and invent some helper utilities for this adaptation:

```
function partialProps(fn,presetArgsObj) {
    return function partiallyApplied(laterArgsObj){
        return fn( Object.assign( {}, presetArgsObj, laterArgsObj ) );
    };
}

function curryProps(fn,arity = 1) {
    return (function nextCurried(prevArgsObj){
        return function curried(nextArgObj = {}){
            var [key] = Object.keys( nextArgObj );
            var allArgsObj = Object.assign(
                {}, prevArgsObj, { [key]: nextArgObj[key] }
            );

            if (Object.keys( allArgsObj ).length >= arity) {
                return fn( allArgsObj );
            }
            else {
                return nextCurried( allArgsObj );
            }
        };
    })( {} );
}
```

Tip

We don't even need a `partialPropsRight(..)` because we don't need to care about what order properties are being mapped; the name mappings make that ordering concern moot!

Here's how to use those helpers:

```
function foo({ x, y, z } = {}) {
    console.log( `x:${x} y:${y} z:${z}` );
}

var f1 = curryProps( foo, 3 );
var f2 = partialProps( foo, { y: 2 } );

f1( {y: 2} )( {x: 1} )( {z: 3} );
// x:1 y:2 z:3

f2( { z: 3, x: 1 } );
// x:1 y:2 z:3
```

Even with currying or partial application, order doesn't matter anymore! We can now specify which arguments we want in whatever sequence makes sense. No more `reverseArgs(..)` or other nuisances. Cool!

 Tip

If this style of function arguments seems useful or interesting to you, check out coverage of the FPO library in Appendix C.

Spreading Properties

Unfortunately, we can only take advantage of currying with named arguments if we have control over the signature of `foo(..)` and define it to destructure its first parameter. What if we wanted to use this technique with a function that had its parameters individually listed (no parameter destructuring!), and we couldn't change that function signature? For example:

```
function bar(x,y,z) {
    console.log( `x:${x} y:${y} z:${z}` );
}
```

Just like the `spreadArgs(..)` utility earlier, we can define a `spreadArgProps(..)` helper that takes the `key: value` pairs out of an object argument and "spreads" the values out as individual arguments.

There are some quirks to be aware of, though. With `spreadArgs(..)`, we were dealing with arrays, where ordering is well defined and obvious. However, with objects, property order is less clear and not necessarily reliable. Depending on how an object is created and properties set, we cannot be absolutely certain what enumeration order properties would come out.

Such a utility needs a way to let you define what order the function in question expects its arguments (e.g., property enumeration order). We can pass an array like `["x","y","z"]` to tell the utility to pull the properties off the object argument in exactly that order.

That's decent, but it's also unfortunate that it then *obligates* us to add that property-name array even for the simplest of functions. Is there any kind of trick we could use to detect what order the parameters are listed for a function, in at least the common simple cases? Fortunately, yes!

JavaScript functions have a `.toString()` method that gives a string representation of the function's code, including the function declaration signature. Dusting off our regular expression parsing skills, we can parse the string representation of the function, and pull out the individually named parameters. The code looks a bit gnarly, but it's good enough to get the job done:

```
function spreadArgProps(
    fn,
    propOrder =
        fn.toString()
        .replace( /^(?:(?:function.*\(([^]*?)\))|(?:([^\(\)]+?)
            \s*=>)|(?:\(([^]*?)\)\s*=>))[^]+$/, "$1$2$3" )
        .split( /\s*,\s*/ )
        .map( v => v.replace( /[=\s].*$/, "" ) )
) {
    return function spreadFn(argsObj){
        return fn( ...propOrder.map( k => argsObj[k] ) );
    };
}
```

Note

This utility's parameter parsing logic is far from bullet-proof; we're using regular expressions to parse code, which is already a faulty premise! But our only goal here is to handle the common cases, which this does reasonably well. We only need a sensible default detection of parameter order for functions with simple parameters (including those with default parameter values). We don't, for example, need to be able to parse out a complex destructured parameter, because we wouldn't likely be using this utility with such a function, anyway. So, this logic gets the job done 80% of the time; it lets us override the propOrder array for any other more complex function signature that wouldn't otherwise be correctly parsed. That's the kind of pragmatic balance this book seeks to find wherever possible.

Let's illustrate using our spreadArgProps(..) utility:

```
function bar(x,y,z) {
    console.log( `x:${x} y:${y} z:${z}` );
}

var f3 = curryProps( spreadArgProps( bar ), 3 );
var f4 = partialProps( spreadArgProps( bar ), { y: 2 } );

f3( {y: 2} )( {x: 1} )( {z: 3} );
// x:1 y:2 z:3

f4( { z: 3, x: 1 } );
// x:1 y:2 z:3
```

While order is no longer a concern, usage of functions defined in this style requires you to know what each argument's exact name is. You can't just remember, "oh, the function goes in as the first argument" anymore. Instead, you have to remember, "the function parameter is called 'fn'." Conventions can create consistency of naming that lessens this burden, but it's still something to be aware of.

Weigh these trade-offs carefully.

No Points

A popular style of coding in the FP world aims to reduce some of the visual clutter by removing unnecessary parameter-argument mapping. This style is formally called tacit programming, or more commonly: point-free style. The term "point" here is referring to a function's parameter input.

Warning

Stop for a moment. Let's make sure we're careful not to take this discussion as an unbounded suggestion that you go overboard trying to be point-free in your FP code at all costs. This should be a technique for improving readability, when used in moderation. But as with most things in software development, you can definitely abuse it. If your code gets harder to understand because of the hoops you have to jump through to be point-free, stop. You won't win a blue ribbon just because you found some clever but esoteric way to remove another "point" from your code.

Let's start with a simple example:

```
function double(x) {
    return x * 2;
}

[1,2,3,4,5].map( function mapper(v){
    return double( v );
} );
// [2,4,6,8,10]
```

Can you see that `mapper(..)` and `double(..)` have the same (or compatible, anyway) signatures? The parameter ("point") v can directly map to the corresponding argument in the `double(..)` call. As such, the `mapper(..)` function wrapper is unnecessary. Let's simplify with point-free style:

```
function double(x) {
    return x * 2;
}

[1,2,3,4,5].map( double );
// [2,4,6,8,10]
```

Let's revisit an example from earlier:

```
["1","2","3"].map( function mapper(v){
    return parseInt( v );
} );
// [1,2,3]
```

In this example, `mapper(..)` is actually serving an important purpose, which is to discard the `index` argument that `map(..)` would pass in, because `parseInt(..)` would incorrectly interpret that value as a `radix` for the parsing.

If you recall from the beginning of this chapter, this was an example where `unary(..)` helps us out:

```
["1","2","3"].map( unary( parseInt ) );
// [1,2,3]
```

Point-free!

The key thing to look for is if you have a function with parameter(s) that is/are directly passed to an inner function call. In both of the preceding examples, mapper(..) had the v parameter that was passed along to another function call. We were able to replace that layer of abstraction with a point-free expression using unary(..).

 Warning

You might have been tempted, as I was, to try map(partialRight(parseInt,10)) to right-partially apply the 10 value as the radix. However, as we saw earlier, partialRight(..) only guarantees that 10 will be the last argument passed in, not that it will be specifically the second argument. Since map(..) itself passes three arguments (value, index, arr) to its mapping function, the 10 value would just be the fourth argument to parseInt(..); it only pays attention to the first two.

Here's another example:

```
// convenience to avoid any potential binding issue
// with trying to use `console.log` as a function
function output(txt) {
    console.log( txt );
}

function printIf( predicate, msg ) {
    if (predicate( msg )) {
        output( msg );
    }
}

function isShortEnough(str) {
```

```
    return str.length <= 5;
}

var msg1 = "Hello";
var msg2 = msg1 + " World";

printIf( isShortEnough, msg1 );          // Hello
printIf( isShortEnough, msg2 );
```

Now let's say you want to print a message only if it's long enough; in other words, if it's !isShortEnough(..). Your first thought is probably this:

```
function isLongEnough(str) {
    return !isShortEnough( str );
}

printIf( isLongEnough, msg1 );
printIf( isLongEnough, msg2 );           // Hello World
```

Easy enough... but "points" now! See how str is passed through? Without re-implementing the str.length check, can we refactor this code to point-free style?

Let's define a not(..) negation helper (often referred to as complement(..) in FP libraries):

```
function not(predicate) {
    return function negated(...args){
        return !predicate( ...args );
    };
}

// or the ES6 => arrow form
var not =
    predicate =>
        (...args) =>
            !predicate( ...args );
```

Next, let's use not(..) to alternatively define isLongEnough(..) without "points":

```
var isLongEnough = not( isShortEnough );

printIf( isLongEnough, msg2 );          // Hello World
```

That's pretty good, isn't it? But we *could* keep going. `printIf(..)` could be refactored to be point-free itself.

We can express the `if` conditional part with a `when(..)` utility:

```
function when(predicate,fn) {
    return function conditional(...args){
        if (predicate( ...args )) {
            return fn( ...args );
        }
    };
}

// or the ES6 => form
var when =
    (predicate,fn) =>
        (...args) =>
            predicate( ...args ) ? fn( ...args ) : undefined;
```

Let's mix `when(..)` with a few other helper utilities we've seen earlier in this chapter, to make the point-free `printIf(..)`:

```
var printIf = uncurry( partialRight( when, output ) );
```

Here's how we did it: we right-partially-applied the `output` method as the second (`fn`) argument for `when(..)`, which leaves us with a function still expecting the first argument (`predicate`). *That* function when called produces another function expecting the message string; it would look like this: `fn(predicate)(str)`.

A chain of multiple (two) function calls like that looks an awful lot like a curried function, so we `uncurry(..)` this result to produce a single function that expects the two `str` and `predicate` arguments together, which matches the original `printIf(predicate,str)` signature.

Here's the whole example put back together (assuming various utilities we've already detailed in this chapter are present):

```
function output(msg) {
    console.log( msg );
}

function isShortEnough(str) {
    return str.length <= 5;
}

var isLongEnough = not( isShortEnough );

var printIf = uncurry( partialRight( when, output ) );

var msg1 = "Hello";
var msg2 = msg1 + " World";

printIf( isShortEnough, msg1 );         // Hello
printIf( isShortEnough, msg2 );

printIf( isLongEnough, msg1 );
printIf( isLongEnough, msg2 );          // Hello World
```

Hopefully the FP practice of point-free style coding is starting to make a little more sense. It'll still take a lot of practice to train yourself to think this way naturally. **And you'll still have to make judgement calls** as to whether point-free coding is worth it, as well as what extent will benefit your code's readability.

What do you think? Points or no points for you?

Note

Want more practice with point-free style coding? We'll revisit this technique in Chapter 4, "Revisiting Points", based on newfound knowledge of function composition.

Summary

Partial application is a technique for reducing the arity (that is, the expected number of arguments to a function) by creating a new function where some of the arguments are preset.

Currying is a special form of partial application where the arity is reduced to 1, with a chain of successive chained function calls, each which takes one argument. Once all arguments have been specified by these function calls, the original function is executed with all the collected arguments. You can also undo a currying.

Other important utilities like `unary(..)`, `identity(..)`, and `constant(..)` are part of the base toolbox for FP.

Point-free is a style of writing code that eliminates unnecessary verbosity of mapping parameters ("points") to arguments, with the goal of making code easier to read/understand.

All of these techniques twist functions around so they can work together more naturally. With your functions shaped compatibly now, the next chapter will teach you how to combine them to model the flows of data through your program.

Chapter 4: Composing Functions

By now, I hope you're feeling much more comfortable with what it means to use functions for functional programming.

A functional programmer sees every function in their program like a simple little Lego piece. They recognize the blue 2x2 brick at a glance, and know exactly how it works and what they can do with it. When they begin building a bigger, more complex Lego model, as they need each next piece, they already have an instinct for which of their many spare pieces to grab.

But sometimes you take the blue 2x2 brick and the gray 4x1 brick and put them together in a certain way, and you realize, "that's a useful piece that I need often".

So now you've come up with a new "piece", a combination of two other pieces, and you can reach for that kind of piece now anytime you need it. It's more effective to recognize and use this compound blue-gray L-brick thing where it's needed than to separately think about assembling the two individual bricks each time.

Functions come in a variety of shapes and sizes. And we can define a certain combination of them to make a new compound function that will be handy in various parts of the program. This process of using functions together is called composition.

Composition is how an FPer models the flow of data through the program. In some senses, it's the most foundational concept in all of FP, because without it, you can't declaratively model data and state changes. In other words, everything else in FP would collapse without composition.

Output to Input

We've already seen a few examples of composition. For example, our discussion of `unary(..)` in Chapter 3 included this expression: `[..].map(unary(parseInt))`. Think about what's happening there.

To compose two functions together, pass the output of the first function call as the input of the second function call. In map(unary(parseInt)), the unary(parseInt) call returns a value (a function); that value is directly passed as an argument to map(..), which returns an array.

To take a step back and visualize the conceptual flow of data, consider:

```
arrayValue <-- map <-- unary <-- parseInt
```

parseInt is the input to unary(..). The output of unary(..) is the input to map(..). The output of map(..) is arrayValue. This is the composition of map(..) and unary(..).

 Note

The right-to-left orientation here is on purpose, though it may seem strange at this point in your learning. We'll come back to explain that more fully later.

Think of this flow of data like a conveyor belt in a candy factory, where each operation is a step in the process of cooling, cutting, and wrapping a piece of candy. We'll use the candy factory metaphor throughout this chapter to explain what composition is.

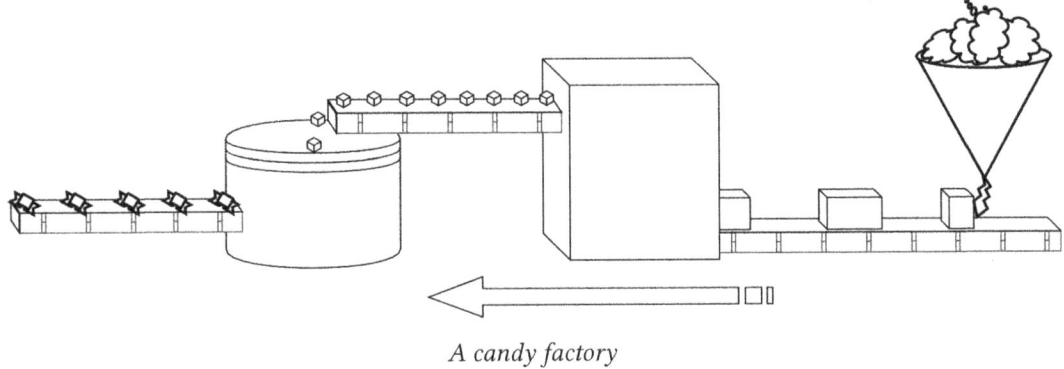

A candy factory

Let's examine composition in action one step at a time. Consider these two utilities you might have in your program:

```js
function words(str) {
    return String( str )
        .toLowerCase()
        .split( /\s|\b/ )
        .filter( function alpha(v){
            return /^[\w]+$/.test( v );
        } );
}

function unique(list) {
    var uniqList = [];

    for (let v of list) {
        // value not yet in the new list?
        if (uniqList.indexOf( v ) === -1 ) {
            uniqList.push( v );
        }
    }

    return uniqList;
}
```

`words(..)` splits a string into an array of words. `unique(..)` takes a list of words and filters it to not have any repeat words in it.

To use these two utilities to analyze a string of text:

```js
var text = "To compose two functions together, pass the \
output of the first function call as the input of the \
second function call.";

var wordsFound = words( text );
var wordsUsed = unique( wordsFound );

wordsUsed;
// ["to","compose","two","functions","together","pass",
// "the","output","of","first","function","call","as",
// "input","second"]
```

We name the array output of words(..) as wordsFound. The input of unique(..) is also an array, so we can pass the wordsFound into it.

Back to the candy factory assembly line: the first machine takes as "input" the melted chocolate, and its "output" is a chunk of formed and cooled chocolate. The next machine a little down the assembly line takes as its "input" the chunk of chocolate, and its "output" is a cut-up piece of chocolate candy. Next, a machine on the line takes small pieces of chocolate candy from the conveyor belt and outputs wrapped candies ready to bag and ship.

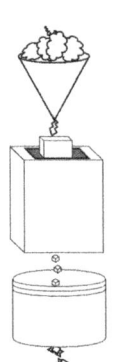

The candy factory is fairly successful with this process, but as with all businesses, management keeps searching for ways to grow.

To keep up with demand for more candy production, they decide to take out the conveyor belt contraption and just stack all three machines on top of one another, so that the output valve of one is connected directly to the input valve of the one below it. There's no longer sprawling wasted space where a chunk of chocolate slowly and noisily rumbles down a conveyor belt from the first machine to the second.

This innovation saves a lot of room on the factory floor, so management is happy they'll get to make more candy each day!

The code equivalent of this improved candy factory configuration is to skip the intermediate step (the wordsFound variable in the earlier snippet), and just use the two function calls together:

```
var wordsUsed = unique( words( text ) );
```

Note

Though we typically read the function calls left-to-right – unique(..) and then words(..) – the order of operations will actually be more right-to-left, or inner-to-outer. words(..) will run first and then unique(..). Later we'll talk about a pattern that matches the order of execution to our natural left-to-right reading, called pipe(..).

The stacked machines are working fine, but it's kind of clunky to have the wires hanging out all over the place. The more of these machine-stacks they create, the more cluttered the factory floor gets. And the effort to assemble and maintain all these machine stacks is awfully time intensive.

One morning, an engineer at the candy factory has a great idea. She figures that it'd be much more efficient if she made an outer box to hide all the wires; on the inside, all three of the machines are hooked up together, and on the outside everything is now neat and tidy. On the top of this fancy new machine is a valve to pour in melted chocolate and on the bottom is a valve that spits out wrapped chocolate candies. Brilliant!

This single compound machine is much easier to move around and install wherever the factory needs it. The workers on the factory floor are even happier because they don't need to fidget with buttons and dials on three individual machines anymore; they quickly prefer using the single fancy machine.

Relating back to the code: we now realize that the pairing of words(..) and unique(..) in that specific order of execution (think: compound Lego) is something we could use in several other parts of our application. So, let's define a compound function that combines them:

```
function uniqueWords(str) {
    return unique( words( str ) );
}
```

uniqueWords(..) takes a string and returns an array. It's a composition of the two functions: unique(..) and words(..); it creates this flow of data:

```
wordsUsed <-- unique <-- words <-- text
```

You probably recognize it by now: the unfolding revolution in candy factory design is function composition.

Machine Making

The candy factory is humming along nicely, and thanks to all the saved space, they now have plenty of room to try out making new kinds of candies. Building on the earlier success, management is keen to keep inventing new fancy compound machines for their growing candy assortment.

But the factory engineers struggle to keep up, because each time a new kind of fancy compound machine needs to be made, they spend quite a bit of time making the new outer box and fitting the individual machines into it.

So the factory engineers contact an industrial machine vendor for help. They're amazed to find out that this vendor offers a **machine-making** machine! As incredible as it sounds, they purchase a machine that can take a couple of the factory's smaller machines – the chocolate cooling one and the cutting one, for example – and wire them together automatically, even wrapping a nice clean bigger box around them. This is surely going to make the candy factory really take off!

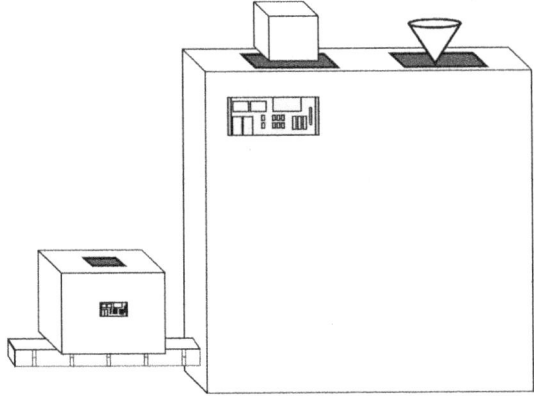

Back to code land, let's consider a utility called `compose2(..)` that creates a composition of two functions automatically, exactly the same way we did manually:

```
function compose2(fn2,fn1) {
    return function composed(origValue){
        return fn2( fn1( origValue ) );
    };
}

// or the ES6 => form
var compose2 =
    (fn2,fn1) =>
        origValue =>
            fn2( fn1( origValue ) );
```

Did you notice that we defined the parameter order as `fn2,fn1`, and furthermore that it's the second function listed (aka `fn1` parameter name) that runs first, then the first function listed (`fn2`)? In other words, the functions compose from right-to-left.

That may seem like a strange choice, but there are some reasons for it. Most typical FP libraries define their `compose(..)` to work right-to-left in terms of ordering, so we're sticking with that convention.

But why? I think the easiest explanation (but perhaps not the most historically accurate) is that we're listing them to match the order they are written in code manually, or rather the order we encounter them when reading from left-to-right.

`unique(words(str))` lists the functions in the left-to-right order `unique, words`, so we make our `compose2(..)` utility accept them in that order, too. The execution order is right-to-left, but the code order is left-to-right. Pay close attention to keep those distinct in your mind.

Now, the more efficient definition of the candy making machine is:

```
var uniqueWords = compose2( unique, words );
```

Composition Variation

It may seem like the `<-- unique <-- words` combination is the only order these two functions can be composed. But we could actually compose them in the opposite order to create a utility with a bit of a different purpose:

```
var letters = compose2( words, unique );

var chars = letters( "How are you Henry?" );
chars;
// ["h","o","w","a","r","e","y","u","n"]
```

This works because the words(..) utility, for value-type safety sake, first coerces its input to a string using String(..). So the array that unique(..) returns – now the input to words(..) – becomes the string "H,o,w, ,a,r,e,y,u,n,?", and then the rest of the behavior in words(..) processes that string into the chars array.

Admittedly, this is a contrived example. But the point is that function compositions are not always unidirectional. Sometimes we put the gray brick on top of the blue brick, and sometimes we put the blue brick on top.

The candy factory better be careful if they try to feed the wrapped candies into the machine that mixes and cools the chocolate!

General Composition

If we can define the composition of two functions, we can just keep going to support composing any number of functions. The general data visualization flow for any number of functions being composed looks like this:

```
finalValue <-- func1 <-- func2 <-- ... <-- funcN <-- origValue
```

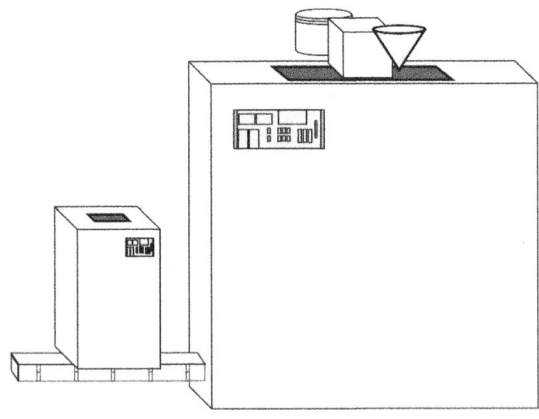

Now the candy factory owns the best machine of all: a machine that can take any number of separate smaller machines and spit out a big fancy machine that does every step in order. That's one heck of a candy operation! It's Willy Wonka's dream!

We can implement a general `compose(..)` utility like this:

```
function compose(...fns) {
    return function composed(result){
        // copy the array of functions
        var list = [...fns];

        while (list.length > 0) {
            // take the last function off the end of the list
            // and execute it
            result = list.pop()( result );
        }

        return result;
    };
}

// or the ES6 => form
var compose =
    (...fns) =>
        result => {
            var list = [...fns];

            while (list.length > 0) {
                // take the last function off the end of the list
                // and execute it
                result = list.pop()( result );
            }

            return result;
        };
```

Warning

...fns is a collected array of arguments, not a passed-in array, and as such, it's local to compose(..). It may be tempting to think the [...fns] would thus be unnecessary. However, in this particular implementation, .pop() inside the inner composed(..) function is mutating the list, so if we didn't make a copy each time, the returned composed function could only be used reliably once. We'll revisit this hazard in Chapter 6.

Now let's look at an example of composing more than two functions. Recalling our uniqueWords(..) composition example, let's add a skipShortWords(..) to the mix:

```
function skipShortWords(words) {
    var filteredWords = [];

    for (let word of words) {
        if (word.length > 4) {
            filteredWords.push( word );
        }
    }

    return filteredWords;
}
```

Let's define biggerWords(..) that includes skipShortWords(..). The manual composition equivalent is skipShortWords(unique(words(text))), so let's do that with compose(..):

```js
var text = "To compose two functions together, pass the \
output of the first function call as the input of the \
second function call.";

var biggerWords = compose( skipShortWords, unique, words );

var wordsUsed = biggerWords( text );

wordsUsed;
// ["compose","functions","together","output","first",
// "function","input","second"]
```

To do something more interesting with composition, let's use `partialRight(..)`, which we first looked at in Chapter 3. We can build a right-partial application of `compose(..)` itself, pre-specifying the second and third arguments (`unique(..)` and `words(..)`, respectively); we'll call it `filterWords(..)`.

Then, we can complete the composition multiple times by calling `filterWords(..)`, but with different first-arguments respectively:

```js
// Note: uses a `<= 4` check instead of the `> 4` check
// that `skipShortWords(..)` uses
function skipLongWords(list) { /* .. */ }

var filterWords = partialRight( compose, unique, words );

var biggerWords = filterWords( skipShortWords );
var shorterWords = filterWords( skipLongWords );

biggerWords( text );
// ["compose","functions","together","output","first",
// "function","input","second"]

shorterWords( text );
// ["to","two","pass","the","of","call","as"]
```

Take a moment to consider what the right-partial application on `compose(..)` gives us. It allows us to specify ahead of time the first step(s) of a composition, and then create specialized variations of that composition with different subsequent steps (`biggerWords(..)` and `shorterWords(..)`). This is one of the most powerful tricks of FP!

You can also `curry(..)` a composition instead of partial application, though because of right-to-left ordering, you might more often want to `curry( reverseArgs(compose), ..)` rather than just `curry( compose, ..)` itself.

 Note

Because `curry(..)` (at least the way we implemented it in Chapter 3) relies on either detecting the arity (`length`) or having it manually specified, and `compose(..)` is a variadic function, you'll need to manually specify the intended arity like `curry(.. , 3)`.

Alternative Implementations

While you may very well never implement your own `compose(..)` to use in production, and rather just use a library's implementation as provided, I've found that understanding how it works under the covers actually helps solidify general FP concepts very well.

So let's examine some different implementation options for `compose(..)`. We'll also see there are some pros/cons to each implementation, especially performance.

We'll be looking at the `reduce(..)` utility in detail in Chapter 9, but for now, just know that it reduces a list (array) to a single finite value. It's like a fancy loop.

For example, if you did an addition-reduction across a list of numbers (such as `[1,2,3,4,5,6]`), you'd loop over them adding them together as you go. The reduction would add `1` to `2`, and add that result to `3`, and then add that result to `4`, and so on, resulting in the final summation: `21`.

The original version of `compose(..)` uses a loop and eagerly (aka, immediately) calculates the result of one call to pass into the next call. This is a reduction of a list of functions, so we can do that same thing with `reduce(..)`:

```
function compose(...fns) {
    return function composed(result){
        return [...fns].reverse().reduce( function reducer(result,fn){
            return fn( result );
        }, result );
    };
}

// or the ES6 => form
var compose = (...fns) =>
    result =>
        [...fns].reverse().reduce(
            (result,fn) =>
                fn( result )
            , result
        );
```

Note

This implementation of `compose(..)` uses `[...fns].reverse().reduce(..)` to reduce from right-to-left. We'll revisit `compose(..)` in Chapter 9, instead using `reduceRight(..)` for that purpose.

Notice that the `reduce(..)` looping happens each time the final `composed(..)` function is run, and that each intermediate `result(..)` is passed along to the next iteration as the input to the next call.

The advantage of this implementation is that the code is more concise and also that it uses a well-known FP construct: `reduce(..)`. And the performance of this implementation is also similar to the original `for`-loop version.

However, this implementation is limited in that the outer composed function (aka, the first function in the composition) can only receive a single argument. Most other implementations pass along all arguments to that first call. If every function in the composition is unary, this is no big deal. But if you need to pass multiple arguments to that first call, you'd want a different implementation.

To fix that first call single-argument limitation, we can still use `reduce(..)` but produce a lazy-evaluation function wrapping:

```
function compose(...fns) {
    return fns.reverse().reduce( function reducer(fn1,fn2){
        return function composed(...args){
            return fn2( fn1( ...args ) );
        };
    } );
}

// or the ES6 => form
var compose =
    (...fns) =>
        fns.reverse().reduce( (fn1,fn2) =>
            (...args) =>
                fn2( fn1( ...args ) )
        );
```

Notice that we return the result of the `reduce(..)` call directly, which is itself a function, not a computed result. *That* function lets us pass in as many arguments as we want, passing them all down the line to the first function call in the composition, then bubbling up each result through each subsequent call.

Instead of calculating the running result and passing it along as the `reduce(..)` looping proceeds, this implementation runs the `reduce(..)` looping **once** up front at composition time, and defers all the function call calculations – referred to as lazy calculation. Each partial result of the reduction is a successively more wrapped function.

When you call the final composed function and provide one or more arguments, all the levels of the big nested function, from the inner most call to the outer, are executed in reverse succession (not via a loop).

The performance characteristics will potentially be different than in the previous `reduce(..)`-based implementation. Here, `reduce(..)` only runs once to produce a big composed function, and then this composed function call simply executes all its nested functions each call. In the former version, `reduce(..)` would be run for every call.

Your mileage may vary on which implementation is better, but keep in mind that this latter implementation isn't limited in argument count the way the former one is.

We could also define `compose(..)` using recursion. The recursive definition for `compose(fn1,fn2, .. fnN)` would look like:

`compose( compose(fn1,fn2, .. fnN-1), fnN );`

> **Note**
>
> We will cover recursion more fully in Chapter 8, so if this approach seems confusing, don't worry for now. Or, go read that chapter then come back and re-read this note. :)

Here's how we implement `compose(..)` with recursion:

```
function compose(...fns) {
    // pull off the last two arguments
    var [ fn1, fn2, ...rest ] = fns.reverse();

    var composedFn = function composed(...args){
        return fn2( fn1( ...args ) );
    };

    if (rest.length == 0) return composedFn;

    return compose( ...rest.reverse(), composedFn );
}

// or the ES6 => form
var compose =
    (...fns) => {
        // pull off the last two arguments
        var [ fn1, fn2, ...rest ] = fns.reverse();
```

```
        var composedFn =
            (...args) =>
                fn2( fn1( ...args ) );

        if (rest.length == 0) return composedFn;

        return compose( ...rest.reverse(), composedFn );
    };
```

I think the benefit of a recursive implementation is mostly conceptual. I personally find it much easier to think about a repetitive action in recursive terms instead of in a loop where I have to track the running result, so I prefer the code to express it that way.

Others will find the recursive approach quite a bit more daunting to mentally juggle. I invite you to make your own evaluations.

Reordered Composition

We talked earlier about the right-to-left ordering of standard `compose(..)` implementations. The advantage is in listing the arguments (functions) in the same order they'd appear if doing the composition manually.

The disadvantage is they're listed in the reverse order that they execute, which could be confusing. It was also more awkward to have to use `partialRight(compose, ..)` to pre-specify the *first* function(s) to execute in the composition.

The reverse ordering, composing from left-to-right, has a common name: `pipe(..)`. This name is said to come from Unix/Linux land, where multiple programs are strung together by "pipe"ing (`|` operator) the output of the first one in as the input of the second, and so on (i.e., `ls -la | grep "foo" | less`).

`pipe(..)` is identical to `compose(..)` except it processes through the list of functions in left-to-right order:

```
function pipe(...fns) {
    return function piped(result){
        var list = [...fns];

        while (list.length > 0) {
            // take the first function from the list
            // and execute it
            result = list.shift()( result );
        }

        return result;
    };
}
```

In fact, we could just define `pipe(..)` as the arguments-reversal of `compose(..)`:

```
var pipe = reverseArgs( compose );
```

That was easy!

Recall this example from general composition earlier:

```
var biggerWords = compose( skipShortWords, unique, words );
```

To express that with `pipe(..)`, we just reverse the order we list them in:

```
var biggerWords = pipe( words, unique, skipShortWords );
```

The advantage of `pipe(..)` is that it lists the functions in order of execution, which can sometimes reduce reader confusion. It may be simpler to read the code: `pipe( words, unique, skipShortWords )`, and recognize that it's executing `words(..)` first, then `unique(..)`, and finally `skipShortWords(..)`.

`pipe(..)` is also handy if you're in a situation where you want to partially apply the *first* function(s) that execute. Earlier we did that with right-partial application of `compose(..)`.

Compare:

```
var filterWords = partialRight( compose, unique, words );

// vs

var filterWords = partial( pipe, words, unique );
```

As you may recall from our first implementation of `partialRight(..)` in Chapter 3, it uses `reverseArgs(..)` under the covers, just as our `pipe(..)` now does. So we get the same result either way.

In this specific case, the slight performance advantage to using `pipe(..)` is, because we're not trying to preserve the right-to-left argument order of `compose(..)`, we don't need to reverse the argument order back, like we do inside `partialRight(..)`. So `partial(pipe, ..)` is a little more efficient here than `partialRight(compose, ..)`.

Abstraction

Abstraction plays heavily into our reasoning about composition, so let's examine it in more detail.

Similar to how partial application and currying (see Chapter 3) allow a progression from generalized to specialized functions, we can abstract by pulling out the generality between two or more tasks. The general part is defined once, so as to avoid repetition. To perform each task's specialization, the general part is parameterized.

For example, consider this (obviously contrived) code:

```
function saveComment(txt) {
    if (txt != "") {
        comments[comments.length] = txt;
    }
}

function trackEvent(evt) {
    if (evt.name !== undefined) {
        events[evt.name] = evt;
    }
}
```

Both of these utilities are storing a value in a data source. That's the generality. The specialty is that one of them sticks the value at the end of an array, while the other sets the value at a property name of an object.

So let's abstract:

```
function storeData(store,location,value) {
    store[location] = value;
}

function saveComment(txt) {
    if (txt != "") {
        storeData( comments, comments.length, txt );
    }
}

function trackEvent(evt) {
    if (evt.name !== undefined) {
        storeData( events, evt.name, evt );
    }
}
```

The general task of referencing a property on an object (or array, thanks to JS's convenient operator overloading of `[ ]`) and setting its value is abstracted into its own function `storeData(..)`. While this utility only has a single line of code right now, one could envision other general behavior that was common across both tasks, such as generating a unique numeric ID or storing a timestamp with the value.

If we repeat the common general behavior in multiple places, we run the maintenance risk of changing some instances but forgetting to change others. There's a principle at play in this kind of abstraction, often referred to as "don't repeat yourself" (DRY).

DRY strives to have only one definition in a program for any given task. An alternative aphorism to motivate DRY coding is that programmers are just generally lazy and don't want to do unnecessary work.

Abstraction can be taken too far. Consider:

```
function conditionallyStoreData(store,location,value,checkFn) {
    if (checkFn( value, store, location )) {
        store[location] = value;
    }
}

function notEmpty(val) { return val != ""; }

function isUndefined(val) { return val === undefined; }

function isPropUndefined(val,obj,prop) {
    return isUndefined( obj[prop] );
}

function saveComment(txt) {
    conditionallyStoreData( comments, comments.length, txt, notEmpty );
}

function trackEvent(evt) {
    conditionallyStoreData( events, evt.name, evt, isPropUndefined );
}
```

In an effort to be DRY and avoid repeating an `if` statement, we moved the conditional into the general abstraction. We also assumed that we *may* have checks for non-empty strings or non-undefined values elsewhere in the program in the future, so we might as well DRY those out, too!

This code *is* more DRY, but to an overkill extent. Programmers must be careful to apply the appropriate levels of abstraction to each part of their program, no more, no less.

Regarding our greater discussion of function composition in this chapter, it might seem like its benefit is this kind of DRY abstraction. But let's not jump to that conclusion, because I think composition actually serves a more important purpose in our code.

Moreover, **composition is helpful even if there's only one occurrence of something** (no repetition to DRY out).

Separation Enables Focus

Aside from generalization vs. specialization, I think there's another more useful definition for abstraction, as revealed by this quote:

> ... abstraction is a process by which the programmer associates a name with a potentially complicated program fragment, which can then be thought of in terms of its purpose of function, rather than in terms of how that function is achieved. By hiding irrelevant details, abstraction reduces conceptual complexity, making it possible for the programmer to focus on a manageable subset of the program text at any particular time.
>
> ---
>
> Michael L. Scott, Programming Language Pragmatics[22]

The point this quote makes is that abstraction – generally, pulling out some piece of code into its own function – serves the primary purpose of separating apart two pieces of functionality so that it's possible to focus on each piece independently of the other.

---

[22]Scott, Michael L. "Chapter 3: Names, Scopes, and Bindings." Programming Language Pragmatics, 4th ed., Morgan Kaufmann, 2015, pp. 115.

Note that abstraction in this sense is not really intended to *hide* details, as if to treat things as black boxes we *never* examine.

In this quote, "irrelevant", in terms of what is hidden, shouldn't be thought of as an absolute qualitative judgement, but rather relative to what you want to focus on at any given moment. In other words, when we separate X from Y, if I want to focus on X, Y is irrelevant at that moment. At another time, if I want to focus on Y, X is irrelevant at that moment.

We're not abstracting to hide details; we're separating details to improve focus.

Recall that at the outset of this book I stated that FP's goal is to create code that is more readable and understandable. One effective way of doing that is untangling complected (read: tightly braided, as in strands of rope) code into separate, simpler (read: loosely bound) pieces of code. In that way, the reader isn't distracted by the details of one part while looking for the details of the other part.

Our higher goal is not to implement something only once, as it is with the DRY mindset. As a matter of fact, sometimes we'll actually repeat ourselves in code.

As we asserted in Chapter 3, the main goal with abstraction is to implement separate things, separately. We're trying to improve focus, because that improves readability.

By separating two ideas, we insert a semantic boundary between them, which affords us the ability to focus on each side independent of the other. In many cases, that semantic boundary is something like the name of a function. The function's implementation is focused on *how* to compute something, and the call-site using that function by name is focused on *what* to do with its output. We abstract the *how* from the *what* so they are separate and separately reason'able.

Another way of describing this goal is with imperative vs. declarative programming style. Imperative code is primarily concerned with explicitly stating *how* to accomplish a task. Declarative code states *what* the outcome should be, and leaves the implementation to some other responsibility.

Declarative code abstracts the *what* from the *how*. Typically declarative coding is favored in readability over imperative, though no program (except of course machine code 1s and 0s) is ever entirely one or the other. The programmer must seek balance between them.

ES6 added many syntactic affordances that transform old imperative operations into newer declarative forms. Perhaps one of the clearest is destructuring. Destructuring is a pattern for assignment that describes how a compound value (object, array) is taken apart into its constituent values.

Here's an example of array destructuring:

```
function getData() {
    return [1,2,3,4,5];
}

// imperative
var tmp = getData();
var a = tmp[0];
var b = tmp[3];

// declarative
var [ a ,,, b ] = getData();
```

The *what* is assigning the first value of the array to a and the fourth value to b. The *how* is getting a reference to the array (tmp) and manually referencing indexes 0 and 3 in assignments to a and b, respectively.

Does the array destructuring *hide* the assignment? Depends on your perspective. I'm asserting that it simply separates the *what* from the *how*. The JS engine still does the assignments, but it prevents you from having to be distracted by *how* it's done.

Instead, you read [a ,,, b] = .. and can see the assignment pattern merely telling you *what* will happen. Array destructuring is an example of declarative abstraction.

Composition as Abstraction

What's all this have to do with function composition? Function composition is also declarative abstraction.

Recall the shorterWords(..) example from earlier. Let's compare an imperative and declarative definition for it:

```
// imperative
function shorterWords(text) {
    return skipLongWords( unique( words( text ) ) );
}
```

```
// declarative
var shorterWords = compose( skipLongWords, unique, words );
```

The declarative form focuses on the *what* – these three functions pipe data from a string to a list of shorter words – and leaves the *how* to the internals of `compose(..)`.

In a bigger sense, the `shorterWords = compose(..)` line explains the *how* for defining a `shorterWords(..)` utility, leaving this declarative line somewhere else in the code to focus only on the *what*:

```
shorterWords( text );
```

Composition abstracts getting a list of shorter words from the steps it takes to do that.

By contrast, what if we hadn't used composition abstraction?

```
var wordsFound = words( text );
var uniqueWordsFound = unique( wordsFound );
skipLongWords( uniqueWordsFound );
```

Or even:

```
skipLongWords( unique( words( text ) ) );
```

Either of these two versions demonstrates a more imperative style as opposed to the prior declarative style. The reader's focus in those two snippets is inextricably tied to the *how* and less on the *what*.

Function composition isn't just about saving code with DRY. Even if the usage of `shorterWords(..)` only occurs in one place – so there's no repetition to avoid! – separating the *how* from the *what* still improves our code.

Composition is a powerful tool for abstraction that transforms imperative code into more readable declarative code.

Revisiting Points

Now that we've thoroughly covered composition (a trick that will be immensely helpful in many areas of FP), let's watch it in action by revisiting point-free style from Chapter 3, "No Points" with a scenario that's a fair bit more complex to refactor:

```
// given: ajax( url, data, cb )

var getPerson = partial( ajax, "http://some.api/person" );
var getLastOrder = partial( ajax, "http://some.api/order", { id: -1 } );

getLastOrder( function orderFound(order){
    getPerson( { id: order.personId }, function personFound(person){
        output( person.name );
    } );
} );
```

The "points" we'd like to remove are the `order` and `person` parameter references.

Let's start by trying to get the `person` "point" out of the `personFound(..)` function. To do so, let's first define:

```
function extractName(person) {
    return person.name;
}
```

Consider that this operation could instead be expressed in generic terms: extracting any property by name off of any object. Let's call such a utility `prop(..)`:

```
function prop(name,obj) {
    return obj[name];
}

// or the ES6 => form
var prop =
    (name,obj) =>
        obj[name];
```

While we're dealing with object properties, let's also define the opposite utility: setProp(..) for setting a property value onto an object.

However, we want to be careful not to just mutate an existing object but rather create a clone of the object to make the change to, and then return it. The reasons for such care will be discussed at length in Chapter 5.

```
function setProp(name,obj,val) {
    var o = Object.assign( {}, obj );
    o[name] = val;
    return o;
}
```

Now, to define an extractName(..) that pulls a "name" property off an object, we'll partially apply prop(..):

```
var extractName = partial( prop, "name" );
```

 Note

Don't miss that extractName(..) here hasn't actually extracted anything yet. We partially applied prop(..) to make a function that's waiting to extract the "name" property from whatever object we pass into it. We could also have done it with curry(prop)("name").

Next, let's narrow the focus on our example's nested lookup calls to this:

```
getLastOrder( function orderFound(order){
    getPerson( { id: order.personId }, outputPersonName );
} );
```

How can we define `outputPersonName(..)`? To visualize what we need, think about the desired flow of data:

```
output <-- extractName <-- person
```

`outputPersonName(..)` needs to be a function that takes an (object) value, passes it into `extractName(..)`, then passes that value to `output(..)`.

Hopefully you recognized that as a `compose(..)` operation. So we can define `outputPersonName(..)` as:

```
var outputPersonName = compose( output, extractName );
```

The `outputPersonName(..)` function we just created is the callback provided to `getPerson(..)`. So we can define a function called `processPerson(..)` that presets the callback argument, using `partialRight(..)`:

```
var processPerson = partialRight( getPerson, outputPersonName );
```

Let's reconstruct the nested lookups example again with our new function:

```
getLastOrder( function orderFound(order){
    processPerson( { id: order.personId } );
} );
```

Phew, we're making good progress!

But we need to keep going and remove the `order` "point". The next step is to observe that `personId` can be extracted from an object (like `order`) via `prop(..)`, just like we did with `name` on the `person` object:

```
var extractPersonId = partial( prop, "personId" );
```

To construct the object (of the form `{ id: .. }`) that needs to be passed to `processPerson(..)`, let's make another utility for wrapping a value in an object at a specified property name, called `makeObjProp(..)`:

```
function makeObjProp(name,value) {
    return setProp( name, {}, value );
}

// or the ES6 => form
var makeObjProp =
    (name,value) =>
        setProp( name, {}, value );
```

> **Tip**
> This utility is known as `objOf(..)` in the Ramda library.

Just as we did with `prop(..)` to make `extractName(..)`, we'll partially apply `makeObjProp(..)` to build a function `personData(..)` that makes our data object:

```
var personData = partial( makeObjProp, "id" );
```

To use `processPerson(..)` to perform the lookup of a person attached to an order value, the conceptual flow of data through operations we need is:

```
processPerson <-- personData <-- extractPersonId <-- order
```

So we'll just use `compose(..)` again to define a `lookupPerson(..)` utility:

```
var lookupPerson =
    compose( processPerson, personData, extractPersonId );
```

And... that's it! Putting the whole example back together without any "points":

```
var getPerson = partial( ajax, "http://some.api/person" );
var getLastOrder =
    partial( ajax, "http://some.api/order", { id: -1 } );
var extractName = partial( prop, "name" );
var outputPersonName = compose( output, extractName );
var processPerson = partialRight( getPerson, outputPersonName );
var personData = partial( makeObjProp, "id" );
var extractPersonId = partial( prop, "personId" );
var lookupPerson =
    compose( processPerson, personData, extractPersonId );

getLastOrder( lookupPerson );
```

Wow. Point-free. And compose(..) turned out to be really helpful in two places!

I think in this case, even though the steps to derive our final answer were a bit drawn out, the end result is much more readable code, because we've ended up explicitly calling out each step.

And even if you didn't like seeing/naming all those intermediate steps, you can preserve point-free but wire the expressions together without individual variables:

```
partial( ajax, "http://some.api/order", { id: -1 } )
(
    compose(
        partialRight(
            partial( ajax, "http://some.api/person" ),
            compose( output, partial( prop, "name" ) )
        ),
        partial( makeObjProp, "id" ),
        partial( prop, "personId" )
    )
);
```

This snippet is less verbose for sure, but I think it's less readable than the previous snippet where each operation is its own variable. Either way, composition helped us with our point-free style.

Summary

Function composition is a pattern for defining a function that routes the output of one function call into another function call, and its output to another, and so on.

Because JS functions can only return single values, the pattern essentially dictates that all functions in the composition (except perhaps the first called) need to be unary, taking only a single input from the output of the previous function.

Instead of listing out each step as a discrete call in our code, function composition using a utility like `compose(..)` or `pipe(..)` abstracts that implementation detail so the code is more readable, allowing us to focus on *what* the composition will be used to accomplish, not *how* it will be performed.

Composition is declarative data flow, meaning our code describes the flow of data in an explicit, obvious, and readable way.

In many ways, composition is the most important foundational pattern, in large part because it's the only way to route data through our programs aside from using side effects; the next chapter explores why such should be avoided wherever possible.

Chapter 5: Reducing Side Effects

In Chapter 2, we discussed how a function can have outputs besides its `return` value. By now you should be very comfortable with the FP definition of a function, so the idea of such side outputs – side effects! – should smell.

We're going to examine the various different forms of side effects and see why they are harmful to our code's quality and readability.

But let me not bury the lede here. The punchline to this chapter: it's impossible to write a program with no side effects. Well, not impossible; you certainly can. But that program won't do anything useful or observable. If you wrote a program with zero side effects, you wouldn't be able to tell the difference between it and an empty program.

The FPer doesn't eliminate all side effects. Rather, the goal is to limit them as much as possible. To do that, we first need to fully understand them.

Effects on the Side, Please

Cause and effect: one of the most fundamental, intuitive observations we humans can make about the world around us. Push a book off the edge of a table, it falls to the ground. You don't need a physics degree to know that the cause was you pushing the book and the effect was gravity pulling it to the ground. There's a clear and direct relationship.

In programming, we also deal entirely in cause and effect. If you call a function (cause), it displays a message on the screen (effect).

When reading a program, it's supremely important that the reader be able to clearly identify each cause and each effect. To any extent where a direct relationship between cause and effect cannot be seen readily upon a read-through of the program, that program's readability is degraded.

Consider:

```
function foo(x) {
    return x * 2;
}

var y = foo( 3 );
```

In this trivial program, it is immediately clear that calling foo (the cause) with value 3 will have the effect of returning the value 6 that is then assigned to y (the effect). There's no ambiguity here.

But now:

```
function foo(x) {
    y = x * 2;
}

var y;

foo( 3 );
```

This program has the exact same outcome. But there's a very big difference. The cause and the effect are disjoint. The effect is indirect. The setting of y in this way is what we call a side effect.

Note
When a function makes a reference to a variable outside itself, this is called a free variable. Not all free variable references will be bad, but we'll want to be very careful with them.

What if I gave you a reference to call a function bar(..) that you cannot see the code for, but I told you that it had no such indirect side effects, only an explicit return value effect?

```
bar( 4 );          // 42
```

Because you know that the internals of `bar(..)` do not create any side effects, you can now reason about any `bar(..)` call like this one in a much more straightforward way. But if you didn't know that `bar(..)` had no side effects, to understand the outcome of calling it, you'd have to go read and dissect all of its logic. This is extra mental tax burden for the reader.

The readability of a side effecting function is worse because it requires more reading to understand the program.

But the problem goes deeper than that. Consider:

```
var x = 1;

foo();

console.log( x );

bar();

console.log( x );

baz();

console.log( x );
```

How sure are you which values are going to be printed at each `console.log(x)`?

The correct answer is: not at all. If you're not sure whether `foo()`, `bar()`, and `baz()` are side-effecting or not, you cannot guarantee what x will be at each step unless you inspect the implementations of each, **and** then trace the program from line 1 forward, keeping track of all the changes in state as you go.

In other words, the final `console.log(x)` is impossible to analyze or predict unless you've mentally executed the whole program up to that point.

Guess who's good at running your program? The JS engine. Guess who's not as good at running your program? The reader of your code. And yet, your choice to write code (potentially) with side effects in one or more of those function calls means that you've burdened the reader with having to mentally execute your program in its entirety up to a certain line, for them to read and understand that line.

If `foo()`, `bar()`, and `baz()` were all free of side effects, they could not affect x, which means we do not need to execute them to mentally trace what happens with x. This is less mental tax, and makes the code more readable.

Hidden Causes

Outputs, changes in state, are the most commonly cited manifestation of side effects. But another readability-harming practice is what some refer to as side causes. Consider:

```
function foo(x) {
    return x + y;
}

var y = 3;

foo( 1 );           // 4
```

y is not changed by `foo(..)`, so it's not the same kind of side effect as we saw before. But now, the calling of `foo(..)` actually depends on the presence and current state of a y. If later, we do:

```
y = 5;

// ..

foo( 1 );           // 6
```

Might we be surprised that the call to `foo(1)` returned different results from call to call?

`foo(..)` has an indirection of cause that is harmful to readability. The reader cannot see, without inspecting `foo(..)`'s implementation carefully, what causes are contributing to the output effect. It *looks* like the argument 1 is the only cause, but it turns out it's not.

To aid readability, all of the causes that will contribute to determining the effect output of foo(..) should be made as direct and obvious inputs to foo(..). The reader of the code will clearly see the cause(s) and effect.

Fixed State

Does avoiding side causes mean the foo(..) function cannot reference any free variables?

Consider this code:

```
function foo(x) {
    return x + bar( x );
}

function bar(x) {
    return x * 2;
}

foo( 3 );            // 9
```

It's clear that for both foo(..) and bar(..), the only direct cause is the x parameter. But what about the bar(x) call? bar is just an identifier, and in JS it's not even a constant (aka, non-reassignable variable) by default. The foo(..) function is relying on the value of bar – a variable that references the second function – as a free variable.

So is this program relying on a side cause?

I say no. Even though it is *possible* to overwrite the bar variable's value with some other function, I am not doing so in this code, nor is it a common practice of mine or precedent to do so. For all intents and purposes, my functions are constants (never reassigned).

Consider:

```
const PI = 3.141592;

function foo(x) {
    return x * PI;
}

foo( 3 );              // 9.424776000000001
```

> **Note**
>
> JavaScript has `Math.PI` built-in, so we're only using the `PI` example in this text as a convenient illustration. In practice, always use `Math.PI` instead of defining your own!

How about the preceding code snippet? Is `PI` a side cause of `foo(..)`?

Two observations will help us answer that question in a reasonable way:

1. Think about every call you might ever make to `foo(3)`. Will it always return that `9.424..` value? **Yes.** Every single time. If you give it the same input (`x`), it will always return the same output.
2. Could you replace every usage of `PI` with its immediate value, and could the program run **exactly** the same as it did before? **Yes.** There's no part of this program that relies on being able to change the value of `PI` -- indeed since it's a `const`, it cannot be reassigned -- so the `PI` variable here is only for readability/maintenance sake. Its value can be inlined without any change in program behavior.

My conclusion: `PI` here is not a violation of the spirit of minimizing/avoiding side effects (or causes). Nor is the `bar(x)` call in the previous snippet.

In both cases, `PI` and `bar` are not part of the state of the program. They're fixed, non-reassigned references. If they don't change throughout the program, we don't have to worry about tracking them as changing state. As such, they don't harm our readability. And they cannot be the source of bugs related to variables changing in unexpected ways.

Note

The use of const here does not, in my opinion, make the case that PI is absolved as a side cause; var PI would lead to the same conclusion. The lack of reassigning PI is what matters, not the inability to do so. We'll discuss const in Chapter 6.

Randomness

You may never have considered it before, but randomness is a side cause. A function that uses Math.random() cannot have predictable output based on its input. So any code that generates unique random IDs/etc. will by definition be considered reliant on the program's side causes.

In computing, we use what's called pseudo-random algorithms for generation. Turns out true randomness is pretty hard, so we just kinda fake it with complex algorithms that produce values that seem observably random. These algorithms calculate long streams of numbers, but the secret is, the sequence is actually predictable if you know the starting point. This starting point is referred to as a seed.

Some languages let you specify the seed value for the random number generation. If you always specify the same seed, you'll always get the same sequence of outputs from subsequent "pseudo-random number" generations. This is incredibly useful for testing purposes, for example, but incredibly dangerous for real-world application usage.

In JS, the randomness of Math.random() calculation is based on an indirect input, because you cannot specify the seed. As such, we have to treat built-in random number generation as a side cause.

I/O Effects

The most common (and essentially unavoidable) form of side cause/effect is input/output (I/O). A program with no I/O is totally pointless, because its work cannot be observed in any way. Useful programs must at a minimum have output, and many also need input. Input is a side cause and output is a side effect.

The typical input for the browser JS programmer is user events (mouse, keyboard), and for output is the DOM. If you work more in Node.js, you may more likely receive input from, and send output to, the file system, network connections, and/or the stdin/stdout streams.

As a matter of fact, these sources can be both input and output, both cause and effect. Take the DOM, for example. We update (side effect) a DOM element to show text or an image to the user, but the current state of the DOM is an implicit input (side cause) to those operations as well.

Side Bugs

The scenarios where side causes and side effects can lead to bugs are as varied as the programs in existence. But let's examine a scenario to illustrate these hazards, in hopes that they help us recognize similar mistakes in our own programs.

Consider:

```js
var users = {};
var userOrders = {};

function fetchUserData(userId) {
    ajax( `http://some.api/user/${userId}`, function onUserData(user){
        users[userId] = user;
    } );
}

function fetchOrders(userId) {
    ajax(
        `http://some.api/orders/${userId}`,
        function onOrders(orders){
            for (let order of orders) {
                // keep a reference to latest order for each user
                users[userId].latestOrder = order;
                userOrders[order.orderId] = order;
            }
        }
```

```
        );
}

function deleteOrder(orderId) {
    var user = users[ userOrders[orderId].userId ];
    var isLatestOrder = (userOrders[orderId] == user.latestOrder);

    // deleting the latest order for a user?
    if (isLatestOrder) {
        hideLatestOrderDisplay();
    }

    ajax(
        `http://some.api/delete/order/${orderId}`,
        function onDelete(success){
            if (success) {
                // deleted the latest order for a user?
                if (isLatestOrder) {
                    user.latestOrder = null;
                }

                userOrders[orderId] = null;
            }
            else if (isLatestOrder) {
                showLatestOrderDisplay();
            }
        }
    );
}
```

I bet for some readers one of the potential bugs here is fairly obvious. If the callback onOrders(..) runs before the onUserData(..) callback, it will attempt to add a latestOrder property to a value (the user object at users[userId]) that's not yet been set.

So one form of "bug" that can occur with logic that relies on side causes/effects is the race condition of two different operations (async or not!) that we expect to run in a certain order but under some cases may run in a different order. There are strategies for ensuring the order of operations, and it's fairly obvious that order is critical in that case.

Another more subtle bug can bite us here. Did you spot it?

Consider this order of calls:

```
fetchUserData( 123 );
onUserData(..);
fetchOrders( 123 );
onOrders(..);

// later

fetchOrders( 123 );
deleteOrder( 456 );
onOrders(..);
onDelete(..);
```

Do you see the interleaving of `fetchOrders(..)` and `onOrders(..)` with the `deleteOrder(..)` and `onDelete(..)` pair? That potential sequencing exposes a weird condition with our side causes/effects of state management.

There's a delay in time (because of the callback) between when we set the `isLatestOrder` flag and when we use it to decide if we should empty the `latestOrder` property of the user data object in `users`. During that delay, if `onOrders(..)` callback fires, it can potentially change which order value that user's `latestOrder` references. When `onDelete(..)` then fires, it will assume it still needs to unset the `latestOrder` reference.

The bug: the data (state) *might* now be out of sync. `latestOrder` will be unset, when potentially it should have stayed pointing at a newer order that came in to `onOrders(..)`.

The worst part of this kind of bug is that you don't get a program-crashing exception like we did with the other bug. We just simply have state that is incorrect; our application's behavior is "silently" broken.

The sequencing dependency between `fetchUserData(..)` and `fetchOrders(..)` is fairly obvious, and straightforwardly addressed. But the potential sequencing dependency between `fetchOrders(..)` and `deleteOrder(..)` is far less obvious. These two seem to be more independent. And ensuring that their order is preserved is more tricky, because you don't know in advance (before the results from `fetchOrders(..)`) whether that sequencing really must be enforced.

Yes, you can recompute the `isLatestOrder` flag once `deleteOrder(..)` fires. But now you have a different problem: your UI state can be out of sync.

If you had called the `hideLatestOrderDisplay()` previously, you'll now need to call the function `showLatestOrderDisplay()`, but only if a new `latestOrder` has in fact been set. So you'll need to track at least three states: was the deleted order the "latest" originally, and is the "latest" set, and are those two orders different? These are solvable problems, of course. But they're not obvious by any means.

All of these hassles are because we decided to structure our code with side causes/-effects on a shared set of state.

Functional programmers detest these sorts of side cause/effect bugs because of how much it hurts our ability to read, reason about, validate, and ultimately **trust** the code. That's why they take the principle to avoid side causes/effects so seriously.

There are multiple different strategies for avoiding/fixing side causes/effects. We'll talk about some later in this chapter, and others in later chapters. I'll say one thing for certain: **writing with side causes/effects is often of our normal default** so avoiding them is going to require careful and intentional effort.

Once Is Enough, Thanks

If you must make side effect changes to state, one class of operations that's useful for limiting the potential trouble is idempotence. If your update of a value is idempotent, then data will be resilient to the case where you might have multiple such updates from different side effect sources.

If you try to research it, the definition of idempotence can be a little confusing; mathematicians use a slightly different meaning than programmers typically do. However, both perspectives are useful for the functional programmer.

First, let's give a counter example that is neither mathematically nor programmingly idempotent:

```
function updateCounter(obj) {
    if (obj.count < 10) {
        obj.count++;
        return true;
    }

    return false;
}
```

This function mutates an object via reference by incrementing `obj.count`, so it produces a side effect on that object. If `updateCounter(o)` is called multiple times – while `o.count` is less than `10`, that is – the program state changes each time. Also, the output of `updateCounter(..)` is a Boolean, which is not suitable to feed back into a subsequent call of `updateCounter(..)`.

Mathematical Idempotence

From the mathematical point of view, idempotence means an operation whose output won't ever change after the first call, if you feed that output back into the operation over and over again. In other words, `foo(x)` would produce the same output as `foo(foo(x))` and `foo(foo(foo(x)))`.

A typical mathematical example is `Math.abs(..)` (absolute value). `Math.abs(-2)` is `2`, which is the same result as `Math.abs(Math.abs(Math.abs(Math.abs(-2))))`. Other idempotent mathematical utilities include:

- `Math.min(..)`
- `Math.max(..)`
- `Math.round(..)`
- `Math.floor(..)`
- `Math.ceil(..)`

Some custom mathematical operations we could define with this same characteristic:

```
function toPower0(x) {
    return Math.pow( x, 0 );
}

function snapUp3(x) {
    return x - (x % 3) + (x % 3 > 0 && 3);
}

toPower0( 3 ) == toPower0( toPower0( 3 ) );              // true

snapUp3( 3.14 ) == snapUp3( snapUp3( 3.14 ) );           // true
```

Mathematical-style idempotence is **not** restricted to mathematical operations. Another place we can illustrate this form of idempotence is with JavaScript primitive type coercions:

```
var x = 42, y = "hello";

String( x ) === String( String( x ) );                   // true

Boolean( y ) === Boolean( Boolean( y ) );                // true
```

Earlier in the text, we explored a common FP tool that fulfills this form of idempotence:

```
identity( 3 ) === identity( identity( 3 ) );    // true
```

Certain string operations are also naturally idempotent, such as:

```
function upper(x) {
    return x.toUpperCase();
}

function lower(x) {
    return x.toLowerCase();
}

var str = "Hello World";

upper( str ) == upper( upper( str ) );            // true

lower( str ) == lower( lower( str ) );            // true
```

We can even design more sophisticated string formatting operations in an idempotent way, such as:

```
function currency(val) {
    var num = parseFloat(
        String( val ).replace( /[^\d.-]+/g, "" )
    );
    var sign = (num < 0) ? "-" : "";
    return `${sign}$${Math.abs( num ).toFixed( 2 )}`;
}

currency( -3.1 );                                       // "-$3.10"

currency( -3.1 ) == currency( currency( -3.1 ) );   // true
```

`currency(..)` illustrates an important technique: in some cases the developer can take extra steps to normalize an input/output operation to ensure the operation is idempotent where it normally wouldn't be.

Wherever possible, restricting side effects to idempotent operations is much better than unrestricted updates.

Programming Idempotence

The programming-oriented definition for idempotence is similar, but less formal. Instead of requiring `f(x) === f(f(x))`, this view of idempotence is just that `f(x);` results in the same program behavior as `f(x); f(x);`. In other words, the result of calling `f(x)` subsequent times after the first call doesn't change anything.

That perspective fits more with our observations about side effects, because it's more likely that such an `f(..)` operation creates an idempotent side effect rather than necessarily returning an idempotent output value.

This idempotence-style is often cited for HTTP operations (verbs) such as GET or PUT. If an HTTP REST API is properly following the specification guidance for idempotence, PUT is defined as an update operation that fully replaces a resource. As such, a client could either send a PUT request once or multiple times (with the same data), and the server would have the same resultant state regardless.

Thinking about this in more concrete terms with programming, let's examine some side effect operations for their idempotence (or lack thereof):

```
// idempotent:
obj.count = 2;
a[a.length - 1] = 42;
person.name = upper( person.name );

// non-idempotent:
obj.count++;
a[a.length] = 42;
person.lastUpdated = Date.now();
```

Remember: the notion of idempotence here is that each idempotent operation (like `obj.count = 2`) could be repeated multiple times and not change the program state beyond the first update. The non-idempotent operations change the state each time.

What about DOM updates?

```
var hist = document.getElementById( "orderHistory" );

// idempotent:
hist.innerHTML = order.historyText;

// non-idempotent:
var update = document.createTextNode( order.latestUpdate );
hist.appendChild( update );
```

The key difference illustrated here is that the idempotent update replaces the DOM element's content. The current state of the DOM element is irrelevant, because it's unconditionally overwritten. The non-idempotent operation adds content to the element; implicitly, the current state of the DOM element is part of computing the next state.

It won't always be possible to define your operations on data in an idempotent way, but if you can, it will definitely help reduce the chances that your side effects will crop up to break your expectations when you least expect it.

Pure Bliss

A function with no side causes/effects is called a pure function. A pure function is idempotent in the programming sense, because it cannot have any side effects. Consider:

```
function add(x,y) {
    return x + y;
}
```

All the inputs (x and y) and outputs (`return ..`) are direct; there are no free variable references. Calling `add(3,4)` multiple times would be indistinguishable from only calling it once. `add(..)` is pure and programming-style idempotent.

However, not all pure functions are idempotent in the mathematical sense, because they don't have to return a value that would be suitable for feeding back in as their own input. Consider:

```
function calculateAverage(nums) {
    var sum = 0;
    for (let num of nums) {
        sum += num;
    }
    return sum / nums.length;
}

calculateAverage( [1,2,4,7,11,16,22] );           // 9
```

The output 9 is not an array, so you cannot pass it back in: calculateAverage(calculateAverage(..)).

As we discussed earlier, a pure function *can* reference free variables, as long as those free variables aren't side causes.

Some examples:

```
const PI = 3.141592;

function circleArea(radius) {
    return PI * radius * radius;
}

function cylinderVolume(radius,height) {
    return height * circleArea( radius );
}
```

circleArea(..) references the free variable PI, but it's a constant so it's not a side cause. cylinderVolume(..) references the free variable circleArea, which is also not a side cause because this program treats it as, in effect, a constant reference to its function value. Both these functions are pure.

Another example where a function can still be pure but reference free variables is with closure:

```
function unary(fn) {
    return function onlyOneArg(arg){
        return fn( arg );
    };
}
```

`unary(..)` itself is clearly pure – its only input is `fn` and its only output is the returned function – but what about the inner function `onlyOneArg(..)`, which closes over the free variable `fn`?

It's still pure because `fn` never changes. In fact, we have full confidence in that fact because lexically speaking, those few lines are the only ones that could possibly reassign `fn`.

Note

`fn` is a reference to a function object, which is by default a mutable value. Somewhere else in the program *could*, for example, add a property to this function object, which technically "changes" the value (mutation, not reassignment). However, because we're not relying on anything about `fn` other than our ability to call it, and it's not possible to affect the callability of a function value, `fn` is still effectively unchanging for our reasoning purposes; it cannot be a side cause.

Another common way to articulate a function's purity is: **given the same input(s), it always produces the same output**. If you pass `3` to `circleArea(..)`, it will always output the same result (`28.274328`).

If a function *can* produce a different output each time it's given the same inputs, it is impure. Even if such a function always `returns` the same value, if it produces an indirect output side effect, the program state is changed each time it's called; this is impure.

Impure functions are undesirable because they make all of their calls harder to reason about. A pure function's call is perfectly predictable. When someone reading the code sees multiple `circleArea(3)` calls, they won't have to spend any extra effort to figure out what its output will be *each time*.

Note

An interesting thing to ponder: is the heat produced by the CPU while performing any given operation an unavoidable side effect of even the most pure functions/programs? What about just the CPU time delay as it spends time on a pure operation before it can do another one?

Purely Relative

We have to be very careful when talking about a function being pure. JavaScript's dynamic value nature makes it all too easy to have non-obvious side causes/effects.

Consider:

```
function rememberNumbers(nums) {
    return function caller(fn){
        return fn( nums );
    };
}

var list = [1,2,3,4,5];

var simpleList = rememberNumbers( list );
```

`simpleList(..)` looks like a pure function, as it's a reference to the inner function `caller(..)`, which just closes over the free variable `nums`. However, there's multiple ways that `simpleList(..)` can actually turn out to be impure.

First, our assertion of purity is based on the array value (referenced both by `list` and `nums`) never changing:

```
function median(nums) {
    return (nums[0] + nums[nums.length - 1]) / 2;
}

simpleList( median );        // 3

// ..

list.push( 6 );

// ..

simpleList( median );        // 3.5
```

When we mutate the array, the `simpleList(..)` call changes its output. So, is `simpleList(..)` pure or impure? Depends on your perspective. It's pure for a given set of assumptions. It could be pure in any program that didn't have the `list.push(6)` mutation.

We could guard against this kind of impurity by altering the definition of `rememberNumbers(..)`. One approach is to duplicate the `nums` array:

```
function rememberNumbers(nums) {
    // make a copy of the array
    nums = [...nums];

    return function caller(fn){
        return fn( nums );
    };
}
```

But an even trickier hidden side effect could be lurking:

```
var list = [1,2,3,4,5];

// make `list[0]` be a getter with a side effect
Object.defineProperty(
    list,
    0,
    {
        get: function(){
            console.log( "[0] was accessed!" );
            return 1;
        }
    }
);

var simpleList = rememberNumbers( list );
// [0] was accessed!
```

A perhaps more robust option is to change the signature of `rememberNumbers(..)` to not receive an array in the first place, but rather the numbers as individual arguments:

```
function rememberNumbers(...nums) {
    return function caller(fn){
        return fn( nums );
    };
}

var simpleList = rememberNumbers( ...list );
// [0] was accessed!
```

The two `...`s have the effect of copying `list` into `nums` instead of passing it by reference.

Note

The console message side effect here comes not from `rememberNumbers(..)` but from the `...list` spreading. So in this case, both `rememberNumbers(..)` and `simpleList(..)` are pure.

But what if the mutation is even harder to spot? Composition of a pure function with an impure function **always** produces an impure function. If we pass an impure function into the otherwise pure `simpleList(..)`, it's now impure:

```
// yes, a silly contrived example :)
function firstValue(nums) {
    return nums[0];
}

function lastValue(nums) {
    return firstValue( nums.reverse() );
}

simpleList( lastValue );    // 5

list;                       // [1,2,3,4,5] -- OK!

simpleList( lastValue );    // 1
```

Note

Despite `reverse()` looking safe (like other array methods in JS) in that it returns a reversed array, it actually mutates the array rather than creating a new one.

We need a more robust definition of `rememberNumbers(..)` to guard against the `fn(..)` mutating its closed over `nums` via reference:

```
function rememberNumbers(...nums) {
    return function caller(fn){
        // send in a copy!
        return fn( [...nums] );
    };
}
```

So is `simpleList(..)` reliably pure yet!? **Nope**. :(

We're only guarding against side effects we can control (mutating by reference). Any function we pass that has other side effects will have polluted the purity of `simpleList(..)`:

```
simpleList( function impureIO(nums){
    console.log( nums.length );
} );
```

In fact, there's no way to define `rememberNumbers(..)` to make a perfectly pure `simpleList(..)` function.

Purity is about confidence. But we have to admit that in many cases, **any confidence we feel is actually relative to the context** of our program and what we know about it. In practice (in JavaScript) the question of function purity is not about being absolutely pure or not, but about a range of confidence in its purity.

The more pure, the better. The more effort you put into making a function pure(r), the higher your confidence will be when you read code that uses it, and that will make that part of the code more readable.

There or Not

So far, we've defined function purity both as a function without side causes/effects and as a function that, given the same input(s), always produces the same output. These are just two different ways of looking at the same characteristics.

But a third way of looking at function purity, and perhaps the most widely accepted definition, is that a pure function has referential transparency.

Referential transparency is the assertion that a function call could be replaced by its output value, and the overall program behavior wouldn't change. In other words, it would be impossible to tell from the program's execution whether the function call was made or its return value was inlined in place of the function call.

From the perspective of referential transparency, both of these programs have identical behavior as they are built with pure functions:

```
function calculateAverage(nums) {
    var sum = 0;
    for (let num of nums) {
        sum += num;
    }
    return sum / nums.length;
}

var numbers = [1,2,4,7,11,16,22];

var avg = calculateAverage( numbers );

console.log( "The average is:", avg );      // The average is: 9


function calculateAverage(nums) {
    var sum = 0;
    for (let num of nums) {
        sum += num;
    }
    return sum / nums.length;
}

var numbers = [1,2,4,7,11,16,22];

var avg = 9;

console.log( "The average is:", avg );      // The average is: 9
```

The only difference between these two snippets is that in the latter one, we skipped the `calculateAverage(nums)` call and just inlined its output (9). Since the rest of the program behaves identically, `calculateAverage(..)` has referential transparency, and is thus a pure function.

Mentally Transparent

The notion that a referentially transparent pure function *can be* replaced with its output does not mean that it *should literally be* replaced. Far from it.

The reasons we build functions into our programs instead of using pre-computed magic constants are not just about responding to changing data, but also about readability with proper abstractions. The function call to calculate the average of that list of numbers makes that part of the program more readable than the line that just assigns the value explicitly. It tells the story to the reader of where avg comes from, what it means, and so on.

What we're really suggesting with referential transparency is that as you're reading a program, once you've mentally computed what a pure function call's output is, you no longer need to think about what that exact function call is doing when you see it in code, especially if it appears multiple times.

That result becomes kinda like a mental `const` declaration, which as you're reading you can transparently swap in and not spend any more mental energy working out.

Hopefully the importance of this characteristic of a pure function is obvious. We're trying to make our programs more readable. One way we can do that is to give the reader less work, by providing assistance to skip over the unnecessary stuff so they can focus on the important stuff.

The reader shouldn't need to keep re-computing some outcome that isn't going to change (and doesn't need to). If you define a pure function with referential transparency, the reader won't have to.

Not So Transparent?

What about a function that has a side effect, but this side effect isn't ever observed or relied upon anywhere else in the program? Does that function still have referential transparency?

Here's one:

```
function calculateAverage(nums) {
    sum = 0;
    for (let num of nums) {
        sum += num;
    }
    return sum / nums.length;
}

var sum;
var numbers = [1,2,4,7,11,16,22];

var avg = calculateAverage( numbers );
```

Did you spot it?

sum is an outer free variable that calculateAverage(..) uses to do its work. But, every time we call calculateAverage(..) with the same list, we're going to get 9 as the output. And this program couldn't be distinguished in terms of behavior from a program that replaced the calculateAverage(nums) call with the value 9. No other part of the program cares about the sum variable, so it's an unobserved side effect.

Is a side cause/effect that's unobserved like this tree:

If a tree falls in the forest, but no one is around to hear it, does it still make a sound?

By the narrowest definition of referential transparency, I think you'd have to say calculateAverage(..) is still a pure function. However, because we're trying to avoid a strictly academic approach in favor of balancing it with pragmatism, I also think this conclusion needs more perspective. Let's explore.

Performance Effects

You'll generally find these kind of side-effects-that-go-unobserved being used to optimize the performance of an operation. For example:

```
var cache = [];

function specialNumber(n) {
    // if we've already calculated this special number,
    // skip the work and just return it from the cache
    if (cache[n] !== undefined) {
        return cache[n];
    }

    var x = 1, y = 1;

    for (let i = 1; i <= n; i++) {
        x += i % 2;
        y += i % 3;
    }

    cache[n] = (x * y) / (n + 1);

    return cache[n];
}

specialNumber( 6 );                // 4
specialNumber( 42 );               // 22
specialNumber( 1E6 );              // 500001
specialNumber( 987654321 );        // 493827162
```

This silly `specialNumber(..)` algorithm is deterministic and thus pure from the definition that it always gives the same output for the same input. It's also pure from the referential transparency perspective – replace any call to `specialNumber(42)` with 22 and the end result of the program is the same.

However, the function has to do quite a bit of work to calculate some of the bigger numbers, especially the `987654321` input. If we needed to get that particular special number multiple times throughout our program, the `cache`ing of the result means that subsequent calls are far more efficient.

Don't be so quick to assume that you could just run the calculation `specialNumber(987654321)` once and manually stick that result in some variable/constant.

Programs are often highly modularized and globally accessible scopes are not usually the way you want to share state between those independent pieces. Having `specialNumber(..)` do its own caching (even though it happens to be using a global variable to do so!) is a more preferable abstraction of that state sharing.

The point is that if `specialNumber(..)` is the only part of the program that accesses and updates the `cache` side cause/effect, the referential transparency perspective observably holds true, and this might be seen as an acceptable pragmatic "cheat" of the pure function ideal.

But should it?

Typically, this sort of performance optimization side effecting is done by hiding the caching of results so they *cannot* be observed by any other part of the program. This process is referred to as memoization. I always think of that word as "memorization"; I have no idea if that's even remotely where it comes from, but it certainly helps me understand the concept better.

Consider:

```
var specialNumber = (function memoization(){
    var cache = [];

    return function specialNumber(n){
        // if we've already calculated this special number,
        // skip the work and just return it from the cache
        if (cache[n] !== undefined) {
            return cache[n];
        }

        var x = 1, y = 1;

        for (let i = 1; i <= n; i++) {
            x += i % 2;
            y += i % 3;
        }

        cache[n] = (x * y) / (n + 1);
```

```
        return cache[n];
    };
})();
```

We've contained the cache side causes/effects of `specialNumber(..)` inside the scope of the `memoization()` IIFE, so now we're sure that no other parts of the program *can* observe them, not just that they *don't* observe them.

That last sentence may seem like a subtle point, but actually I think it might be **the most important point of the entire chapter**. Read it again.

Recall this philosophical musing:

If a tree falls in the forest, but no one is around to hear it, does it still make a sound?

Going with the metaphor, what I'm getting at is: whether the sound is made or not, it would be better if we never create a scenario where the tree can fall without us being around; we'll always hear the sound when a tree falls.

The purpose of reducing side causes/effects is not per se to have a program where they aren't observed, but to design a program where fewer of them are possible, because this makes the code easier to reason about. A program with side causes/effects that *just happen* to not be observed is not nearly as effective in this goal as a program that *cannot* observe them.

If side causes/effects can happen, the writer and reader must mentally juggle them. Make it so they can't happen, and both writer and reader will find more confidence over what can and cannot happen in any part.

Purifying

The first best option in writing functions is that you design them from the beginning to be pure. But you'll spend plenty of time maintaining existing code, where those kinds of decisions were already made; you'll run across a lot of impure functions.

If possible, refactor the impure function to be pure. Sometimes you can just shift the side effects out of a function to the part of the program where the call of that function happens. The side effect wasn't eliminated, but it was made more obvious by showing up at the call-site.

Consider this trivial example:

```
function addMaxNum(arr) {
    var maxNum = Math.max( ...arr );
    arr.push( maxNum + 1 );
}

var nums = [4,2,7,3];

addMaxNum( nums );

nums;           // [4,2,7,3,8]
```

The nums array needs to be modified, but we don't have to obscure that side effect by containing it in addMaxNum(..). Let's move the push(..) mutation out, so that addMaxNum(..) becomes a pure function, and the side effect is now more obvious:

```
function addMaxNum(arr) {
    var maxNum = Math.max( ...arr );
    return maxNum + 1;
}

var nums = [4,2,7,3];

nums.push(
    addMaxNum( nums )
);

nums;           // [4,2,7,3,8]
```

 Note

Another technique for this kind of task could be to use an immutable data structure, which we cover in the next chapter.

But what can you do if you have an impure function where the refactoring is not as easy?

You need to figure what kind of side causes/effects the function has. It may be that the side causes/effects come variously from lexical free variables, mutations-by-reference, or even `this` binding. We'll look at approaches that address each of these scenarios.

Containing Effects

If the nature of the concerned side causes/effects is with lexical free variables, and you have the option to modify the surrounding code, you can encapsulate them using scope.

Recall:

```
var users = {};

function fetchUserData(userId) {
    ajax( `http://some.api/user/${userId}`, function onUserData(user){
        users[userId] = user;
    } );
}
```

One option for purifying this code is to create a wrapper around both the variable and the impure function. Essentially, the wrapper has to receive as input "the entire universe" of state it can operate on.

```
function safer_fetchUserData(userId,users) {
    // simple, naive ES6+ shallow object copy, could also
    // be done w/ various libs or frameworks
    users = Object.assign( {}, users );

    fetchUserData( userId );

    // return the copied state
    return users;


    // ************************

    // original untouched impure function:
    function fetchUserData(userId) {
        ajax(
            `http://some.api/user/${userId}`,
            function onUserData(user){
                users[userId] = user;
            }
        );
    }
}
```

 Warning

`safer_fetchUserData(..)` is *more* pure, but is not strictly pure in that it still relies on the I/O of making an Ajax call. There's no getting around the fact that an Ajax call is an impure side effect, so we'll just leave that detail unaddressed.

Both `userId` and `users` are input for the original `fetchUserData`, and `users` is also output. The `safer_fetchUserData(..)` takes both of these inputs, and returns `users`. To make sure we're not creating a side effect on the outside when `users` is mutated, we make a local copy of `users`.

This technique has limited usefulness mostly because if you cannot modify a function itself to be pure, you're not that likely to be able to modify its surrounding code either. However, it's helpful to explore it if possible, as it's the simplest of our fixes.

Regardless of whether this will be a practical technique for refactoring to pure functions, the more important take-away is that function purity only need be skin deep. That is, the **purity of a function is judged from the outside**, regardless of what goes on inside. As long as a function's usage behaves pure, it is pure. Inside a pure function, impure techniques can be used – in moderation! – for a variety of reasons, including most commonly, for performance. It's not necessarily, as they say, "turtles all the way down".

Be very careful, though. Any part of the program that's impure, even if it's wrapped with and only ever used via a pure function, is a potential source of bugs and confusion for readers of the code. The overall goal is to reduce side effects wherever possible, not just hide them.

Covering Up Effects

Many times you will be unable to modify the code to encapsulate the lexical free variables inside the scope of a wrapper function. For example, the impure function may be in a third-party library file that you do not control, containing something like:

```
var nums = [];
var smallCount = 0;
var largeCount = 0;

function generateMoreRandoms(count) {
    for (let i = 0; i < count; i++) {
        let num = Math.random();

        if (num >= 0.5) {
            largeCount++;
        }
        else {
            smallCount++;
        }
```

```
        nums.push( num );
    }
}
```

The brute-force strategy to *quarantine* the side causes/effects when using this utility in the rest of our program is to create an interface function that performs the following steps:

1. Capture the to-be-affected current states
2. Set initial input states
3. Run the impure function
4. Capture the side effect states
5. Restore the original states
6. Return the captured side effect states

```
function safer_generateMoreRandoms(count,initial) {
    // (1) Save original state
    var orig = {
        nums,
        smallCount,
        largeCount
    };

    // (2) Set up initial pre-side effects state
    nums = [...initial.nums];
    smallCount = initial.smallCount;
    largeCount = initial.largeCount;

    // (3) Beware impurity!
    generateMoreRandoms( count );

    // (4) Capture side effect state
    var sides = {
        nums,
```

```
        smallCount,
        largeCount
    };

    // (5) Restore original state
    nums = orig.nums;
    smallCount = orig.smallCount;
    largeCount = orig.largeCount;

    // (6) Expose side effect state directly as output
    return sides;
}
```

And to use safer_generateMoreRandoms(..):

```
var initialStates = {
    nums: [0.3, 0.4, 0.5],
    smallCount: 2,
    largeCount: 1
};

safer_generateMoreRandoms( 5, initialStates );
// { nums: [0.3,0.4,0.5,0.8510024448959794,0.04206799238...

nums;            // []
smallCount;      // 0
largeCount;      // 0
```

That's a lot of manual work to avoid a few side causes/effects; it'd be a lot easier if we just didn't have them in the first place. But if we have no choice, this extra effort is well worth it to avoid surprises in our programs.

> **Note**
>
> This technique really only works when you're dealing with synchronous code. Asynchronous code can't reliably be managed with this approach because it can't prevent surprises if other parts of the program access/modify the state variables in the interim.

Evading Effects

When the nature of the side effect to be dealt with is a mutation of a direct input value (object, array, etc.) via reference, we can again create an interface function to interact with instead of the original impure function.

Consider:

```
function handleInactiveUsers(userList,dateCutoff) {
    for (let i = 0; i < userList.length; i++) {
        if (userList[i].lastLogin == null) {
            // remove the user from the list
            userList.splice( i, 1 );
            i--;
        }
        else if (userList[i].lastLogin < dateCutoff) {
            userList[i].inactive = true;
        }
    }
}
```

Both the `userList` array itself, plus the objects in it, are mutated. One strategy to protect against these side effects is to do a deep (well, just not shallow) copy first:

```
function safer_handleInactiveUsers(userList,dateCutoff) {
    // make a copy of both the list and its user objects
    let copiedUserList = userList.map( function mapper(user){
        // copy a `user` object
        return Object.assign( {}, user );
    } );

    // call the original function with the copy
    handleInactiveUsers( copiedUserList, dateCutoff );

    // expose the mutated list as a direct output
    return copiedUserList;
}
```

The success of this technique will be dependent on the thoroughness of the *copy* you make of the value. Using [...userList] would not work here, since that only creates a shallow copy of the userList array itself. Each element of the array is an object that needs to be copied, so we need to take extra care. Of course, if those objects have objects inside them (they might!), the copying needs to be even more robust.

`this` Revisited

Another variation of the via-reference side cause/effect is with this-aware functions having this as an implicit input. See Chapter 2, "What's This" for more info on why the this keyword is problematic for FPers.

Consider:

```
var ids = {
    prefix: "_",
    generate() {
        return this.prefix + Math.random();
    }
};
```

Our strategy is similar to the previous section's discussion: create an interface function that forces the generate() function to use a predictable this context:

```
function safer_generate(context) {
    return ids.generate.call( context );
}

// **********************

safer_generate( { prefix: "foo" } );
// "foo0.8988802158307285"
```

These strategies are in no way fool-proof; the safest protection against side causes/effects is to not do them. But if you're trying to improve the readability and confidence level of your program, reducing the side causes/effects wherever possible is a huge step forward.

Essentially, we're not really eliminating side causes/effects, but rather containing and limiting them, so that more of our code is verifiable and reliable. If we later run into program bugs, we know that the parts of our code still using side causes/effects are the most likely culprits.

Summary

Side effects are harmful to code readability and quality because they make your code much harder to understand. Side effects are also one of the most common *causes* of bugs in programs, because juggling them is hard. Idempotence is a strategy for restricting side effects by essentially creating one-time-only operations.

Pure functions are how we best avoid side effects. A pure function is one that always returns the same output given the same input, and has no side causes or side effects. Referential transparency further states that – more as a mental exercise than a literal action – a pure function's call could be replaced with its output and the program would not have altered behavior.

Refactoring an impure function to be pure is the preferred option. But if that's not possible, try encapsulating the side causes/effects, or creating a pure interface against them.

No program can be entirely free of side effects. But prefer pure functions in as many places as that's practical. Collect impure functions side effects together as much as possible, so that it's easier to identify and audit these most likely culprits of bugs when they arise.

Chapter 6: Value Immutability

In Chapter 5, we talked about the importance of reducing side causes/effects: the ways that your application's state can change unexpectedly and cause surprises (bugs). The fewer places we have with such landmines, the more confidence we have over our code, and the more readable it will be. Our topic for this chapter follows directly from that same effort.

If programming-style idempotence is about defining a value change operation so that it can only affect state once, we now turn our attention to the goal of reducing the number of change occurrences from one to zero.

Let's now explore value immutability, the notion that in our programs we use only values that cannot be changed.

Primitive Immutability

Values of the primitive types (`number`, `string`, `boolean`, `null`, and `undefined`) are already immutable; there's nothing you can do to change them:

```
// invalid, and also makes no sense
2 = 2.5;
```

However, JS does have a peculiar behavior which seems like it allows mutating such primitive type values: "boxing". When you access a property on certain primitive type values – specifically `number`, `string`, and `boolean` – under the covers JS automatically wraps (aka "boxes") the value in its object counterpart (`Number`, `String`, and `Boolean`, respectively).

Consider:

```
var x = 2;

x.length = 4;

x;              // 2
x.length;       // undefined
```

Numbers do not normally have a `length` property available, so the `x.length = 4` setting is trying to add a new property, and it silently fails (or is ignored/discarded, depending on your point-of-view); x continues to hold the simple primitive 2 number.

But the fact that JS allows the `x.length = 4` statement to run at all can seem troubling, if for no other reason than its potential confusion to readers. The good news is, if you use strict mode (`"use strict";`), such a statement will throw an error.

What if you try to mutate the explicitly boxed object representation of such a value?

```
var x = new Number( 2 );

// works fine
x.length = 4;
```

x in this snippet is holding a reference to an object, so custom properties can be added and changed without issue.

The immutability of simple primitives like `numbers` probably seems fairly obvious. But what about `string` values? JS developers have a very common misconception that strings are like arrays and can thus be changed. JS syntax even hints at them being "array like" with the `[ ]` access operator. However, strings are also immutable:

```js
var s = "hello";

s[1];                // "e"

s[1] = "E";
s.length = 10;

s;                   // "hello"
```

Despite being able to access `s[1]` like it's an array, JS strings are not real arrays. Setting `s[1] = "E"` and `s.length = 10` both silently fail, just as `x.length = 4` did before. In strict mode, these assignments will fail, because both the `1` property and the `length` property are read-only on this primitive `string` value.

Interestingly, even the boxed `String` object value will act (mostly) immutable as it will throw errors in strict mode if you change existing properties:

```js
"use strict";

var s = new String( "hello" );

s[1] = "E";          // error
s.length = 10;       // error

s[42] = "?";         // OK

s;                   // "hello"
```

Value to Value

We'll unpack this idea more throughout the chapter, but just to start with a clear understanding in mind: value immutability does not mean we can't have values change over the course of our program. A program without changing state is not a very interesting one! It also doesn't mean that our variables can't hold different values. These are all common misconceptions about value immutability.

Value immutability means that *when* we need to change the state in our program, we must create and track a new value rather than mutate an existing value.

For example:

```
function addValue(arr) {
    var newArr = [ ...arr, 4 ];
    return newArr;
}

addValue( [1,2,3] );    // [1,2,3,4]
```

Notice that we did not change the array that `arr` references, but rather created a new array (`newArr`) that contains the existing values plus the new 4 value.

Analyze `addValue(..)` based on what we discussed in Chapter 5 about side causes/effects. Is it pure? Does it have referential transparency? Given the same array, will it always produce the same output? Is it free of both side causes and side effects? **Yes.**

Imagine the `[1,2,3]` array represents a sequence of data from some previous operations and we stored in some variable. It is our current state. If we want to compute what the next state of our application is, we call `addValue(..)`. But we want that act of next-state computation to be direct and explicit. So the `addValue(..)` operation takes a direct input, returns a direct output, and avoids the side effect of mutating the original array that `arr` references.

This means we can calculate the new state of `[1,2,3,4]` and be fully in control of that transition of states. No other part of our program can unexpectedly transition us to that state early, or to another state entirely, like `[1,2,3,5]`. By being disciplined about our values and treating them as immutable, we drastically reduce the surface area of surprise, making our programs easier to read, reason about, and ultimately trust.

The array that `arr` references is actually mutable. We just chose not to mutate it, so we practiced the spirit of value immutability.

We can use the copy-instead-of-mutate strategy for objects, too. Consider:

```
function updateLastLogin(user) {
    var newUserRecord = Object.assign( {}, user );
    newUserRecord.lastLogin = Date.now();
    return newUserRecord;
}

var user = {
    // ..
};

user = updateLastLogin( user );
```

Non-Local

Non-primitive values are held by reference, and when passed as arguments, it's the reference that's copied, not the value itself.

If you have an object or array in one part of the program, and pass it to a function that resides in another part of the program, that function can now affect the value via this reference copy, mutating it in possibly unexpected ways.

In other words, if passed as arguments, non-primitive values become non-local. Potentially the entire program has to be considered to understand whether such a value will be changed or not.

Consider:

```
var arr = [1,2,3];

foo( arr );

console.log( arr[0] );
```

Ostensibly, you're expecting `arr[0]` to still be the value 1. But is it? You don't know, because `foo(..)` *might* mutate the array using the reference copy you pass to it.

We already saw a trick in the previous chapter to avoid such a surprise:

```
var arr = [1,2,3];

foo( [...arr] );          // ha! a copy!

console.log( arr[0] );    // 1
```

In a little bit, we'll see another strategy for protecting ourselves from a value being mutated out from underneath us unexpectedly.

Reassignment

How would you describe what a "constant" is? Think about that for a moment before you move on to the next paragraph.

* * * *

Some of you may have conjured descriptions like, "a value that can't change", "a variable that can't be changed", or something similar. These are all approximately in the neighborhood, but not quite at the right house. The precise definition we should use for a constant is: a variable that cannot be reassigned.

This nitpicking is really important, because it clarifies that a constant actually has nothing to do with the value, except to say that whatever value a constant holds, that variable cannot be reassigned any other value. But it says nothing about the nature of the value itself.

Consider:

```
var x = 2;
```

Like we discussed earlier, the value 2 is an unchangeable (immutable) primitive. If I change that code to:

```
const x = 2;
```

The presence of the const keyword, known familiarly as a "constant declaration", actually does nothing at all to change the nature of 2; it's already unchangeable, and it always will be.

It's true that this later line will fail with an error:

```
// try to change `x`, fingers crossed!
x = 3;          // Error!
```

But again, we're not changing anything about the value. We're attempting to reassign the variable x. The values involved are almost incidental.

To prove that const has nothing to do with the nature of the value, consider:

```
const x = [ 2 ];
```

Is the array a constant? **No.** x is a constant because it cannot be reassigned. But this later line is totally OK:

```
x[0] = 3;
```

Why? Because the array is still totally mutable, even though x is a constant.

The confusion around const and "constant" only dealing with assignments and not value semantics is a long and dirty story. It seems a high degree of developers in just about every language that has a const stumble over the same sorts of confusions. Java in fact deprecated const and introduced a new keyword final at least in part to separate itself from the confusion over "constant" semantics.

Setting aside the confusion detractions, what importance does const hold for the FPer, if not to have anything to do with creating an immutable value?

Intent

The use of `const` tells the reader of your code that *that* variable will not be reassigned. As a signal of intent, `const` is often highly lauded as a welcome addition to JavaScript and a universal improvement in code readability.

In my opinion, this is mostly hype; there's not much substance to these claims. I see only the mildest of faint benefit in signaling your intent in this way. And when you match that up against decades of precedent around confusion about it implying value immutability, I don't think `const` comes close to carrying its own weight.

To back up my assertion, let's consider scope. `const` creates a block scoped variable, meaning that variable only exists in that one localized block:

```
// lots of code

{
    const x = 2;

    // a few lines of code
}

// lots of code
```

Typically, blocks are considered best designed to be only a few lines long. If you have blocks of more than say 10 lines, most developers will advise you to refactor. So `const x = 2` only applies to those next nine lines of code at most.

No other part of the program can ever affect the assignment of x. **Period.**

My claim is that program has basically the same magnitude of readability as this one:

```
// lots of code

{
    let x = 2;

    // a few lines of code
}

// lots of code
```

If you look at the next few lines of code after `let x = 2;`, you'll be able to easily tell that x is in fact *not* reassigned. That to me is a **much stronger signal** – actually not reassigning it! – than the use of some confusable `const` declaration to say "won't reassign it".

Moreover, let's consider what this code is likely to communicate to a reader at first glance:

```
const magicNums = [1,2,3,4];
```

Isn't it at least possible (probable?) that the reader of your code will assume (wrongly) that your intent is to never mutate the array? That seems like a reasonable inference to me. Imagine their confusion if later you do in fact allow the array value referenced by `magicNums` to be mutated. Might that surprise them?

Worse, what if you intentionally mutate `magicNums` in some way that turns out to not be obvious to the reader? Subsequently in the code, they see a usage of `magicNums` and assume (again, wrongly) that it's still `[1,2,3,4]` because they read your intent as, "not gonna change this".

I think you should use `var` or `let` for declaring variables to hold values that you intend to mutate. I think that actually is a **much clearer signal** of your intent than using `const`.

But the troubles with `const` don't stop there. Remember we asserted at the top of the chapter that to treat values as immutable means that when our state needs to change, we have to create a new value instead of mutating it? What are you going to do with that new array once you've created it? If you declared your reference to it using `const`, you can't reassign it.

```
const magicNums = [1,2,3,4];

// later:
magicNums = magicNums.concat( 42 );   // oops, can't reassign!
```

So... what next?

In this light, I see `const` as actually making our efforts to adhere to FP harder, not easier. My conclusion: `const` is not all that useful. It creates unnecessary confusion and restricts us in inconvenient ways. I only use `const` for simple constants like:

```
const PI = 3.141592;
```

The value `3.141592` is already immutable, and I'm clearly signaling, "this `PI` will always be used as stand-in placeholder for this literal value." To me, that's what `const` is good for. And to be frank, I don't use many of those kinds of declarations in my typical coding.

I've written and seen a lot of JavaScript, and I just think it's an imagined problem that very many of our bugs come from accidental reassignment.

One of the reasons FPers so highly favor `const` and avoid reassignment is because of equational reasoning. Though this topic is more related to other languages than JS and goes beyond what we'll get into here, it is a valid point. However, I prefer the pragmatic view over the more academic one.

For example, I've found measured use of variable reassignment can be useful in simplifying the description of intermediate states of computation. When a value goes through multiple type coercions or other transformations, I don't generally want to come up with new variable names for each representation:

```js
var a = "420";

// later

a = Number( a );

// later

a = [ a ];
```

If after changing from `"420"` to `420`, the original `"420"` value is no longer needed, then I think it's more readable to reassign `a` rather than come up with a new variable name like `aNum`.

The thing we really should worry more about is not whether our variables get reassigned, but **whether our values get mutated**. Why? Because values are portable; lexical assignments are not. You can pass an array to a function, and it can be changed without you realizing it. But a reassignment will never be unexpectedly caused by some other part of your program.

It's Freezing in Here

There's a cheap and simple way to turn a mutable object/array/function into an "immutable value" (of sorts):

```js
var x = Object.freeze( [2] );
```

The `Object.freeze(..)` utility goes through all the properties/indices of an object/array and marks them as read-only, so they cannot be reassigned. It's sorta like declaring properties with a `const`, actually! `Object.freeze(..)` also marks the properties as non-reconfigurable, and it marks the object/array itself as non-extensible (no new properties can be added). In effect, it makes the top level of the object immutable.

Top level only, though. Be careful!

```
var x = Object.freeze( [ 2, 3, [4, 5] ] );

// not allowed:
x[0] = 42;

// oops, still allowed:
x[2][0] = 42;
```

`Object.freeze(..)` provides shallow, naive immutability. You'll have to walk the entire object/array structure manually and apply `Object.freeze(..)` to each sub-object/array if you want a deeply immutable value.

But contrasted with `const` which can confuse you into thinking you're getting an immutable value when you aren't, `Object.freeze(..)` *actually* gives you an immutable value.

Recall the protection example from earlier:

```
var arr = Object.freeze( [1,2,3] );

foo( arr );

console.log( arr[0] );          // 1
```

Now `arr[0]` is quite reliably 1.

This is so important because it makes reasoning about our code much easier when we know we can trust that a value doesn't change when passed somewhere that we do not see or control.

Performance

Whenever we start creating new values (arrays, objects, etc.) instead of mutating existing ones, the obvious next question is: what does that mean for performance?

If we have to reallocate a new array each time we need to add to it, that's not only churning CPU time and consuming extra memory; the old values (if no longer referenced) are also being garbage collected. That's even more CPU burn.

Is that an acceptable trade-off? It depends. No discussion or optimization of code performance should happen **without context.**

If you have a single state change that happens once (or even a couple of times) in the whole life of the program, throwing away an old array/object for a new one is almost certainly not a concern. The churn we're talking about will be so small – probably mere microseconds at most – as to have no practical effect on the performance of your application. Compared to the minutes or hours you will save not having to track down and fix a bug related to unexpected value mutation, there's not even a contest here.

Then again, if such an operation is going to occur frequently, or specifically happen in a *critical path* of your application, then performance – consider both performance and memory! – is a totally valid concern.

Think about a specialized data structure that's like an array, but that you want to be able to make changes to and have each change behave implicitly as if the result was a new array. How could you accomplish this without actually creating a new array each time? Such a special array data structure could store the original value and then track each change made as a delta from the previous version.

Internally, it might be like a linked-list tree of object references where each node in the tree represents a mutation of the original value. Actually, this is conceptually similar to how **Git** version control works.

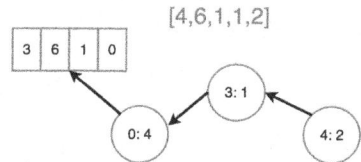

Mutations tree for immutable data structure

In this conceptual illustration, an original array [3,6,1,0] first has the mutation of value 4 assigned to position 0 (resulting in [4,6,1,0]), then 1 is assigned to position 3 (now [4,6,1,1]), finally 2 is assigned to position 4 (result: [4,6,1,1,2]). The key idea is that at each mutation, only the change from the previous version is recorded, not a duplication of the entire original data structure. This approach is much more efficient in both memory and CPU performance, in general.

Imagine using this hypothetical specialized array data structure like this:

```
var state = specialArray( 4, 6, 1, 1 );

var newState = state.set( 4, 2 );

state === newState;                     // false

state.get( 2 );                         // 1
state.get( 4 );                         // undefined

newState.get( 2 );                      // 1
newState.get( 4 );                      // 2

newState.slice( 2, 5 );                 // [1,1,2]
```

The `specialArray(..)` data structure would internally keep track of each mutation operation (like `set(..)`) as a *diff*, so it won't have to reallocate memory for the original values (4, 6, 1, and 1) just to add the 2 value to the end of the list. But importantly, `state` and `newState` point at different versions (or views) of the array value, so **the value immutability semantic is preserved**.

Inventing your own performance-optimized data structures is an interesting challenge. But pragmatically, you should probably use a library that already does this well. One great option is Immutable.js[23], which provides a variety of data structures, including `List` (like array) and `Map` (like object).

Consider the previous `specialArray` example but using `Immutable.List`:

---

[23] http://facebook.github.io/immutable-js

```
var state = Immutable.List.of( 4, 6, 1, 1 );

var newState = state.set( 4, 2 );

state === newState;                 // false

state.get( 2 );                     // 1
state.get( 4 );                     // undefined

newState.get( 2 );                  // 1
newState.get( 4 );                  // 2

newState.toArray().slice( 2, 5 );   // [1,1,2]
```

A powerful library like Immutable.js employs sophisticated performance optimizations. Handling all the details and corner-cases manually without such a library would be quite difficult.

When changes to a value are few or infrequent and performance is less of a concern, I'd recommend the lighter-weight solution, sticking with built-in `Object.freeze(..)` as discussed earlier.

Treatment

What if we receive a value to our function and we're not sure if it's mutable or immutable? Is it ever OK to just go ahead and try to mutate it? **No.** As we asserted at the beginning of this chapter, we should treat all received values as immutable – to avoid side effects and remain pure – regardless of whether they are or not.

Recall this example from earlier:

```
function updateLastLogin(user) {
    var newUserRecord = Object.assign( {}, user );
    newUserRecord.lastLogin = Date.now();
    return newUserRecord;
}
```

This implementation treats `user` as a value that should not be mutated; whether it *is* immutable or not is irrelevant to reading this part of the code. Contrast that with this implementation:

```
function updateLastLogin(user) {
    user.lastLogin = Date.now();
    return user;
}
```

That version is a lot easier to write, and even performs better. But not only does this approach make `updateLastLogin(..)` impure, it also mutates a value in a way that makes both the reading of this code, as well as the places it's used, more complicated.

We should treat `user` as immutable, always, because at this point of reading the code we do not know where the value comes from, or what potential issues we may cause if we mutate it.

Nice examples of this approach can be seen in various built-in methods of the JS array, such as `concat(..)` and `slice(..)`:

```
var arr = [1,2,3,4,5];

var arr2 = arr.concat( 6 );

arr;                    // [1,2,3,4,5]
arr2;                   // [1,2,3,4,5,6]

var arr3 = arr2.slice( 1 );

arr2;                   // [1,2,3,4,5,6]
arr3;                   // [2,3,4,5,6]
```

Other array prototype methods that treat the value instance as immutable and return a new array instead of mutating: `map(..)` and `filter(..)`. The `reduce(..)`/`reduceRight(..)` utilities also avoid mutating the instance, though they don't by default return a new array.

Unfortunately, for historical reasons, quite a few other array methods are impure mutators of their instance: `splice(..)`, `pop(..)`, `push(..)`, `shift(..)`, `unshift(..)`, `reverse(..)`, `sort(..)`, and `fill(..)`.

It should not be seen as *forbidden* to use these kinds of utilities, as some claim. For reasons such as performance optimization, sometimes you will want to use them. But you should never use such a method on an array value that is not already local to the function you're working in, to avoid creating a side effect on some other remote part of the code.

Recall one of the implementations of `compose(..)` from Chapter 4:

```
function compose(...fns) {
    return function composed(result){
        // copy the array of functions
        var list = [...fns];

        while (list.length > 0) {
            // take the last function off the end of the list
            // and execute it
            result = list.pop()( result );
        }

        return result;
    };
}
```

The `...fns` gather parameter is making a new local array from the passed-in arguments, so it's not an array that we could create an outside side effect on. It would be reasonable then to assume that it's safe for us to mutate it locally. But the subtle gotcha here is that the inner `composed(..)` which closes over `fns` is not "local" in this sense.

Consider this different version which doesn't make a copy:

```
function compose(...fns) {
    return function composed(result){
        while (fns.length > 0) {
            // take the last function off the end of the list
            // and execute it
            result = fns.pop()( result );
        }

        return result;
    };
}

var f = compose( x => x / 3, x => x + 1, x => x * 2 );

f( 4 );     // 3

f( 4 );     // 4 <-- uh oh!
```

The second usage of f(..) here wasn't correct, since we mutated that fns during the first call, which affected any subsequent uses. Depending on the circumstances, making a copy of an array like list = [...fns] may or may not be necessary. But I think it's safest to assume you need it – even if only for readability sake! – unless you can prove you don't, rather than the other way around.

Be disciplined and always treat *received values* as immutable, whether they are or not. That effort will improve the readability and trustability of your code.

Summary

Value immutability is not about unchanging values. It's about creating and tracking new values as the state of the program changes, rather than mutating existing values. This approach leads to more confidence in reading the code, because we limit the places where our state can change in ways we don't readily see or expect.

const declarations (constants) are commonly mistaken for their ability to signal intent and enforce immutability. In reality, const has basically nothing to do with value immutability, and its usage will likely create more confusion than it solves.

Instead, `Object.freeze(..)` provides a nice built-in way of setting shallow value immutability on an array or object. In many cases, this will be sufficient.

For performance-sensitive parts of the program, or in cases where changes happen frequently, creating a new array or object (especially if it contains lots of data) is undesirable, for both processing and memory concerns. In these cases, using immutable data structures from a library like **Immutable.js** is probably the best idea.

The importance of value immutability on code readability is less in the inability to change a value, and more in the discipline to treat a value as immutable.

Chapter 7: Closure vs. Object

A number of years ago, Anton van Straaten crafted what has become a rather famous and oft-cited koan[24] to illustrate and provoke an important tension between closure and objects:

> The venerable master Qc Na was walking with his student, Anton. Hoping to prompt the master into a discussion, Anton said "Master, I have heard that objects are a very good thing - is this true?" Qc Na looked pityingly at his student and replied, "Foolish pupil - objects are merely a poor man's closures."
>
> Chastised, Anton took his leave from his master and returned to his cell, intent on studying closures. He carefully read the entire "Lambda: The Ultimate..." series of papers and its cousins, and implemented a small Scheme interpreter with a closure-based object system. He learned much, and looked forward to informing his master of his progress.
>
> On his next walk with Qc Na, Anton attempted to impress his master by saying "Master, I have diligently studied the matter, and now understand that objects are truly a poor man's closures." Qc Na responded by hitting Anton with his stick, saying "When will you learn? Closures are a poor man's object." At that moment, Anton became enlightened.
>
> – Anton van Straaten 6/4/2003
>
> http://people.csail.mit.edu/gregs/ll1-discuss-archive-html/msg03277.html

The original posting, while brief, has more context to the origin and motivations, and I strongly suggest you read that post to properly set your mindset for approaching this chapter.

Many people I've observed read this koan smirk at its clever wit but then move on without it changing much about their thinking. However, the purpose of a koan

---

[24]https://www.merriam-webster.com/dictionary/koan

(from the Zen Buddhist perspective) is to prod the reader into wrestling with the contradictory truths therein. So, go back and read it again. Now read it again.

Which is it? Is a closure a poor man's object, or is an object a poor man's closure? Or neither? Or both? Is merely the take-away that closures and objects are in some way equivalent?

And what does any of this have to do with functional programming? Pull up a chair and ponder for a while. This chapter will be an interesting detour, an excursion if you will.

The Same Page

First, let's make sure we're all on the same page when we refer to closures and objects. We're obviously in the context of how JavaScript deals with these two mechanisms, and specifically talking about simple function closure (see Chapter 2, "Keeping Scope") and simple objects (collections of key-value pairs).

For the record, here's an illustration of a simple function closure:

```
function outer() {
    var one = 1;
    var two = 2;

    return function inner(){
        return one + two;
    };
}

var three = outer();

three();            // 3
```

And an illustration of a simple object:

```js
var obj = {
    one: 1,
    two: 2
};

function three(outer) {
    return outer.one + outer.two;
}

three( obj );           // 3
```

Many people conjure lots of extra things when you mention "closure", such as the asynchronous callbacks or even the module pattern with encapsulation and information hiding. Similarly, "object" brings to mind classes, `this`, prototypes, and a whole slew of other utilities and patterns.

As we go along, we'll carefully address the parts of this external context that matter, but for now, try to just stick to the simplest interpretations of "closure" and "object" as illustrated here; it'll make our exploration less confusing.

Look Alike

It may not be obvious how closures and objects are related. So let's explore their similarities first.

To frame this discussion, let me just briefly assert two things:

1. A programming language without closures can simulate them with objects instead.
2. A programming language without objects can simulate them with closures instead.

In other words, we can think of closures and objects as two different representations of a thing.

State

Consider this code from before:

```
function outer() {
    var one = 1;
    var two = 2;

    return function inner(){
        return one + two;
    };
}

var obj = {
    one: 1,
    two: 2
};
```

Both the scope closed over by `inner()` and the object `obj` contain two elements of state: one with value 1 and two with value 2. Syntactically and mechanically, these representations of state are different. But conceptually, they're actually quite similar.

As a matter of fact, it's fairly straightforward to represent an object as a closure, or a closure as an object. Go ahead, try it yourself:

```
var point = {
    x: 10,
    y: 12,
    z: 14
};
```

Did you come up with something like?

```
function outer() {
    var x = 10;
    var y = 12;
    var z = 14;

    return function inner(){
        return [x,y,z];
    }
};

var point = outer();
```

Note

The `inner()` function creates and returns a new array (aka, an object!) each time it's called. That's because JS doesn't afford us any capability to `return` multiple values without encapsulating them in an object. That's not technically a violation of our object-as-closure task, because it's just an implementation detail of exposing/transporting values; the state tracking itself is still object-free. With ES6+ array destructuring, we can declaratively ignore this temporary intermediate array on the other side: `var [x,y,z] = point()`. From a developer ergonomics perspective, the values are stored individually and tracked via closure instead of objects.

What if we have nested objects?

```
var person = {
    name: "Kyle Simpson",
    address: {
        street: "123 Easy St",
        city: "JS'ville",
        state: "ES"
    }
};
```

We could represent that same kind of state with nested closures:

```
function outer() {
    var name = "Kyle Simpson";
    return middle();

    // *********************

    function middle() {
        var street = "123 Easy St";
        var city = "JS'ville";
        var state = "ES";

        return function inner(){
            return [name,street,city,state];
        };
    }
}

var person = outer();
```

Let's practice going the other direction, from closure to object:

```
function point(x1,y1) {
    return function distFromPoint(x2,y2){
        return Math.sqrt(
            Math.pow( x2 - x1, 2 ) +
            Math.pow( y2 - y1, 2 )
        );
    };
}

var pointDistance = point( 1, 1 );

pointDistance( 4, 5 );      // 5
```

distFromPoint(..) is closed over x1 and y1, but we could instead explicitly pass those values as an object:

```
function pointDistance(point,x2,y2) {
    return Math.sqrt(
        Math.pow( x2 - point.x1, 2 ) +
        Math.pow( y2 - point.y1, 2 )
    );
};

pointDistance(
    { x1: 1, y1: 1 },
    4,  // x2
    5   // y2
);
// 5
```

The `point` object state explicitly passed in replaces the closure that implicitly held that state.

Behavior, Too!

It's not just that objects and closures represent ways to express collections of state, but also that they can include behavior via functions/methods. Bundling data with its behavior has a fancy name: encapsulation.

Consider:

```
function person(name,age) {
    return happyBirthday(){
        age++;
        console.log(
            `Happy ${age}th Birthday, ${name}!`
        );
    }
}

var birthdayBoy = person( "Kyle", 36 );

birthdayBoy();          // Happy 37th Birthday, Kyle!
```

The inner function happyBirthday() has closure over name and age so that the functionality therein is kept with the state.

We can achieve that same capability with a this binding to an object:

```
var birthdayBoy = {
    name: "Kyle",
    age: 36,
    happyBirthday() {
        this.age++;
        console.log(
            `Happy ${this.age}th Birthday, ${this.name}!`
        );
    }
};

birthdayBoy.happyBirthday();
// Happy 37th Birthday, Kyle!
```

We're still expressing the encapsulation of state data with the happyBirthday() function, but with an object instead of a closure. And we don't have to explicitly pass in an object to a function (as with earlier examples); JavaScript's this binding easily creates an implicit binding.

Another way to analyze this relationship: a closure associates a single function with a set of state, whereas an object holding the same state can have any number of functions to operate on that state.

As a matter of fact, you could even expose multiple methods with a single closure as the interface. Consider a traditional object with two methods:

```
var person = {
    firstName: "Kyle",
    lastName: "Simpson",
    first() {
        return this.firstName;
    },
    last() {
        return this.lastName;
    }
}

person.first() + " " + person.last();
// Kyle Simpson
```

Just using closure without objects, we could represent this program as:

```
function createPerson(firstName,lastName) {
    return API;

    // ********************

    function API(methodName) {
        switch (methodName) {
            case "first":
                return first();
                break;
            case "last":
                return last();
                break;
        };
    }

    function first() {
        return firstName;
    }

    function last() {
```

```
        return lastName;
    }
}

var person = createPerson( "Kyle", "Simpson" );

person( "first" ) + " " + person( "last" );
// Kyle Simpson
```

While these programs look and feel a bit different ergonomically, they're actually just different implementation variations of the same program behavior.

(Im)mutability

Many people will initially think that closures and objects behave differently with respect to mutability; closures protect from external mutation while objects do not. But, it turns out, both forms have identical mutation behavior.

That's because what we care about, as discussed in Chapter 6, is **value** mutability, and this is a characteristic of the value itself, regardless of where or how it's assigned:

```
function outer() {
    var x = 1;
    var y = [2,3];

    return function inner(){
        return [ x, y[0], y[1] ];
    };
}

var xyPublic = {
    x: 1,
    y: [2,3]
};
```

The value stored in the x lexical variable inside outer() is immutable – remember, primitives like 2 are by definition immutable. But the value referenced by y, an array, is definitely mutable. The exact same goes for the x and y properties on xyPublic.

We can reinforce the point that objects and closures have no bearing on mutability by pointing out that y is itself an array, and thus we need to break this example down further:

```
function outer() {
    var x = 1;
    return middle();

    // *******************

    function middle() {
        var y0 = 2;
        var y1 = 3;

        return function inner(){
            return [ x, y0, y1 ];
        };
    }
}

var xyPublic = {
    x: 1,
    y: {
        0: 2,
        1: 3
    }
};
```

If you think about it as "turtles (aka, objects) all the way down", at the lowest level, all state data is primitives, and all primitives are value-immutable.

Whether you represent this state with nested objects, or with nested closures, the values being held are all immutable.

Isomorphic

The term "isomorphic" gets thrown around a lot in JavaScript these days, and it's usually used to refer to code that can be used/shared in both the server and the browser. I wrote a blog post a while back that calls bogus on that usage of this word "isomorphic", which actually has an explicit and important meaning that's being clouded.

Here's some selections from a part of that post:

> What does isomorphic mean? Well, we could talk about it in mathematical terms, or sociology, or biology. The general notion of isomorphism is that you have two things which are similar in structure but not the same.
>
> In all those usages, isomorphism is differentiated from equality in this way: two values are equal if they're exactly identical in all ways, but they are isomorphic if they are represented differently but still have a 1-to-1, bi-directional mapping relationship.
>
> In other words, two things A and B would be isomorphic if you could map (convert) from A to B and then go back to A with the inverse mapping.

Recall in Chapter 2, "Brief Math Review", we discussed the mathematical definition of a function as being a mapping between inputs and outputs. We pointed out this is technically called a morphism. An isomorphism is a special case of bijective (aka, 2-way) morphism that requires not only that the mapping must be able to go in either direction, but also that the behavior is identical in either form.

But instead of thinking about numbers, let's relate isomorphism to code. Again quoting my blog post:

> [W]hat would isomorphic JS be if there were such a thing? Well, it could be that you have one set of JS code that is converted to another set of JS code, and that (importantly) you could convert from the latter back to the former if you wanted.

As we asserted earlier with our examples of closures-as-objects and objects-as-closures, these representative alternations go either way. In this respect, they are isomorphisms to each other.

Put simply, closures and objects are isomorphic representations of state (and its associated functionality).

The next time you hear someone say "X is isomorphic to Y", what they mean is, "X and Y can be converted from either one to the other in either direction, and not lose information."

Under the Hood

So, we can think of objects as an isomorphic representation of closures from the perspective of code we could write. But we can also observe that a closure system could actually be implemented – and likely is – with objects!

Think about it this way: in the following code, how is JS keeping track of the x variable for `inner()` to keep referencing, well after `outer()` has already run?

```
function outer() {
    var x = 1;

    return function inner(){
        return x;
    };
}
```

We could imagine that the scope – the set of all variables defined – of `outer()` is implemented as an object with properties. So, conceptually, somewhere in memory, there's something like:

```
scopeOfOuter = {
    x: 1
};
```

And then for the `inner()` function, when created, it gets an (empty) scope object called `scopeOfInner`, which is linked via its `[[Prototype]]` to the `scopeOfOuter` object, sorta like this:

```
scopeOfInner = {};
Object.setPrototypeOf( scopeOfInner, scopeOfOuter );
```

Then, inside `inner()`, when it makes reference to the lexical variable x, it's actually more like:

```
return scopeOfInner.x;
```

`scopeOfInner` doesn't have an x property, but it's `[[Prototype]]`-linked to `scopeOfOuter`, which does have an x property. Accessing `scopeOfOuter.x` via prototype delegation results in the 1 value being returned.

In this way, we can sorta see why the scope of `outer()` is preserved (via closure) even after it finishes: because the `scopeOfInner` object is linked to the `scopeOfOuter` object, thereby keeping that object and its properties alive and well.

Now, this is all conceptual. I'm not literally saying the JS engine uses objects and prototypes. But it's entirely plausible that it *could* work similarly.

Many languages do in fact implement closures via objects. And other languages implement objects in terms of closures. But we'll let the reader use their imagination on how that would work.

Two Roads Diverged in a Wood...

So closures and objects are equivalent, right? Not quite. I bet they're more similar than you thought before you started this chapter, but they still have important differences.

These differences should not be viewed as weaknesses or arguments against usage; that's the wrong perspective. They should be viewed as features and advantages that make one or the other more suitable (and readable!) for a given task.

Structural Mutability

Conceptually, the structure of a closure is not mutable.

In other words, you can never add to or remove state from a closure. Closure is a characteristic of where variables are declared (fixed at author/compile time), and is not sensitive to any runtime conditions – assuming you use strict mode and/or avoid using cheats like eval(..), of course!

Note

The JS engine could technically cull a closure to weed out any variables in its scope that are no longer going to be used, but this is an advanced optimization that's transparent to the developer. Whether the engine actually does these kinds of optimizations, I think it's safest for the developer to assume that closure is per-scope rather than per-variable. If you don't want it to stay around, don't close over it!

However, objects by default are quite mutable. You can freely add or remove (delete) properties/indices from an object, as long as that object hasn't been frozen (Object.freeze(..)).

It may be an advantage of the code to be able to track more (or less!) state depending on the runtime conditions in the program.

For example, let's imagine tracking the keypress events in a game. Almost certainly, you'll think about using an array to do this:

```
function trackEvent(evt,keypresses = []) {
    return [ ...keypresses, evt ];
}

var keypresses = trackEvent( newEvent1 );

keypresses = trackEvent( newEvent2, keypresses );
```

> **Note**
>
> Did you spot why I didn't push(..) directly to keypresses? Because in FP, we typically want to treat arrays as immutable data structures that can be re-created and added to, but not directly changed. We trade out the evil of side-effects for an explicit reassignment (more on that later).

Though we're not changing the structure of the array, we could if we wanted to. More on this in a moment.

But an array is not the only way to track this growing "list" of evt objects. We could use closure:

```
function trackEvent(evt,keypresses = () => []) {
    return function newKeypresses() {
        return [ ...keypresses(), evt ];
    };
}

var keypresses = trackEvent( newEvent1 );

keypresses = trackEvent( newEvent2, keypresses );
```

Do you spot what's happening here?

Each time we add a new event to the "list", we create a new closure wrapped around the existing keypresses() function (closure), which captures the current evt. When we call the keypresses() function, it will successively call all the nested functions, building up an intermediate array of all the individually closed-over evt objects. Again, closure is the mechanism that's tracking all the state; the array you see is only an implementation detail of needing a way to return multiple values from a function.

So which one is better suited for our task? No surprise here, the array approach is probably a lot more appropriate. The structural immutability of a closure means our only option is to wrap more closure around it. Objects are by default extensible, so we can just grow the array as needed.

By the way, even though I'm presenting this structural (im)mutability as a clear difference between closure and object, the way we're using the object as an immutable value is actually more similar than not.

Creating a new array for each addition to the array is treating the array as structurally immutable, which is conceptually symmetrical to closure being structurally immutable by its very design.

Privacy

Probably one of the first differences you think of when analyzing closure vs. object is that closure offers "privacy" of state through nested lexical scoping, whereas objects expose everything as public properties. Such privacy has a fancy name: information hiding.

Consider lexical closure hiding:

```
function outer() {
    var x = 1;

    return function inner(){
        return x;
    };
}

var xHidden = outer();

xHidden();           // 1
```

Now the same state in public:

```
var xPublic = {
    x: 1
};

xPublic.x;              // 1
```

There are some obvious differences around general software engineering principles – consider abstraction, the module pattern with public and private APIs, etc. – but let's try to constrain our discussion to the perspective of FP; this is, after all, a book about functional programming!

Visibility

It may seem that the ability to hide information is a desired characteristic of state tracking, but I believe the FPer might argue the opposite.

One of the advantages of managing state as public properties on an object is that it's easier to enumerate (and iterate!) all the data in your state. Imagine you wanted to process each keypress event (from the earlier example) to save it to a database, using a utility like:

```
function recordKeypress(keypressEvt) {
    // database utility
    DB.store( "keypress-events", keypressEvt );
}
```

If you already have an array – just an object with public numerically named properties – this is very straightforward using a built-in JS array utility `forEach(..)`:

```
keypresses.forEach( recordKeypress );
```

But if the list of keypresses is hidden inside closure, you'll have to expose a utility on the public API of the closure with privileged access to the hidden data.

For example, we can give our closure-`keypresses` example its own `forEach`, like built-in arrays have:

```
function trackEvent(
    evt,
    keypresses = {
        list() { return []; },
        forEach() {}
    }
) {
    return {
        list() {
            return [ ...keypresses.list(), evt ];
        },
        forEach(fn) {
            keypresses.forEach( fn );
            fn( evt );
        }
    };
}

// ..

keypresses.list();          // [ evt, evt, .. ]

keypresses.forEach( recordKeypress );
```

The visibility of an object's state data makes using it more straightforward, whereas closure obscures the state making us work harder to process it.

Change Control

If the lexical variable x is hidden inside a closure, the only code that has the freedom to reassign it is also inside that closure; it's impossible to modify x from the outside.

As we saw in Chapter 6, that fact alone improves the readability of code by reducing the surface area that the reader must consider to predict the behavior of any given variable.

The local proximity of lexical reassignment is a big reason why I don't find `const` as a feature that helpful. Scopes (and thus closures) should in general be pretty small, and that means there will only be a few lines of code that can affect reassignment. In `outer()` above, we can quickly inspect to see that no line of code reassigns x, so for all intents and purposes it's acting as a constant.

This kind of guarantee is a powerful contributor to our confidence in the purity of a function, for example.

On the other hand, `xPublic.x` is a public property, and any part of the program that gets a reference to `xPublic` has the ability, by default, to reassign `xPublic.x` to some other value. That's a lot more lines of code to consider!

That's why in Chapter 6, we looked at `Object.freeze(..)` as a quick-n-dirty means of making all of an object's properties read-only (`writable: false`), so that they can't be reassigned unpredictably.

Unfortunately, `Object.freeze(..)` is both all-or-nothing and irreversible.

With closure, you have some code with the privilege to change, and the rest of the program is restricted. When you freeze an object, no part of the code will be able to reassign. Moreover, once an object is frozen, it can't be thawed out, so the properties will remain read-only for the duration of the program.

In places where I want to allow reassignment but restrict its surface area, closures are a more convenient and flexible form than objects. In places where I want no reassignment, a frozen object is a lot more convenient than repeating `const` declarations all over my function.

Many FPers take a hard-line stance on reassignment: it shouldn't be used. They will tend to use `const` to make all closure variables read-only, and they'll use `Object.freeze(..)` or full immutable data structures to prevent property reassignment. Moreover, they'll try to reduce the amount of explicitly declared/tracked variables and properties wherever possible, preferring value transfer – function chains, `return` value passed as argument, etc. – instead of intermediate value storage.

This book is about "Functional-Light" programming in JavaScript, and this is one of those cases where I diverge from the core FP crowd.

I think variable reassignment can be quite useful, and when used appropriately, quite readable in its explicitness. It's certainly been my experience that debugging is a lot easier when you can insert a `debugger` or breakpoint, or track a watch expression.

Cloning State

As we learned in Chapter 6, one of the best ways we prevent side effects from eroding the predictability of our code is to make sure we treat all state values as immutable, regardless of whether they are actually immutable (frozen) or not.

If you're not using a purpose-built library to provide sophisticated immutable data structures, the simplest approach will suffice: duplicate your objects/arrays each time before making a change.

Arrays are easy to clone shallowly – just use ... array spread:

```
var a = [ 1, 2, 3 ];

var b = [...a];
b.push( 4 );

a;          // [1,2,3]
b;          // [1,2,3,4]
```

Objects can be shallow-cloned relatively easily too:

```
var o = {
    x: 1,
    y: 2
};

// in ES2018+, using object spread:
var p = { ...o };
p.y = 3;

// in ES6/ES2015+:
var p = Object.assign( {}, o );
p.y = 3;
```

If the values in an object/array are themselves non-primitives (objects/arrays), to get deep cloning you'll have to walk each layer manually to clone each nested object.

Otherwise, you'll have copies of shared references to those sub-objects, and that's likely to create havoc in your program logic.

Did you notice that this cloning is possible only because all these state values are visible and can thus be easily copied? What about a set of state wrapped up in a closure; how would you clone that state?

That's much more tedious. Essentially, you'd have to do something similar to our custom `forEach` API method earlier: provide a function inside each layer of the closure with the privilege to extract/copy the hidden values, creating new equivalent closures along the way.

Even though that's theoretically possible – another exercise for the reader! – it's far less practical to implement than you're likely to justify for any real program.

Objects have a clear advantage when it comes to representing state that we need to be able to clone.

Performance

One reason objects may be favored over closures, from an implementation perspective, is that in JavaScript objects are often lighter-weight in terms of memory and even computation.

But be careful with that as a general assertion: there are plenty of things you can do with objects that will erase any performance gains you may get from ignoring closure and moving to object-based state tracking.

Let's consider a scenario with both implementations. First, the closure-style implementation:

```
function StudentRecord(name,major,gpa) {
    return function printStudent(){
        return `${name}, Major: ${major}, GPA: ${gpa.toFixed(1)}`;
    };
}

var student = StudentRecord( "Kyle Simpson", "CS", 4 );

// later

student();
// Kyle Simpson, Major: CS, GPA: 4.0
```

The inner function `printStudent()` closes over three variables: `name`, `major`, and `gpa`. It maintains this state wherever we transfer a reference to that function – we call it `student()` in this example.

Now for the object (and `this`) approach:

```
function StudentRecord(){
    return `${this.name}, Major: ${this.major}, \
GPA: ${this.gpa.toFixed(1)}`;
}

var student = StudentRecord.bind( {
    name: "Kyle Simpson",
    major: "CS",
    gpa: 4
} );

// later

student();
// Kyle Simpson, Major: CS, GPA: 4.0
```

The `student()` function – technically referred to as a "bound function" – has a hard-bound `this` reference to the object literal we passed in, such that any later call to `student()` will use that object for its `this`, and thus be able to access its encapsulated state.

Both implementations have the same outcome: a function with preserved state. But what about the performance; what differences will there be?

Note

Accurately and actionably judging performance of a snippet of JS code is a very dodgy affair. We won't get into all the details here, but I urge you to read *You Don't Know JS: Async & Performance*, specifically Chapter 6, "Benchmarking & Tuning", for more details.

If you were writing a library that created a pairing of state with its function – either the call to `StudentRecord(..)` in the first snippet or the call to `StudentRecord.bind(..)` in the second snippet – you're likely to care most about how those two perform. Inspecting the code, we can see that the former has to create a new function expression each time. The second one uses `bind(..)`, which is not as obvious in its implications.

One way to think about what `bind(..)` does under the covers is that it creates a closure over a function, like this:

```
function bind(orinFn,thisObj) {
    return function boundFn(...args) {
        return origFn.apply( thisObj, args );
    };
}

var student = bind( StudentRecord, { name: "Kyle.." } );
```

In this way, it looks like both implementations of our scenario create a closure, so the performance is likely to be about the same.

However, the built-in `bind(..)` utility doesn't really have to create a closure to accomplish the task. It simply creates a function and manually sets its internal `this` to the specified object. That's potentially a more efficient operation than if we did the closure ourselves.

The kind of performance savings we're talking about here is miniscule on an individual operation. But if your library's critical path is doing this hundreds or thousands of times or more, that savings can add up quickly. Many libraries – Bluebird being one such example – have ended up optimizing by removing closures and going with objects, in exactly this means.

Outside of the library use-case, the pairing of the state with its function usually only happens relatively few times in the critical path of an application. By contrast, typically the usage of the function+state – calling `student()` in either snippet – is more common.

If that's the case for some given situation in your code, you should probably care more about the performance of the latter versus the former.

Bound functions have historically had pretty lousy performance in general, but have recently been much more highly optimized by JS engines. If you benchmarked these variations a couple of years ago, it's entirely possible you'd get different results repeating the same test with the latest engines.

A bound function is now likely to perform at least as good if not better as the equivalent closed-over function. So that's another tick in favor of objects over closures.

I just want to reiterate: these performance observations are not absolutes, and the determination of what's best for a given scenario is very complex. Do not just casually apply what you've heard from others or even what you've seen on some other earlier project. Carefully examine whether objects or closures are appropriately efficient for the task.

Summary

> *The truth of this chapter cannot be written out.*
> *One must read this chapter to find its truth.*

Coining some Zen wisdom here was my attempt at being clever. But you deserve a proper summary of this chapter's message.

Objects and closures are isomorphic to each other, which means that they can be used somewhat interchangeably to represent state and behavior in your program.

Representation as a closure has certain benefits, like granular change control and automatic privacy. Representation as an object has other benefits, like easier cloning of state.

The critically thinking FPer should be able to conceive any segment of state and behavior in the program with either representation, and pick the representation that's most appropriate for the task at hand.

Chapter 8: Recursion

Did you have fun down our little closures/objects rabbit hole in the previous chapter? Welcome back!

On the next page, we're going to jump into the topic of recursion.

(rest of the page intentionally left blank)

Let's talk about recursion. Before we dive in, consult the previous page for the formal definition.

Weak joke, I know. :)

Recursion is one of those programming techniques that most developers admit can be very powerful, but also most of them don't like to use it. I'd put it in the same category as regular expressions, in that sense. Powerful, but confusing, and thus seen as *not worth the effort*.

I'm a big fan of recursion, and you can, too! Unfortunately, many examples of recursion focus on trivial academic tasks like generating Fibonacci sequences. If you're needing those kinds of numbers in your program – and let's face it, that's not very common! – you'll likely miss the big picture.

As a matter of fact, recursion is one of the most important ways that FP developers avoid imperative looping and reassignment, by offloading the implementation details to the language and engine. When used properly, recursion is powerfully declarative for complex problems.

Sadly, recursion gets far less attention, especially in JS, than it should, in large part because of some very real performance (speed and memory) limitations. Our goal in this chapter is to dig deeper and find practical reasons that recursion should be front and center in our FP.

Definition

Recursion is when a function calls itself, and that call does the same, and this cycle continues until a base condition is satisfied and the call loop unwinds.

 Warning
If you don't ensure that a base condition is *eventually* met, recursion will run forever, and crash or lock up your program; the base condition is pretty important to get right!

But... that definition is too confusing in its written form. We can do better. Consider this recursive function:

```
function foo(x) {
    if (x < 5) return x;
    return foo( x / 2 );
}
```

Let's visualize what happens with this function when we call `foo( 16 )`:

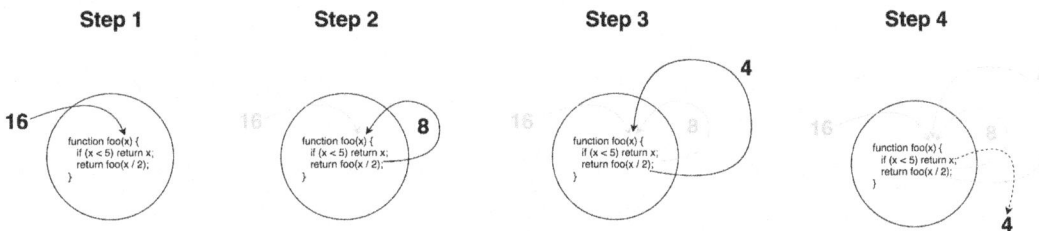

Steps of recursive function calls

In step 2, `x / 2` produces 8, and that's passed in as the argument to a recursive `foo(..)` call. In step 3, same thing, `x / 2` produces 4, and that's passed in as the argument to yet another `foo(..)` call. That part is hopefully fairly straightforward.

But where someone may often get tripped up is what happens in step 4. Once we've satisfied the base condition where x (value 4) is `< 5`, we no longer make any more recursive calls, and just (effectively) do `return 4`. Specifically the dotted line return of 4 in this figure simplifies what's happening there, so let's dig into that last step and visualize it as these three sub-steps:

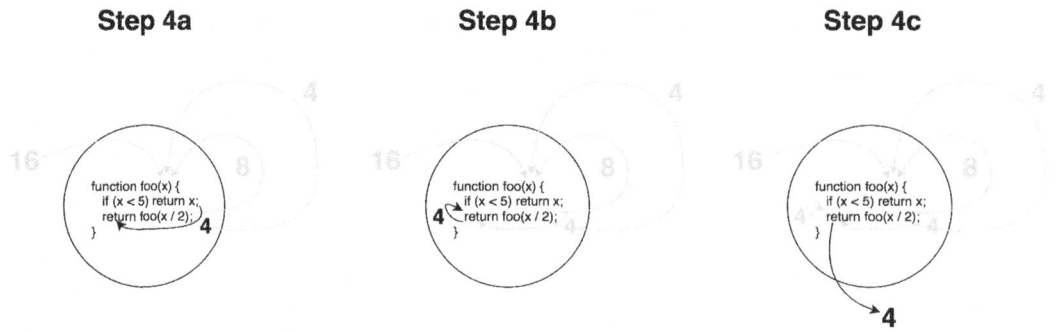

Steps of recursive return

Once the base condition is satisfied, the returned value cascades back through all of the current function calls (and thus `returns`), eventually `returning` the final result out.

Another way to visualize this recursion is by considering the function calls in the order they happen (commonly referred to as the call stack):

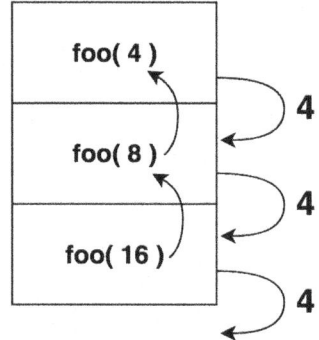

Recursive function call stack

More on the call stack later in this chapter.

Another recursion example:

```
function isPrime(num,divisor = 2){
    if (num < 2 || (num > 2 && num % divisor == 0)) {
        return false;
    }
    if (divisor <= Math.sqrt( num )) {
        return isPrime( num, divisor + 1 );
    }

    return true;
}
```

This prime checking basically works by trying each integer from 2 up to the square root of the num being checked, to see if any of them divide evenly (% mod returning 0) into the number. If any do, it's not a prime. Otherwise, it must be prime. The divisor + 1 uses the recursion to iterate through each possible divisor value.

One of the most famous examples of recursion is calculating a Fibonacci number, where the sequence is defined as:

```
fib( 0 ): 0
fib( 1 ): 1
fib( n ):
    fib( n - 2 ) + fib( n - 1 )
```

Note

The first several numbers of this sequence are: 0, 1, 1, 2, 3, 5, 8, 13, 21, 34, ... Each number is the addition of the previous two numbers in the sequence.

The definition of Fibonacci expressed directly in code:

```
function fib(n) {
    if (n <= 1) return n;
    return fib( n - 2 ) + fib( n - 1 );
}
```

`fib(..)` calls itself recursively twice, which is typically referred to as binary recursion. We'll talk more about binary recursion later.

We'll use `fib(..)` variously throughout this chapter to illustrate ideas around recursion, but one downside to this particular form is that there's an awful lot of duplicated work. `fib(n-1)` and `fib(n-2)` don't share any of their work with each other, but overlap with each other almost entirely, over the entire integer space down to 0.

We briefly touched on memoization in Chapter 5, "Performance Effects". Here, memoization would allow the `fib(..)` of any given number to be computed only once, instead of being recomputed many times. We won't go further into that topic here, but that performance caveat is important to keep in mind with any algorithm, recursive or not.

Mutual Recursion

When a function calls itself, specifically, this is referred to as direct recursion. That's what we saw in the previous section with `foo(..)`, `isPrime(..)`, and `fib(..)`. When two or more functions call each other in a recursive cycle, this is referred to as mutual recursion.

These two functions are mutually recursive:

```
function isOdd(v) {
    if (v === 0) return false;
    return isEven( Math.abs( v ) - 1 );
}

function isEven(v) {
    if (v === 0) return true;
    return isOdd( Math.abs( v ) - 1 );
}
```

Yes, this is a silly way to calculate if a number is odd or even. But it illustrates the idea that certain algorithms can be defined in terms of mutual recursion.

Recall the binary recursive `fib(..)` from the previous section; we could instead have expressed it with mutual recursion:

```
function fib_(n) {
    if (n == 1) return 1;
    else return fib( n - 2 );
}

function fib(n) {
    if (n == 0) return 0;
    else return fib( n - 1 ) + fib_( n );
}
```

 Note

This mutually recursive `fib(..)` implementation is adapted from research presented in "Fibonacci Numbers Using Mutual Recursion"[25].

While these mutual recursion examples shown are rather contrived, there are more complex use cases where mutual recursion can be very helpful. Counting the number of leaves in a tree data structure is one example, and recursive descent parsing (of source code, by a compiler) is another.

---

[25]https://www.researchgate.net/publication/246180510_Fibonacci_Numbers_Using_Mutual_Recursion

Why Recursion?

Now that we've defined and illustrated recursion, we should examine why it is useful.

The most commonly cited reason that recursion fits the spirit of FP is because it trades (much of) the explicit tracking of state with implicit state on the call stack. Typically, recursion is most useful when the problem requires conditional branching and back-tracking, and managing that kind of state in a purely iterative environment can be quite tricky; at a minimum, the code is highly imperative and harder to read and verify. But tracking each level of branching as its own scope on the call stack often significantly cleans up the readability of the code.

Simple iterative algorithms can trivially be expressed as recursion:

```
function sum(total,...nums) {
    for (let num of nums) {
        total = total + num;
    }

    return total;
}

// vs

function sum(num1,...nums) {
    if (nums.length == 0) return num1;
    return num1 + sum( ...nums );
}
```

It's not just that the `for`-loop is eliminated in favor of the call stack, but that the incremental partial sums (the intermittent state of `total`) are tracked implicitly across the `return`s of the call stack instead of reassigning `total` each iteration. FPers will often prefer to avoid reassignment of local variables where it's possible to avoid.

In a basic algorithm like this kind of summation, this difference is minor and nuanced. But the more sophisticated your algorithm, the more you will likely see the payoff of recursion instead of imperative state tracking.

Declarative Recursion

Mathematicians use the Σ symbol as a placeholder to represent the summation of a list of numbers. The primary reason they do that is because it's more cumbersome (and less readable!) if they're working with more complex formulas and they have to write out the summation manually, like 1 + 3 + 5 + 7 + 9 + ... Using the notation is declarative math!

Recursion is declarative for algorithms in the same sense that Σ is declarative for mathematics. Recursion expresses that a problem solution exists, but doesn't necessarily require the reader of the code to understand how that solution works. Let's consider two approaches to finding the highest even number passed as an argument:

```
function maxEven(...nums) {
    var maxNum = -Infinity;

    for (let num of nums) {
        if (num % 2 == 0 && num > maxNum) {
            maxNum = num;
        }
    }

    if (maxNum !== -Infinity) {
        return maxNum;
    }
}
```

This implementation is not particularly intractable, but it's also not readily apparent what its nuances are. How obvious is it that maxEven(), maxEven(1), and maxEven(1,13) all return undefined? Is it quickly clear why the final if statement is necessary?

Let's instead consider a recursive approach, to compare. We could notate the recursion this way:

```
maxEven( nums ):
    maxEven( nums.0, maxEven( ...nums.1 ) )
```

In other words, we can define the max-even of a list of numbers as the max-even of the first number compared to the max-even of the rest of the numbers. For example:

```
maxEven( 1, 10, 3, 2 ):
    maxEven( 1, maxEven( 10, maxEven( 3, maxEven( 2 ) ) ) )
```

To implement this recursive definition in JS, one approach is:

```
function maxEven(num1,...restNums) {
    var maxRest = restNums.length > 0 ?
            maxEven( ...restNums ) :
            undefined;

    return (num1 % 2 != 0 || num1 < maxRest) ?
        maxRest :
        num1;
}
```

So what advantages does this approach have?

First, the signature is a little different than before. I intentionally called out `num1` as the first argument name, collecting the rest of the arguments into `restNums`. But why? We could just have collected them all into a single `nums` array and then referred to `nums[0]`.

This function signature is an intentional hint at the recursive definition. It reads like this:

```
maxEven( num1, ...restNums ):
    maxEven( num1, maxEven( ...restNums ) )
```

Do you see the symmetry between the signature and the recursive definition?

When we can make the recursive definition more apparent even in the function signature, we improve the declarativeness of the function. And if we can then mirror the recursive definition from the signature to the function body, it gets even better.

But I'd say the most obvious improvement is that the distraction of the imperative `for`-loop is suppressed. All the looping logic is abstracted into the recursive call stack, so that stuff doesn't clutter the code. We're free then to focus on the logic of finding a max-even by comparing two numbers at a time – the important part anyway!

Mentally, what's happening is similar to when a mathematician uses a Σ summation in a larger equation. We're saying, "the max-even of the rest of the list is calculated by `maxEven(...restNums)`, so we'll just assume that part and move on."

Additionally, we reinforce that notion with the `restNums.length > 0` guard, because if there are no more numbers to consider, the natural result is that `maxRest` would have to be `undefined`. We don't need to devote any extra mental attention to that part of the reasoning. This base condition (no more numbers to consider) is clearly evident.

Next, we turn our attention to checking `num1` against `maxRest` – the main logic of the algorithm is how to determine which of two numbers, if any, is a max-even. If `num1` is not even (`num1 % 2 != 0`), or it's less than `maxRest`, then `maxRest` *has* to be `returned`, even if it's `undefined`. Otherwise, `num1` is the answer.

The case I'm making is that this reasoning while reading an implementation is more straightforward, with fewer nuances or noise to distract us, than the imperative approach; it's **more declarative** than the `for`-loop with `-Infinity` version.

Tip

We should point out that another (likely better!) way to model this besides manual iteration or recursion would be with list operations (see Chapter 9), with a `filter(..)` to include only evens and then a `reduce(..)` to find the max. We only used this example to illustrate the more declarative nature of recursion over manual iteration.

Binary Tree Recursion

Here's another recursion example: calculating the depth of a binary tree. In fact, almost every operation you'll do with trees is implemented most easily with recursion, because manually tracking the stack up and down is highly imperative and error-prone.

The depth of a binary tree is the longest path down (either left or right) through the nodes of the tree. Another way to define that is recursively – the depth of a tree at any node is 1 (the current node) plus the greater of depths from either its left or right child trees:

```
depth( node ):
    1 + max( depth( node.left ), depth( node.right ) )
```

Translating that straightforwardly to a binary recursive function:

```
function depth(node) {
    if (node) {
        let depthLeft = depth( node.left );
        let depthRight = depth( node.right );
        return 1 + max( depthLeft, depthRight );
    }

    return 0;
}
```

I'm not going to list out the imperative form of this algorithm, but trust me, it's a lot messier. This recursive approach is nicely and gracefully declarative. It follows the recursive definition of the algorithm very closely with very little distraction.

Not all problems are cleanly recursive. This is not some silver bullet that you should try to apply everywhere. But recursion can be very effective at evolving the expression of a problem from more imperative to more declarative.

Stack

Let's revisit the `isOdd(..)`/`isEven(..)` recursion from earlier:

```
function isOdd(v) {
    if (v === 0) return false;
    return isEven( Math.abs( v ) - 1 );
}

function isEven(v) {
    if (v === 0) return true;
    return isOdd( Math.abs( v ) - 1 );
}
```

In most browsers, if you try this you'll get an error:

```
isOdd( 33333 );          // RangeError: Maximum call stack size exceeded
```

What's going on with this error? The engine throws this error because it's trying to protect your program from running the system out of memory. To explain that, we need to peek a little below the hood at what's going on in the JS engine when function calls happen.

Each function call sets aside a small chunk of memory called a stack frame. The stack frame holds certain important information about the current state of processing statements in a function, including the values in any variables. The reason this information needs to be stored in memory (in a stack frame) is because the function may call out to another function, which pauses the current function. When the other function finishes, the engine needs to resume the exact state from when it was paused.

When the second function call starts, it needs a stack frame as well, bringing the count to 2. If that function calls another, we need a third stack frame. And so on. The word "stack" speaks to the notion that each time a function is called from the previous one, the next frame is *stacked* on top. When a function call finishes, its frame is popped off the stack.

Consider this program:

```
function foo() {
    var z = "foo!";
}

function bar() {
    var y = "bar!";
    foo();
}

function baz() {
    var x = "baz!";
    bar();
}

baz();
```

Visualizing this program's stack frames step by step:

Step 1

baz()
var x;

Step 2

bar()
var y;

baz()
var x;

Step 3

foo()
var z;

bar()
var y;

baz()
var x;

Call stack frames

 Note

If these functions didn't call each other, but were just called sequentially – like `baz(); bar(); foo();`, where each one finishes before the next one starts – the frames won't stack up; each function call finishes and removes its frame from the stack before the next one is added.

OK, so a little bit of memory is needed for each function call. No big deal under most normal program conditions, right? But it quickly becomes a big deal once you introduce recursion. While you'd almost certainly never manually stack thousands (or even hundreds!) of calls of different functions together in one call stack, you'll easily see tens of thousands or more recursive calls stack up.

The `isOdd(..)`/`isEven(..)` pairing throws a `RangeError` because the engine steps in at an arbitrary limit when it thinks the call stack has grown too much and should be stopped. This is not likely a limit based on actual memory levels nearing zero, but rather a prediction by the engine that if this kind of program was left running, memory usage would be runaway. It is impossible to know or prove that a program will eventually stop, so the engine has to make an informed guess.

This limit is implementation dependent. The specification doesn't say anything about it at all, so it's not *required*. But practically all JS engines do have a limit, because having no limit would create an unstable device that's susceptible to poorly written or malicious code. Each engine in each different device environment is going to enforce its own limits, so there's no way to predict or guarantee how far we can run up the function call stack.

What this limit means to us as developers is that there's a practical limitation on the usefulness of recursion in solving problems on non-trivially sized data sets. In fact, I think this kind of limitation might be the single biggest reason that recursion is a second-class citizen in the developer's toolbox. Regrettably, recursion is an afterthought rather than a primary technique.

Tail Calls

Recursion far predates JS, and so do these memory limitations. Back in the 1960s, developers were wanting to use recursion and running up against hard limits of device memory of their powerful computers that were far lower than we have on our watches today.

Fortunately, a powerful observation was made in those early days that still offers hope. The technique is called *tail calls*.

The idea is that if a call from function `baz()` to function `bar()` happens at the very end of function `baz()`'s execution – referred to as a tail call – the stack frame for baz() isn't needed anymore. That means that either the memory can be reclaimed, or even better, simply reused to handle function bar()'s execution. Visualizing:

Call stack frames with tail calls

Tail calls are not really directly related to recursion, per se; this notion holds for any function call. But your manual non-recursion call stacks are unlikely to go beyond maybe 10 levels deep in most cases, so the chances of tail calls impacting your program's memory footprint are pretty low.

Tail calls really shine in the recursion case, because it means that a recursive stack could run "forever", and the only performance concern would be computation, not fixed memory limitations. Tail call recursion can run in O(1) fixed memory usage.

These sorts of techniques are often referred to as Tail Call Optimizations (TCO), but it's important to distinguish the ability to detect a tail call to run in fixed memory space, from the techniques that optimize this approach. Technically, tail calls themselves are not a performance optimization as most people would think, as they might actually run slower than normal calls. TCO is about optimizing tail calls to run more efficiently.

Proper Tail Calls (PTC)

JavaScript has never required (nor forbidden) tail calls, until ES6. ES6 mandates recognition of tail calls, of a specific form referred to as Proper Tail Calls (PTC), and the guarantee that code in PTC form will run without unbounded stack memory growth. Practically speaking, this means we should not get `RangeErrors` thrown if we adhere to PTC.

First, PTC in JavaScript requires strict mode. You should already be using strict mode, but if you aren't, this is yet another reason you should already be using strict mode. Did I mention, yet, you should already be using strict mode!?

Second, a *proper* tail call looks like this:

```
return foo( .. );
```

In other words, the function call is the last thing to execute in the surrounding function, and whatever value it returns is explicitly `returned`. In this way, JS can be absolutely guaranteed that the current stack frame won't be needed anymore.

These *are not* PTC:

```
foo();
return;

// or

var x = foo( .. );
return x;

// or

return 1 + foo( .. );
```

Note

A JS engine, or a smart transpiler, *could* do some code reorganization to treat `var x = foo(); return x;` effectively the same as `return foo();`, which would then make it eligible for PTC. But that is not required by the specification.

The `1 +` part is definitely processed *after* `foo(..)` finishes, so the stack frame has to be kept around.

However, this *is* PTC:

```
return x ? foo( .. ) : bar( .. );
```

After the x condition is computed, either `foo(..)` or `bar(..)` will run, and in either case, the return value will always be `return`ed back. That's PTC form.

Binary (or multiple) recursion – as shown earlier, two (or more!) recursive calls made at each level – can never be fully PTC as-is, because all the recursion has to be in tail call position to avoid the stack growth; at most, only one recursive call can appear in PTC position.

Earlier, we showed an example of refactoring from binary recursion to mutual recursion. It may be possible to achieve PTC from a multiple-recursive algorithm by splitting each into separate function calls, where each is expressed respectively in PTC form. However, that type of intricate refactoring is highly dependent on the scenario, and beyond the scope of what we can cover in this text.

Rearranging Recursion

If you want to use recursion but your problem set could grow enough eventually to exceed the stack limit of the JS engine, you're going to need to rearrange your recursive calls to take advantage of PTC (or avoid nested calls entirely). There are several refactoring strategies that can help, but there are of course trade-offs to be aware of.

As a word of caution, always keep in mind that code readability is our overall most important goal. If recursion along with some combination of the strategies described here results in code that is harder to read/understand, **don't use recursion**; find another more readable approach.

Replacing the Stack

The main problem with recursion is its memory usage, keeping around the stack frames to track the state of a function call while it dispatches to the next recursive call iteration. If we can figure out how to rearrange our usage of recursion so that the stack frame doesn't need to be kept, then we can express recursion with PTC and take advantage of the JS engine's optimized handling of tail calls.

Let's recall the summation example from earlier:

```
function sum(num1,...nums) {
    if (nums.length == 0) return num1;
    return num1 + sum( ...nums );
}
```

This isn't in PTC form because after the recursive call to `sum(...nums)` is finished, the `total` variable is added to that result. So, the stack frame has to be preserved to keep track of the `total` partial result while the rest of the recursion proceeds.

The key recognition point for this refactoring strategy is that we could remove our dependence on the stack by doing the addition *now* instead of *after*, and then forward-passing that partial result as an argument to the recursive call. In other words, instead of keeping `total` in the current function's stack frame, push it into the stack frame of the next recursive call; that frees up the current stack frame to be removed/reused.

To start, we could alter our `sum(..)` function's signature to have a new first parameter as the partial result:

```
function sum(result,num1,...nums) {
    // ..
}
```

Now, we should pre-calculate the addition of `result` and `num1`, and pass that along:

```
"use strict";

function sum(result,num1,...nums) {
    result = result + num1;
    if (nums.length == 0) return result;
    return sum( result, ...nums );
}
```

Now our `sum(..)` is in PTC form! Yay!

But the downside is we now have altered the signature of the function that makes using it stranger. The caller essentially has to pass `0` as the first argument ahead of the rest of the numbers they want to sum:

```
sum( /*initialResult=*/0, 3, 1, 17, 94, 8 );          // 123
```

That's unfortunate.

Typically, people will solve this by naming their awkward-signature recursive function differently, then defining an interface function that hides the awkwardness:

```
"use strict";

function sumRec(result,num1,...nums) {
    result = result + num1;
    if (nums.length == 0) return result;
    return sumRec( result, ...nums );
}

function sum(...nums) {
    return sumRec( /*initialResult=*/0, ...nums );
}

sum( 3, 1, 17, 94, 8 );                               // 123
```

That's better. Still unfortunate that we've now created multiple functions instead of just one. Sometimes you'll see developers "hide" the recursive function as an inner function, like this:

```
"use strict";

function sum(...nums) {
    return sumRec( /*initialResult=*/0, ...nums );

    function sumRec(result,num1,...nums) {
        result = result + num1;
        if (nums.length == 0) return result;
        return sumRec( result, ...nums );
    }
}

sum( 3, 1, 17, 94, 8 );                               // 123
```

The downside here is that we'll re-create that inner `sumRec(..)` function each time the outer `sum(..)` is called. So, we can go back to them being side-by-side functions, but hide them both inside an IIFE, and expose just the one we want to:

```
"use strict";

var sum = (function IIFE(){

    return function sum(...nums) {
        return sumRec( /*initialResult=*/0, ...nums );
    }

    function sumRec(result,num1,...nums) {
        result = result + num1;
        if (nums.length == 0) return result;
        return sumRec( result, ...nums );
    }

})();

sum( 3, 1, 17, 94, 8 );                         // 123
```

OK, we've got PTC and we've got a nice clean signature for our `sum(..)` that doesn't require the caller to know about our implementation details. Yay!

But... wow, our simple recursive function has a lot more noise now. The readability has definitely been reduced. That's unfortunate to say the least. Sometimes, that's just the best we can do.

Luckily, in some other cases, like the present one, there's a better way. Let's reset back to this version:

```
"use strict";

function sum(result,num1,...nums) {
    result = result + num1;
    if (nums.length == 0) return result;
    return sum( result, ...nums );
}

sum( /*initialResult=*/0, 3, 1, 17, 94, 8 );        // 123
```

What you might observe is that `result` is a number just like `num1`, which means that we can always treat the first number in our list as our running total; that includes even the first call. All we need is to rename those params to make this clear:

```
"use strict";

function sum(num1,num2,...nums) {
    num1 = num1 + num2;
    if (nums.length == 0) return num1;
    return sum( num1, ...nums );
}

sum( 3, 1, 17, 94, 8 );                              // 123
```

Awesome. That's much better, huh!? I think this pattern achieves a good balance between declarative/reasonable and performant.

Let's try refactoring with PTC once more, revisiting our earlier `maxEven(..)` (currently not PTC). We'll observe that similar to keeping the sum as the first argument, we can narrow the list of numbers one at a time, keeping the first argument as the highest even we've come across thus far.

For clarity, the algorithm strategy (similar to what we discussed earlier) we might use:

1. Start by comparing the first two numbers, `num1` and `num2`.
2. Is `num1` even, and is `num1` greater than `num2`? If so, keep `num1`.

3. If num2 is even, keep it (store in num1).
4. Otherwise, fall back to undefined (store in num1).
5. If there are more nums to consider, recursively compare them to num1.
6. Finally, just return whatever value is left in num1.

Our code can follow these steps almost exactly:

```
"use strict";

function maxEven(num1,num2,...nums) {
    num1 =
        (num1 % 2 == 0 && !(maxEven( num2 ) > num1)) ?
            num1 :
            (num2 % 2 == 0 ? num2 : undefined);

    return nums.length == 0 ?
        num1 :
        maxEven( num1, ...nums )
}
```

Note

The first maxEven(..) call is not in PTC position, but because it only passes in num2, it only recurses just that one level then returns right back out; this is only a trick to avoid repeating the % logic. As such, this call won't increase the growth of the recursive stack, any more than if that call was to an entirely different function. The second maxEven(..) call is the legitimate recursive call, and it is in fact in PTC position, meaning our stack won't grow as the recursion proceeds.

It should be repeated that this example is only to illustrate the approach to moving recursion to the PTC form to optimize the stack (memory) usage. The more direct way to express a max-even algorithm might indeed be a filtering of the nums list for evens first, followed then by a max bubbling or even a sort.

Refactoring recursion into PTC is admittedly a little intrusive on the simple declarative form, but it still gets the job done reasonably. Unfortunately, some kinds of recursion won't work well even with an interface function, so we'll need different strategies.

Continuation Passing Style (CPS)

In JavaScript, the word *continuation* is often used to mean a function callback that specifies the next step(s) to execute after a certain function finishes its work. Organizing code so that each function receives another function to execute at its end is referred to as Continuation Passing Style (CPS).

Some forms of recursion cannot practically be refactored to pure PTC, especially multiple recursion. Recall the `fib(..)` function earlier, and even the mutual recursion form we derived. In both cases, there are multiple recursive calls, which effectively defeats PTC memory optimizations.

However, you can perform the first recursive call, and wrap the subsequent recursive calls in a continuation function to pass into that first call. Even though this would mean ultimately many more functions will need to be executed in the stack, as long all of them, continuations included, are in PTC form, stack memory usage will not grow unbounded.

We could do this for `fib(..)`:

```
"use strict";

function fib(n,cont = identity) {
    if (n <= 1) return cont( n );
    return fib(
        n - 2,
        n2 => fib(
            n - 1,
            n1 => cont( n2 + n1 )
        )
    );
}
```

Pay close attention to what's happening here. First, we default the cont(..) continuation function as our identity(..) utility from Chapter 3; remember, it simply returns whatever is passed to it.

Moreover, not just one but two continuation functions are added to the mix. The first one receives the n2 argument, which eventually receives the computation of the fib(n-2) value. The next inner continuation receives the n1 argument, which eventually is the fib(n-1) value. Once both n2 and n1 values are known, they can be added together (n2 + n1), and that value is passed along to the next cont(..) continuation step.

Perhaps this will help mentally sort out what's going on: just like in the previous discussion when we passed partial results along instead of returning them back after the recursive stack, we're doing the same here, but each step gets wrapped in a continuation, which defers its computation. That trick allows us to perform multiple steps where each is in PTC form.

In static languages, CPS is often an opportunity for tail calls the compiler can automatically identify and rearrange recursive code to take advantage of. Unfortunately, that doesn't really apply to the nature of JS.

In JavaScript, you'd likely need to write the CPS form yourself. It's clunkier, for sure; the declarative notation-like form has certainly been obscured. But overall, this form is still more declarative than the for-loop imperative implementation.

Warning

One major caveat that should be noted is that in CPS, creating the extra inner continuation functions still consumes memory, but of a different sort. Instead of piling up stack frames, the closures just consume free memory (typically, from the heap). Engines don't seem to apply the RangeError limits in these cases, but that doesn't mean your memory usage is fixed in scale.

Trampolines

Where CPS creates continuations and passes them along, another technique for alleviating memory pressure is called trampolines. In this style of code, CPS-like continuations are created, but instead of passed in, they are shallowly returned.

Instead of functions calling functions, the stack never goes beyond depth of one, because each function just returns the next function that should be called. A loop simply keeps running each returned function until there are no more functions to run.

One advantage with trampolines is you aren't limited to environments that support PTC; another is that each function call is regular, not PTC optimized, so it may run quicker.

Let's sketch out a `trampoline(..)` utility:

```
function trampoline(fn) {
    return function trampolined(...args) {
        var result = fn( ...args );

        while (typeof result == "function") {
            result = result();
        }

        return result;
    };
}
```

As long as a function is returned, the loop keeps going, executing that function and capturing its return, then checking its type. Once a non-function comes back, the trampoline assumes the function calling is complete, and just gives back the value.

Because each continuation needs to return another continuation, we'll need to use the earlier trick of forward-passing the partial result as an argument. Here's how we could use this utility with our earlier example of summation of a list of numbers:

```
var sum = trampoline(
    function sum(num1,num2,...nums) {
        num1 = num1 + num2;
        if (nums.length == 0) return num1;
        return () => sum( num1, ...nums );
    }
);

var xs = [];
for (let i=0; i<20000; i++) {
    xs.push( i );
}

sum( ...xs );                           // 199990000
```

The downside is that a trampoline requires you to wrap your recursive function in the trampoline driving function; moreover, just like CPS, closures are created for each continuation. However, unlike CPS, each continuation function returned runs and finishes right away, so the engine won't have to accumulate a growing amount of closure memory while the call stack depth of the problem is exhausted.

Beyond execution and memory performance, the advantage of trampolines over CPS is that they're less intrusive on the declarative recursion form, in that you don't have to change the function signature to receive a continuation function argument. Trampolines are not ideal, but they can be effective in your balancing act between imperative looping code and declarative recursion.

Summary

Recursion is when a function recursively calls itself. Heh. A recursive definition for recursion. Get it!?

Direct recursion is a function that makes at least one call to itself, and it keeps dispatching to itself until it satisfies a base condition. Multiple recursion (like binary recursion) is when a function calls itself multiple times. Mutual recursion is when two or more functions recursively loop by *mutually* calling each other.

The upside of recursion is that it's more declarative and thus typically more readable. The downside is usually performance, but more memory constraints even than execution speed.

Tail calls alleviate the memory pressure by reusing/discarding stack frames. JavaScript requires strict mode and proper tail calls (PTC) to take advantage of this "optimization". There are several techniques we can mix-n-match to refactor a non-PTC recursive function to PTC form, or at least avoid the memory constraints by flattening the stack.

Remember: recursion should be used to make code more readable. If you misuse or abuse recursion, the readability will end up worse than the imperative form. Don't do that!

Chapter 9: List Operations

If you can do something awesome, keep doing it repeatedly.

We've already seen several brief references earlier in the text to some utilities that we now want to take a very close look at, namely `map(..)`, `filter(..)`, and `reduce(..)`. In JavaScript, these utilities are typically used as methods on the array (aka, "list") prototype, so we would naturally refer to them as array or list operations.

Before we talk about the specific array methods, we want to examine conceptually what these operations are used for. It's equally important in this chapter that you understand *why* list operations are important as it is to understand *how* list operations work. Make sure you approach this chapter with that detail in mind.

The vast majority of common illustrations of these operations, both outside of this book and here in this chapter, depict trivial tasks performed on lists of values (like doubling each number in an array); it's a cheap and easy way to get the point across.

But don't just gloss over these simple examples and miss the deeper point. Some of the most important FP value in understanding list operations comes from being able to model a sequence of tasks – a series of statements that wouldn't otherwise *look* like a list – as a list operation instead of performing them individually.

This isn't just a trick to write more terse code. What we're after is to move from imperative to declarative style, to make the code patterns more readily recognizable and thus more readable.

But there's something **even more important to grasp**. With imperative code, each intermediate result in a set of calculations is stored in variable(s) through assignment. The more of these imperative patterns your code relies on, the harder it is to verify that there aren't mistakes – in the logic, accidental mutation of values, or hidden side causes/effects lurking.

By chaining and/or composing list operations together, the intermediate results are tracked implicitly and largely protected from these hazards.

Note

More than previous chapters, to keep the many following code snippets as brief as possible, we'll rely heavily on the ES6 => form. However, my advice on => from Chapter 2 still applies for general coding.

Non-FP List Processing

As a quick preamble to our discussion in this chapter, I want to call out a few operations which may seem related to JavaScript arrays and FP list operations, but which aren't. These operations will not be covered here, because they are not consistent with general FP best practices:

- `forEach(..)`
- `some(..)`
- `every(..)`

`forEach(..)` is an iteration helper, but it's designed for each function call to operate with side effects; you can probably guess why that's not an endorsed FP list operation for our discussion!

`some(..)` and `every(..)` do encourage the use of pure functions (specifically, predicate functions like `filter(..)` expects), but they inevitably reduce a list to a `true`/`false` result, essentially like a search or matching. These two utilities don't really fit the mold of how we want to model our code with FP, so we're going to skip covering them here.

Map

We'll start our exploration of FP list operations with one of the most basic and fundamental: `map(..)`.

A mapping is a transformation from one value to another value. For example, if you start with the number 2 and you multiply it by 3, you have mapped it to

6. It's important to note that we're not talking about mapping transformation as implying *in-place* mutation or reassignment; instead, we're looking at how mapping transformation projects a new value from one location to the other.

In other words:

```
var x = 2, y;

// transformation / projection
y = x * 3;

// mutation / reassignment
x = x * 3;
```

If we define a function for this multiplying by 3, that function acts as a mapping (transformer) function:

```
var multipleBy3 = v => v * 3;

var x = 2, y;

// transformation / projection
y = multiplyBy3( x );
```

We can naturally extend mapping from a single value transformation to a collection of values. map(..) is an operation that transforms all the values of a list as it projects them to a new list:

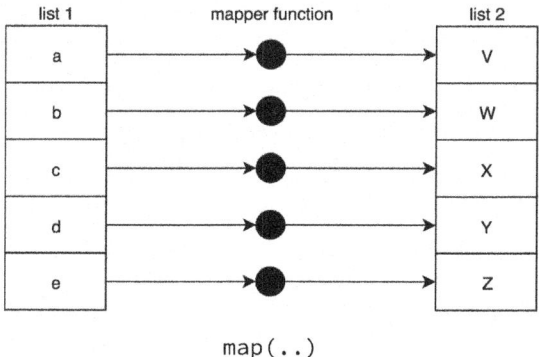

To implement `map(..)`:

```
function map(mapperFn,arr) {
    var newList = [];

    for (let [idx,v] of arr.entries()) {
        newList.push(
            mapperFn( v, idx, arr )
        );
    }

    return newList;
}
```

Note

The parameter order `mapperFn, arr` may feel backwards at first, but this convention is much more common in FP libraries because it makes these utilities easier to compose (with currying).

The `mapperFn(..)` is naturally passed the list item to map/transform, but also an `idx` and `arr`. We're doing that to keep consistency with the built-in array `map(..)`. These extra pieces of information can be very useful in some cases.

But in other cases, you may want to use a `mapperFn(..)` that only the list item should be passed to, because the extra arguments might change its behavior. In Chapter 3, "All For One", we introduced `unary(..)`, which limits a function to only accept a single argument (no matter how many are passed).

Recall the example from Chapter 3 about limiting `parseInt(..)` to a single argument to be used safely as a `mapperFn(..)`, which we can also utilize with the standalone `map(..)`:

```
map( ["1","2","3"], unary( parseInt ) );
// [1,2,3]
```

Note

The JavaScript array prototype operations (`map(..)`, `filter(..)`, and `reduce(..)`) all accept an optional last argument to use for `this` binding of the function. As we discussed in Chapter 2, "What's This?", `this`-based coding should generally be avoided wherever possible in terms of being consistent with the best practices of FP. As such, our example implementations in this chapter do not support such a `this`-binding feature.

Beyond the obvious numeric or string operations you could perform against a list of those respective value types, here are some other examples of mapping operations. We can use `map(..)` to transform a list of functions into a list of their return values:

```
var one = () => 1;
var two = () => 2;
var three = () => 3;

[one,two,three].map( fn => fn() );
// [1,2,3]
```

Or we can first transform a list of functions by composing each of them with another function, and then execute them:

```
var increment = v => ++v;
var decrement = v => --v;
var square = v => v * v;

var double = v => v * 2;

[increment,decrement,square]
.map( fn => compose( fn, double ) )
.map( fn => fn( 3 ) );
// [7,5,36]
```

Something interesting to observe about `map(..)`: we typically would assume that the list is processed left-to-right, but there's nothing about the concept of `map(..)`

that really requires that. Each transformation is supposed to be independent of every other transformation.

Mapping in a general sense could even been parallelized in an environment that supports that, which for a large list could drastically improve performance. We don't see JavaScript actually doing that because there's nothing that requires you to pass a pure function as mapperFn(..), even though you **really ought to**. If you were to pass an impure function and JS were to run different calls in different orders, it would quickly cause havoc.

Even though theoretically, individual mapping operations are independent, JS has to assume that they're not. That's a bummer.

Sync vs. Async

The list operations we're discussing in this chapter all operate synchronously on a list of values that are all already present; map(..) as conceived here is an eager operation. But another way of thinking about the mapper function is as an event handler which is invoked for each new value encountered in the list.

Imagine something fictional like this:

```
var newArr = arr.map();

arr.addEventListener( "value", multiplyBy3 );
```

Now, any time a value is added to arr, the multiplyBy3(..) event handler – mapper function – is called with the value, and its transformation is added to newArr.

What we're hinting at is that arrays, and the array operations we perform on them, are the eager synchronous versions, whereas these same operations can also be modeled on a "lazy list" (aka, stream) that receives its values over time. We'll dive into this topic in Chapter 10.

Mapping vs. Eaching

Some advocate using map(..) as a general form of forEach(..)-iteration, where essentially the value received is passed through untouched, but then some side effect can be performed:

```
[1,2,3,4,5]
.map( function mapperFn(v){
    console.log( v );           // side effect!
    return v;
} )
..
```

The reason this technique can seem useful is that the map(..) returns the array so you can keep chaining more operations after it; the return value of forEach(..) is undefined. However, I think you should avoid using map(..) in this way, because it's a net confusion to use a core FP operation in a decidedly un-FP way.

You've heard the old adage about using the right tool for the right job, right? Hammer for a nail, screwdriver for a screw... This is slightly different: it's use the right tool *in the right way*.

A hammer is meant to be held in your hand; if you instead hold it in your mouth and try to hammer the nail, you're not gonna be very effective. map(..) is intended to map values, not create side effects.

A Word: Functors

We've mostly tried to stay away from invented terminology in FP as much as possible in this book. We have used official terms at times, but mostly when we can derive some sense of meaning from them in regular everyday conversation.

I'm going to very briefly break that pattern and use a word that might be a little intimidating: functor. The reason I want to talk about functors here is because we now already understand what they do, and because that term is used heavily throughout the rest of FP literature; indeed, functors are foundational ideas in FP that come straight from the mathematical principles (category theory). You being at least familiar with and not scared by this term will be beneficial.

A functor is a value that has a utility for using an operator function on that value, which preserves composition.

If the value in question is compound, meaning it's comprised of individual values – as is the case with arrays, for example! – a functor uses the operator function on each individual value. Moreover, the functor utility creates a new compound value holding the results of all the individual operator function calls.

This is all a fancy way of describing what we just looked at with `map(..)`. The `map(..)` function takes its associated value (an array) and a mapping function (the operator function), and executes the mapping function for each individual value in the array. Finally, it returns a new array with all the newly mapped values in it.

Another example: a string functor would be a string plus a utility that executes some operator function across all the characters in the string, returning a new string with the processed letters. Consider this highly contrived example:

```
function uppercaseLetter(c) {
    var code = c.charCodeAt( 0 );

    // lowercase letter?
    if (code >= 97 && code <= 122) {
        // uppercase it!
        code = code - 32;
    }

    return String.fromCharCode( code );
}

function stringMap(mapperFn,str) {
    return [...str].map( mapperFn ).join( "" );
}

stringMap( uppercaseLetter, "Hello World!" );
// HELLO WORLD!
```

`stringMap(..)` allows a string to be a functor. You can define a mapping function for any data structure; as long as the utility follows these rules, the data structure is a functor.

Filter

Imagine I bring an empty basket with me to the grocery store to visit the fruit section; there's a big display of fruit (apples, oranges, and bananas). I'm really hungry so I want to get as much fruit as they have available, but I really only prefer the round fruits (apples and oranges). So I sift through each fruit one by one, and I walk away with a basket full of just the apples and oranges.

Let's say we call this process *filtering*. Would you more naturally describe my shopping as starting with an empty basket and **filtering in** (selecting, including) only the apples and oranges, or starting with the full display of fruits and **filtering out** (skipping, excluding) the bananas as my basket is filled with fruit?

If you cook spaghetti in a pot of water, and then pour it into a strainer (aka filter) over the sink, are you filtering in the spaghetti or filtering out the water? If you put coffee grounds into a filter and make a cup of coffee, did you filter in the coffee into your cup, or filter out the coffee grounds?

Does your view of filtering depend on whether the stuff you want is "kept" in the filter or passes through the filter?

What about on airline/hotel websites, when you specify options to "filter your results"? Are you filtering in the results that match your criteria, or are you filtering out everything that doesn't match? Think carefully: this example might have a different semantic than the previous ones.

Filtering Confusion

Depending on your perspective, filtering is either exclusionary or inclusionary. This conceptual conflation is unfortunate.

I think the most common interpretation of filtering – outside of programming, anyway – is that you filter out unwanted stuff. Unfortunately, in programming, we have essentially flipped this semantic to be more like filtering in wanted stuff.

The `filter(..)` list operation takes a function to decide if each value in the original array should be in the new array or not. This function needs to return `true` if a value should make it, and `false` if it should be skipped. A function that returns true/false for this kind of decision making goes by the special name: predicate function.

If you think of true as indicating a positive signal, the definition of filter(..) is that you are saying "keep" (to filter in) a value rather than saying "discard" (to filter out) a value.

To use filter(..) as an exclusionary action, you have to twist your brain to think of positively signaling an exclusion by returning false, and passively letting a value pass through by returning true.

The reason this semantic mismatch matters is because of how you will likely name the function used as predicateFn(..), and what that means for the readability of code. We'll come back to this point shortly.

Here's how to visualize a filter(..) operation across a list of values:

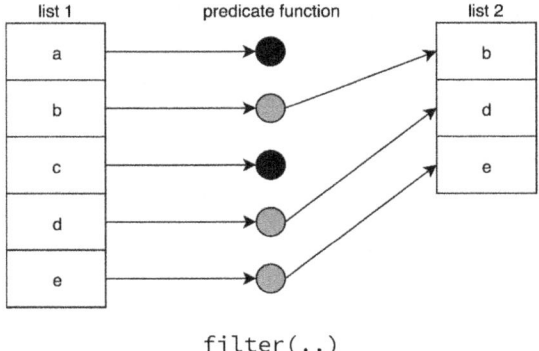

filter(..)

To implement filter(..):

```
function filter(predicateFn,arr) {
    var newList = [];

    for (let [idx,v] of arr.entries()) {
        if (predicateFn( v, idx, arr )) {
            newList.push( v );
        }
    }
}
```

```
        return newList;
}
```

Notice that just like `mapperFn(..)` before, `predicateFn(..)` is passed not only the value but also the `idx` and `arr`. Use `unary(..)` to limit its arguments as necessary.

Just as with `map(..)`, `filter(..)` is provided as a built-in utility on JS arrays.

Let's consider a predicate function like this:

```
var whatToCallIt = v => v % 2 == 1;
```

This function uses `v % 2 == 1` to return `true` or `false`. The effect here is that an odd number will return `true`, and an even number will return `false`. So, what should we call this function? A natural name might be:

```
var isOdd = v => v % 2 == 1;
```

Consider how you might use `isOdd(..)` with a simple value check somewhere in your code:

```
var midIdx;

if (isOdd( list.length )) {
    midIdx = (list.length + 1) / 2;
}
else {
    midIdx = list.length / 2;
}
```

Makes sense, right? But, let's consider using it with the built-in array `filter(..)` to filter a list of values:

```
[1,2,3,4,5].filter( isOdd );
// [1,3,5]
```

If you described the `[1,3,5]` result, would you say, "I filtered out the even numbers", or would you say "I filtered in the odd numbers"? I think the former is a more natural way of describing it. But the code reads the opposite. The code reads, almost literally, that we "filtered (in) each number that is odd".

I personally find this semantic confusing. There's no question there's plenty of precedent for experienced developers. But if you just start with a fresh slate, this expression of the logic seems kinda like not speaking without a double negative – aka, speaking with a double negative.

We could make this easier by renaming `isOdd(..)` to `isEven(..)`:

```
var isEven = v => v % 2 == 1;

[1,2,3,4,5].filter( isEven );
// [1,3,5]
```

Yay! But that function makes no sense with its name, in that it returns `false` when it's even:

```
isEven( 2 );          // false
```

Yuck.

Recall that in Chapter 3, "No Points", we defined a `not(..)` operator that negates a predicate function. Consider:

```
var isEven = not( isOdd );

isEven( 2 );          // true
```

But we can't use *this* `isEven(..)` with `filter(..)` the way it's currently defined, because our logic will be reversed; we'll end up with evens, not odds. We'd need to do:

```
[1,2,3,4,5].filter( not( isEven ) );
// [1,3,5]
```

That defeats the whole purpose, though, so let's not do that. We're just going in circles.

Filtering-Out & Filtering-In

To clear up all this confusion, let's define a `filterOut(..)` that actually **filters out** values by internally negating the predicate check. While we're at it, we'll alias `filterIn(..)` to the existing `filter(..)`:

```
var filterIn = filter;

function filterOut(predicateFn,arr) {
    return filterIn( not( predicateFn ), arr );
}
```

Now we can use whichever filtering makes most sense at any point in our code:

```
isOdd( 3 );                              // true
isEven( 2 );                             // true

filterIn( isOdd, [1,2,3,4,5] );          // [1,3,5]
filterOut( isEven, [1,2,3,4,5] );        // [1,3,5]
```

I think using `filterIn(..)` and `filterOut(..)` (known as `reject(..)` in Ramda) will make your code a lot more readable than just using `filter(..)` and leaving the semantics conflated and confusing for the reader.

Reduce

While `map(..)` and `filter(..)` produce new lists, typically this third operator (`reduce(..)`) combines (aka "reduces") the values of a list down to a single finite (non-list) value, like a number or string. However, later in this chapter, we'll look at how you can push reduce(..) to use it in more advanced ways. reduce(..) is one of the most important FP tools; it's like a Swiss Army all-in-one knife with all its usefulness.

A combination/reduction is abstractly defined as taking two values and making them into one value. Some FP contexts refer to this as "folding", as if you're folding two values together into one value. That's a helpful visualization, I think.

Just like with mapping and filtering, the manner of the combination is entirely up to you, and generally dependent on the types of values in the list. For example, numbers will typically be combined through arithmetic, strings through concatenation, and functions through composition.

Sometimes a reduction will specify an initialValue and start its work by combining it with the first value in the list, cascading down through each of the rest of the values in the list. That looks like this:

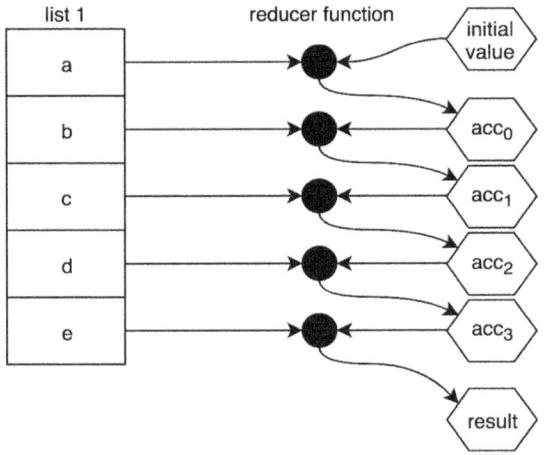

reduce(..) *with initial value specified*

Alternatively, you can omit the initialValue in which case the first value of the list will act in place of the initialValue and the combining will start with the second value in the list, like this:

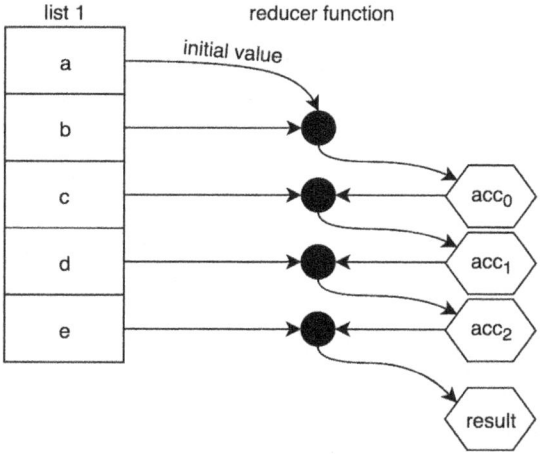

reduce(..) *with no initial value specified*

 Warning

In JavaScript, if there's not at least one value in the reduction (either in the array or specified as initialValue), an error is thrown. Be careful not to omit the initialValue if the list for the reduction could possibly be empty under any circumstance.

The function you pass to reduce(..) to perform the reduction is typically called a reducer. A reducer has a different signature from the mapper and predicate functions we looked at earlier. Reducers primarily receive the current reduction result as well as the next value to reduce it with. The current result at each step of the reduction is often referred to as the accumulator.

For example, consider the steps involved in multiply-reducing the numbers 5, 10, and 15, with an initialValue of 3:

1. 3 * 5 = 15
2. 15 * 10 = 150
3. 150 * 15 = 2250

Expressed in JavaScript using the built-in reduce(..) method on arrays:

```
[5,10,15].reduce( (product,v) => product * v, 3 );
// 2250
```

But a standalone implementation of `reduce(..)` might look like this:

```
function reduce(reducerFn,initialValue,arr) {
    var acc, startIdx;

    if (arguments.length == 3) {
        acc = initialValue;
        startIdx = 0;
    }
    else if (arr.length > 0) {
        acc = arr[0];
        startIdx = 1;
    }
    else {
        throw new Error( "Must provide at least one value." );
    }

    for (let idx = startIdx; idx < arr.length; idx++) {
        acc = reducerFn( acc, arr[idx], idx, arr );
    }

    return acc;
}
```

Just as with `map(..)` and `filter(..)`, the reducer function is also passed the lesser-common `idx` and `arr` arguments in case that's useful to the reduction. I would say I don't typically use these, but I guess it's nice to have them available.

Recall in Chapter 4, we discussed the `compose(..)` utility and showed an implementation with `reduce(..)`:

```
function compose(...fns) {
    return function composed(result){
        return [...fns].reverse().reduce( function reducer(result,fn){
            return fn( result );
        }, result );
    };
}
```

To illustrate `reduce(..)`-based composition differently, consider a reducer that will compose functions left-to-right (like `pipe(..)` does), to use in an array chain:

```
var pipeReducer = (composedFn,fn) => pipe( composedFn, fn );

var fn =
    [3,17,6,4]
    .map( v => n => v * n )
    .reduce( pipeReducer );

fn( 9 );            // 11016  (9 * 3 * 17 * 6 * 4)
fn( 10 );           // 12240  (10 * 3 * 17 * 6 * 4)
```

`pipeReducer(..)` is unfortunately not point-free (see Chapter 3, "No Points"), but we can't just pass `pipe(..)` as the reducer itself, because it's variadic; the extra arguments (`idx` and `arr`) that `reduce(..)` passes to its reducer function would be problematic.

Earlier we talked about using `unary(..)` to limit a `mapperFn(..)` or `predicateFn(..)` to just a single argument. It might be handy to have a `binary(..)` that does something similar but limits to two arguments, for a `reducerFn(..)` function:

```
var binary =
    fn =>
        (arg1,arg2) =>
            fn( arg1, arg2 );
```

Using `binary(..)`, our previous example is a little cleaner:

```
var pipeReducer = binary( pipe );

var fn =
    [3,17,6,4]
    .map( v => n => v * n )
    .reduce( pipeReducer );

fn( 9 );                // 11016  (9 * 3 * 17 * 6 * 4)
fn( 10 );               // 12240  (10 * 3 * 17 * 6 * 4)
```

Unlike `map(..)` and `filter(..)` whose order of passing through the array wouldn't actually matter, `reduce(..)` definitely uses left-to-right processing. If you want to reduce right-to-left, JavaScript provides a `reduceRight(..)`, with all other behaviors the same as `reduce(..)`:

```
var hyphenate = (str,char) => `${str}-${char}`;

["a","b","c"].reduce( hyphenate );
// "a-b-c"

["a","b","c"].reduceRight( hyphenate );
// "c-b-a"
```

Where `reduce(..)` works left-to-right and thus acts naturally like `pipe(..)` in composing functions, `reduceRight(..)`'s right-to-left ordering is natural for performing a `compose(..)`-like operation. So, let's revisit `compose(..)` from Chapter 4, but implement it using `reduceRight(..)`:

```
function compose(...fns) {
    return function composed(result){
        return fns.reduceRight( function reducer(result,fn){
            return fn( result );
        }, result );
    };
}
```

Now, we don't need to do `[...fns].reverse()`; we just reduce from the other direction!

Map as Reduce

The `map(..)` operation is iterative in its nature, so it can also be represented as a reduction (`reduce(..)`). The trick is to realize that the `initialValue` of `reduce(..)` can be itself an (empty) array, in which case the result of a reduction can be another list!

```
var double = v => v * 2;

[1,2,3,4,5].map( double );
// [2,4,6,8,10]

[1,2,3,4,5].reduce(
    (list,v) => (
        list.push( double( v ) ),
        list
    ), []
);
// [2,4,6,8,10]
```

Note

> We're cheating with this reducer: using a side effect by allowing `list.push(..)` to mutate the list that was passed in. In general, that's not a good idea, obviously, but since we know the `[]` list is being created and passed in, it's less dangerous. You could be more formal – yet less performant! – by creating a new list with the val `concat(..)`d onto the end. We'll come back to this cheat in Appendix A.

Implementing `map(..)` with `reduce(..)` is not on its surface an obvious step or even an improvement. However, this ability will be a crucial recognition for more advanced techniques covered in Appendix A.

Filter as Reduce

Just as `map(..)` can be done with `reduce(..)`, so can `filter(..)`:

```
var isOdd = v => v % 2 == 1;

[1,2,3,4,5].filter( isOdd );
// [1,3,5]

[1,2,3,4,5].reduce(
    (list,v) => (
        isOdd( v ) ? list.push( v ) : undefined,
        list
    ), []
);
// [1,3,5]
```

 Note

> More impure reducer cheating here. Instead of `list.push(..)`, we could have done `list.concat(..)` and returned the new list. We'll come back to this cheat in Appendix A.

Advanced List Operations

Now that we feel somewhat comfortable with the foundational list operations `map(..)`, `filter(..)`, and `reduce(..)`, let's look at a few more-sophisticated operations you may find useful in various situations. These are generally utilities you'll find in various FP libraries.

Unique

Filtering a list to include only unique values, based on `indexOf(..)` searching (which uses `===` strict equality comparison):

```
var unique =
    arr =>
        arr.filter(
            (v,idx) =>
                arr.indexOf( v ) == idx
        );
```

This technique works by observing that we should only include the first occurrence of an item from `arr` into the new list; when running left-to-right, this will only be true if its `idx` position is the same as the `indexOf(..)` found position.

Another way to implement `unique(..)` is to run through `arr` and include an item into a new (initially empty) list if that item cannot already be found in the new list. For that processing, we use `reduce(..)`:

```
var unique =
    arr =>
        arr.reduce(
            (list,v) =>
                list.indexOf( v ) == -1 ?
                    ( list.push( v ), list ) : list
        , [] );
```

Note

There are many other ways to implement this algorithm using more imperative approaches like loops, and many of them are likely "more efficient" performance-wise. However, the advantage of either of these presented approaches is that they use existing built-in list operations, which makes them easier to chain/compose alongside other list operations. We'll talk more about those concerns later in this chapter.

`unique(..)` nicely produces a new list with no duplicates:

```
unique( [1,4,7,1,3,1,7,9,2,6,4,0,5,3] );
// [1, 4, 7, 3, 9, 2, 6, 0, 5]
```

Flatten

From time to time, you may have (or produce through some other operations) an array that's not just a flat list of values – for instance, it might include nested arrays, as shown here:

```
[ [1, 2, 3], 4, 5, [6, [7, 8]] ]
```

What if you'd like to transform it as follows?

```
[ 1, 2, 3, 4, 5, 6, 7, 8 ]
```

The operation we're looking for is typically called `flatten(..)`, and it could be implemented like this using our Swiss Army knife `reduce(..)`:

```
var flatten =
    arr =>
        arr.reduce(
            (list,v) =>
                list.concat( Array.isArray( v ) ? flatten( v ) : v )
        , [] );
```

Note

This implementation choice relies on recursion as we saw in Chapter 8.

To use `flatten(..)` with an array of arrays (of any nested depth):

```
flatten( [[0,1],2,3,[4,[5,6,7],[8,[9,[10,[11,12],13]]]]] );
// [0,1,2,3,4,5,6,7,8,9,10,11,12,13]
```

You might like to limit the recursive flattening to a certain depth. We can handle this by adding an optional `depth` limit argument to the implementation:

```
var flatten =
    (arr,depth = Infinity) =>
        arr.reduce(
            (list,v) =>
                list.concat(
                    depth > 0 ?
                        (depth > 1 && Array.isArray( v ) ?
                            flatten( v, depth - 1 ) :
                            v
                        ) :
                        [v]
                )
        , [] );
```

Illustrating the results with different flattening depths:

```
flatten( [[0,1],2,3,[4,[5,6,7],[8,[9,[10,[11,12],13]]]]], 0 );
// [[0,1],2,3,[4,[5,6,7],[8,[9,[10,[11,12],13]]]]]

flatten( [[0,1],2,3,[4,[5,6,7],[8,[9,[10,[11,12],13]]]]], 1 );
// [0,1,2,3,4,[5,6,7],[8,[9,[10,[11,12],13]]]]

flatten( [[0,1],2,3,[4,[5,6,7],[8,[9,[10,[11,12],13]]]]], 2 );
// [0,1,2,3,4,5,6,7,8,[9,[10,[11,12],13]]]

flatten( [[0,1],2,3,[4,[5,6,7],[8,[9,[10,[11,12],13]]]]], 3 );
// [0,1,2,3,4,5,6,7,8,9,[10,[11,12],13]]

flatten( [[0,1],2,3,[4,[5,6,7],[8,[9,[10,[11,12],13]]]]], 4 );
// [0,1,2,3,4,5,6,7,8,9,10,[11,12],13]

flatten( [[0,1],2,3,[4,[5,6,7],[8,[9,[10,[11,12],13]]]]], 5 );
// [0,1,2,3,4,5,6,7,8,9,10,11,12,13]
```

Mapping, Then Flattening

One of the most common usages of `flatten(..)` behavior is when you've mapped a list of elements where each transformed value from the original list is now itself a list of values. For example:

```
var firstNames = [
    { name: "Jonathan", variations: [ "John", "Jon", "Jonny" ] },
    { name: "Stephanie", variations: [ "Steph", "Stephy" ] },
    { name: "Frederick", variations: [ "Fred", "Freddy" ] }
];

firstNames
.map( entry => [ entry.name, ...entry.variations ] );
// [ ["Jonathan","John","Jon","Jonny"], ["Stephanie","Steph","Stephy"],
//   ["Frederick","Fred","Freddy"] ]
```

The return value is an array of arrays, which might be more awkward to work with. If we want a single dimension list with all the names, we can then `flatten(..)` that result:

```
flatten(
    firstNames
    .map( entry => [ entry.name, ...entry.variations ] )
);
// ["Jonathan","John","Jon","Jonny","Stephanie","Steph","Stephy",
//  "Frederick","Fred","Freddy"]
```

Besides being slightly more verbose, the disadvantage of doing the `map(..)` and `flatten(..)` as separate steps is primarily around performance; this approach processes the list twice, and creates an intermediate list that's then thrown away.

FP libraries typically define a `flatMap(..)` (often also called `chain(..)`) that does the mapping-then-flattening combined. For consistency and ease of composition (via currying), the `flatMap(..)` (aka `chain(..)`) utility typically matches the `mapperFn, arr` parameter order that we saw earlier with the standalone `map(..)`, `filter(..)`, and `reduce(..)` utilities:

```
flatMap( entry => [ entry.name, ...entry.variations ], firstNames );
// ["Jonathan","John","Jon","Jonny","Stephanie","Steph","Stephy",
//  "Frederick","Fred","Freddy"]
```

The naive implementation of `flatMap(..)` with both steps done separately:

```
var flatMap =
    (mapperFn,arr) =>
        flatten( arr.map( mapperFn ), 1 );
```

Note

We use 1 for the flattening-depth because the typical definition of `flatMap(..)` is that the flattening is shallow on just the first level.

Since this approach still processes the list twice resulting in worse performance, we can combine the operations manually, using `reduce(..)`:

```
var flatMap =
    (mapperFn,arr) =>
        arr.reduce(
            (list,v) =>
                // note: concat(..) used here since it automatically
                // flattens an array into the concatenation
                list.concat( mapperFn( v ) )
        , [] );
```

While there's some convenience and performance gained with a `flatMap(..)` utility, there may very well be times when you need other operations like `filter(..)`ing mixed in. If that's the case, doing the `map(..)` and `flatten(..)` separately might still be more appropriate.

Zip

So far, the list operations we've examined have operated on a single list. But some cases will need to process multiple lists. One well-known operation alternates selection of values from each of two input lists into sub-lists, called `zip(..)`:

```
zip( [1,3,5,7,9], [2,4,6,8,10] );
// [ [1,2], [3,4], [5,6], [7,8], [9,10] ]
```

Values 1 and 2 were selected into the sub-list `[1,2]`, then 3 and 4 into `[3,4]`, and so on. The definition of `zip(..)` requires a value from each of the two lists. If the two lists are of different lengths, the selection of values will continue until the shorter list has been exhausted, with the extra values in the other list ignored.

An implementation of `zip(..)`:

```
function zip(arr1,arr2) {
    var zipped = [];
    arr1 = [...arr1];
    arr2 = [...arr2];

    while (arr1.length > 0 && arr2.length > 0) {
        zipped.push( [ arr1.shift(), arr2.shift() ] );
    }

    return zipped;
}
```

The `[...arr1]` and `[...arr2]` copies ensure `zip(..)` is pure by not causing side effects on the received array references.

Note

There are some decidedly un-FP things going on in this implementation. There's an imperative `while`-loop and mutations of lists with both `shift()` and `push(..)`. Earlier in the book, I asserted that it's reasonable for pure functions to use impure behavior inside them (usually for performance), as long as the effects are fully self-contained. This implementation is safely pure.

Merge

Merging two lists by interleaving values from each source looks like this:

```
mergeLists( [1,3,5,7,9], [2,4,6,8,10] );
// [1,2,3,4,5,6,7,8,9,10]
```

It may not be obvious, but this result seems similar to what we get if we compose `flatten(..)` and `zip(..)`:

```
zip( [1,3,5,7,9], [2,4,6,8,10] );
// [ [1,2], [3,4], [5,6], [7,8], [9,10] ]

flatten( [ [1,2], [3,4], [5,6], [7,8], [9,10] ] );
// [1,2,3,4,5,6,7,8,9,10]

// composed:
flatten( zip( [1,3,5,7,9], [2,4,6,8,10] ) );
// [1,2,3,4,5,6,7,8,9,10]
```

However, recall that `zip(..)` only selects values until the shorter of two lists is exhausted, ignoring the leftover values; merging two lists would most naturally retain those extra values. Also, `flatten(..)` works recursively on nested lists, but you might expect list-merging to only work shallowly, keeping nested lists.

So, let's define a `mergeLists(..)` that works more like we'd expect:

```
function mergeLists(arr1,arr2) {
    var merged = [];
    arr1 = [...arr1];
    arr2 = [...arr2];

    while (arr1.length > 0 || arr2.length > 0) {
        if (arr1.length > 0) {
            merged.push( arr1.shift() );
        }
        if (arr2.length > 0) {
            merged.push( arr2.shift() );
        }
    }

    return merged;
}
```

Note

Various FP libraries don't define a `mergeLists(..)` but instead define a `merge(..)` that merges properties of two objects; the results of such a `merge(..)` will differ from our `mergeLists(..)`.

Alternatively, here are a couple of options to implement the list merging as a reducer:

```
// via @rwaldron
var mergeReducer =
    (merged,v,idx) =>
        (merged.splice( idx * 2, 0, v ), merged);


// via @WebReflection
var mergeReducer =
    (merged,v,idx) =>
        merged
            .slice( 0, idx * 2 )
            .concat( v, merged.slice( idx * 2 ) );
```

And using a `mergeReducer(..)`:

```
[1,3,5,7,9]
.reduce( mergeReducer, [2,4,6,8,10] );
// [1,2,3,4,5,6,7,8,9,10]
```

 Tip
We'll use the `mergeReducer(..)` trick later in the chapter.

Method vs. Standalone

A common source of frustration for FPers in JavaScript is unifying their strategy for working with utilities when some of them are provided as standalone functions (think about the various FP utilities we've derived in previous chapters) and others are methods of the array prototype (like the ones we've seen in this chapter).

The pain of this problem becomes more evident when you consider combining multiple operations:

```
[1,2,3,4,5]
.filter( isOdd )
.map( double )
.reduce( sum, 0 );                    // 18

// vs.

reduce(
    map(
        filter( [1,2,3,4,5], isOdd ),
        double
    ),
    sum,
    0
);                                    // 18
```

Both API styles accomplish the same task, but they have very different ergonomics. Many FPers will prefer the latter to the former, but the former is unquestionably more common in JavaScript. One thing specifically that's disliked about the latter is the nesting of the calls. The preference for the method chain style – typically called a fluent API style, as in jQuery and other tools – is that it's compact/concise and it reads in declarative top-down order.

The visual order for that manual composition of the standalone style is neither strictly left-to-right (top-to-bottom) nor right-to-left (bottom-to-top); it's inner-to-outer, which harms the readability.

Automatic composition normalizes the reading order as right-to-left (bottom-to-top) for both styles. So, to explore the implications of the style differences, let's examine composition specifically; it seems like it should be straightforward, but it's a little awkward in both cases.

Composing Method Chains

The array methods receive the implicit `this` argument, so despite their appearance, they can't be treated as unary; that makes composition more awkward. To cope, we'll first need a `this`-aware version of `partial(..)`:

```
var partialThis =
    (fn,...presetArgs) =>
        // intentionally `function` to allow `this`-binding
        function partiallyApplied(...laterArgs){
            return fn.apply( this, [...presetArgs, ...laterArgs] );
        };
```

We'll also need a version of `compose(..)` that calls each of the partially applied methods in the context of the chain – the input value it's being "passed" (via implicit `this`) from the previous step:

```
var composeChainedMethods =
    (...fns) =>
        result =>
            fns.reduceRight(
                (result,fn) =>
                    fn.call( result )
                , result
            );
```

And using these two `this`-aware utilities together:

```
composeChainedMethods(
   partialThis( Array.prototype.reduce, sum, 0 ),
   partialThis( Array.prototype.map, double ),
   partialThis( Array.prototype.filter, isOdd )
)
( [1,2,3,4,5] );                          // 18
```

Note

The three `Array.prototype.XXX`-style references are grabbing references to the built-in `Array.prototype.*` methods so that we can reuse them with our own arrays.

Composing Standalone Utilities

Standalone `compose(..)`-style composition of these utilities doesn't need all the `this` contortions, which is its most favorable argument. For example, we could define standalones as:

```
var filter = (arr,predicateFn) => arr.filter( predicateFn );

var map = (arr,mapperFn) => arr.map( mapperFn );

var reduce = (arr,reducerFn,initialValue) =>
    arr.reduce( reducerFn, initialValue );
```

But this particular standalone approach, with the `arr` as the first parameter, suffers from its own awkwardness; the cascading array context is the first argument rather than the last, so we have to use right-partial application to compose them:

```
compose(
    partialRight( reduce, sum, 0 ),
    partialRight( map, double ),
    partialRight( filter, isOdd )
)
( [1,2,3,4,5] );                        // 18
```

That's why FP libraries typically define `filter(..)`, `map(..)`, and `reduce(..)` to instead receive the array last, not first. They also typically automatically curry the utilities:

```
var filter = curry(
    (predicateFn,arr) =>
        arr.filter( predicateFn )
);

var map = curry(
    (mapperFn,arr) =>
        arr.map( mapperFn )
);

var reduce = curry(
    (reducerFn,initialValue,arr) =>
        arr.reduce( reducerFn, initialValue )
);
```

Working with the utilities defined in this way, the composition flow is a bit nicer:

```
compose(
    reduce( sum )( 0 ),
    map( double ),
    filter( isOdd )
)
( [1,2,3,4,5] );                        // 18
```

The cleanliness of this approach is in part why FPers prefer the standalone utility style instead of instance methods. But your mileage may vary.

Adapting Methods to Standalones

In the previous definition of `filter(..)`/`map(..)`/`reduce(..)`, you might have spotted the common pattern across all three: they all dispatch to the corresponding native array method. So, can we generate these standalone adaptations with a utility? Yes! Let's make a utility called `unboundMethod(..)` to do just that:

```
var unboundMethod =
    (methodName,argCount = 2) =>
        curry(
            (...args) => {
                var obj = args.pop();
                return obj[methodName]( ...args );
            },
            argCount
        );
```

And to use this utility:

```
var filter = unboundMethod( "filter", 2 );
var map = unboundMethod( "map", 2 );
var reduce = unboundMethod( "reduce", 3 );

compose(
    reduce( sum )( 0 ),
    map( double ),
    filter( isOdd )
)
( [1,2,3,4,5] );                     // 18
```

Note

unboundMethod(..) is called invoker(..) in Ramda.

Adapting Standalones to Methods

If you prefer to work with only array methods (fluent chain style), you have two choices. You can:

1. Extend the built-in Array.prototype with additional methods.

2. Adapt a standalone utility to work as a reducer function and pass it to the `reduce(..)` instance method.

Don't do (1). It's never a good idea to extend built-in natives like `Array.prototype` – unless you define a subclass of `Array`, but that's beyond our discussion scope here. In an effort to discourage bad practices, we won't go any further into this approach.

Let's **focus on (2)** instead. To illustrate this point, we'll convert the recursive `flatten(..)` standalone utility from earlier:

```
var flatten =
    arr =>
        arr.reduce(
            (list,v) =>
                // note: concat(..) used here since it automatically
                // flattens an array into the concatenation
                list.concat( Array.isArray( v ) ? flatten( v ) : v )
        , [] );
```

Let's pull out the inner `reducer(..)` function as the standalone utility (and adapt it to work without the outer `flatten(..)`):

```
// intentionally a function to allow recursion by name
function flattenReducer(list,v) {
    // note: concat(..) used here since it automatically
    // flattens an array into the concatenation
    return list.concat(
        Array.isArray( v ) ? v.reduce( flattenReducer, [] ) : v
    );
}
```

Now, we can use this utility in an array method chain via `reduce(..)`:

```
[ [1, 2, 3], 4, 5, [6, [7, 8]] ]
.reduce( flattenReducer, [] )
// ..
```

Looking for Lists

So far, most of the examples have been rather trivial, based on simple lists of numbers or strings. Let's now talk about where list operations can start to shine: modeling an imperative series of statements declaratively.

Consider this base example:

```
var getSessionId = partial( prop, "sessId" );
var getUserId = partial( prop, "uId" );

var session, sessionId, user, userId, orders;

session = getCurrentSession();
if (session != null) sessionId = getSessionId( session );
if (sessionId != null) user = lookupUser( sessionId );
if (user != null) userId = getUserId( user );
if (userId != null) orders = lookupOrders( userId );
if (orders != null) processOrders( orders );
```

First, let's observe that the five variable declarations and the running series of `if` conditionals guarding the function calls are effectively one big composition of these six calls `getCurrentSession()`, `getSessionId(..)`, `lookupUser(..)`, `getUserId(..)`, `lookupOrders(..)`, and `processOrders(..)`. Ideally, we'd like to get rid of all these variable declarations and imperative conditionals.

Unfortunately, the `compose(..)`/`pipe(..)` utilities we explored in Chapter 4 don't by themselves offer a convenient way to express the `!= null` conditionals in the composition. Let's define a utility to help:

```
var guard =
    fn =>
        arg =>
            arg != null ? fn( arg ) : arg;
```

This guard(..) utility lets us map the five conditional-guarded functions:

```
[ getSessionId, lookupUser, getUserId, lookupOrders, processOrders ]
.map( guard )
```

The result of this mapping is an array of functions that are ready to compose (actually, pipe, in this listed order). We could spread this array to pipe(..), but because we're already doing list operations, let's do it with a reduce(..), using the session value from getCurrentSession() as the initial value:

```
.reduce(
    (result,nextFn) => nextFn( result )
    , getCurrentSession()
)
```

Next, let's observe that getSessionId(..) and getUserId(..) can be expressed as a mapping from the respective values "sessId" and "uId":

```
[ "sessId", "uId" ].map( propName => partial( prop, propName ) )
```

But to use these, we'll need to interleave them with the other three functions (lookupUser(..), lookupOrders(..), and processOrders(..)) to get the array of five functions to guard/compose as discussed before.

To do the interleaving, we can model this as list merging. Recall mergeReducer(..) from earlier in the chapter:

```
var mergeReducer =
    (merged,v,idx) =>
        (merged.splice( idx * 2, 0, v ), merged);
```

We can use `reduce(..)` (our Swiss Army knife, remember!?) to "insert" `lookupUser(..)` in the array between the generated functions `getSessionId(..)` and `getUserId(..)`, by merging two lists:

```
.reduce( mergeReducer, [ lookupUser ] )
```

Then we'll concatenate `lookupOrders(..)` and `processOrders(..)` onto the end of the running functions array:

```
.concat( lookupOrders, processOrders )
```

To review, the generated list of five functions is expressed as:

```
[ "sessId", "uId" ].map( propName => partial( prop, propName ) )
.reduce( mergeReducer, [ lookupUser ] )
.concat( lookupOrders, processOrders )
```

Finally, to put it all together, take this list of functions and tack on the guarding and composition from earlier:

```
[ "sessId", "uId" ].map( propName => partial( prop, propName ) )
.reduce( mergeReducer, [ lookupUser ] )
.concat( lookupOrders, processOrders )
.map( guard )
.reduce(
    (result,nextFn) => nextFn( result )
    , getCurrentSession()
);
```

Gone are all the imperative variable declarations and conditionals, and in their place we have clean and declarative list operations chained together.

I know this version is likely harder for most readers to understand right now than the original. Don't worry, that's natural. The original imperative form is one you're probably much more familiar with.

Part of your evolution to become a functional programmer is to develop a recognition of FP patterns such as list operations, and that takes lots of exposure and practice. Over time, these will jump out of the code more readily as your sense of code readability shifts to declarative style.

Before we move on from this topic, let's take a reality check: the example here is heavily contrived. Not all code segments will be straightforwardly modeled as list operations. The pragmatic take-away is to develop the instinct to look for these opportunities, but not get too hung up on code acrobatics; some improvement is better than none. Always step back and ask if you're **improving or harming** code readability.

Fusion

As FP list operations permeate the way you think about code, you'll very likely start recognizing chains of combined behavior, like:

```
..
.filter(..)
.map(..)
.reduce(..);
```

And more often than not, you're also probably going to end up with chains with multiple adjacent instances of each operation, like:

```
someList
.filter(..)
.filter(..)
.map(..)
.map(..)
.map(..)
.reduce(..);
```

The good news is the chain-style is declarative and it's easy to read the specific steps that will happen, in order. The downside is that each of these operations loops over the entire list, meaning performance can suffer unnecessarily, especially if the list is longer.

With the alternative standalone style, you might see code like this:

```
map(
    fn3,
    map(
        fn2,
        map( fn1, someList )
    )
);
```

With this style, the operations are listed from bottom-to-top, and we still loop over the list three times.

Fusion deals with combining adjacent operators to reduce the number of times the list is iterated over. We'll focus here on collapsing adjacent map(..)s as it's the most straightforward to explain.

Imagine this scenario:

```
var removeInvalidChars = str => str.replace( /[^\w]*/g, "" );

var upper = str => str.toUpperCase();

var elide = str =>
    str.length > 10 ?
        str.substr( 0, 7 ) + "..." :
        str;

var words = "Mr. Jones isn't responsible for this disaster!"
    .split( /\s/ );

words;
// ["Mr.","Jones","isn't","responsible","for","this","disaster!"]

words
.map( removeInvalidChars )
.map( upper )
.map( elide );
// ["MR","JONES","ISNT","RESPONS...","FOR","THIS","DISASTER"]
```

Think about each value that goes through this flow of transformations. The first value in the words list starts out as `"Mr."`, becomes `"Mr"`, then `"MR"`, and then passes through `elide(..)` unchanged. Another piece of data flows: `"responsible"` -> `"responsible"` -> `"RESPONSIBLE"` -> `"RESPONS..."`.

In other words, you could think of these data transformations like this:

```
elide( upper( removeInvalidChars( "Mr." ) ) );
// "MR"

elide( upper( removeInvalidChars( "responsible" ) ) );
// "RESPONS..."
```

Did you catch the point? We can express the three separate steps of the adjacent `map(..)` calls as a composition of the transformers, since they are all unary functions and each returns the value that's suitable as input to the next. We can fuse the mapper functions using `compose(..)`, and then pass the composed function to a single `map(..)` call:

```
words
.map(
    compose( elide, upper, removeInvalidChars )
);
// ["MR","JONES","ISNT","RESPONS...","FOR","THIS","DISASTER"]
```

This is another case where `pipe(..)` can be a more convenient form of composition, for its ordering readability:

```
words
.map(
    pipe( removeInvalidChars, upper, elide )
);
// ["MR","JONES","ISNT","RESPONS...","FOR","THIS","DISASTER"]
```

What about fusing two or more `filter(..)` predicate functions? Typically treated as unary functions, they seem suitable for composition. But the wrinkle is they each return a different kind of value (`boolean`) than the next one would want as input. Fusing adjacent `reduce(..)` calls is also possible, but reducers are not unary so that's a bit more challenging; we need more sophisticated tricks to pull this kind of fusion off. We'll cover these advanced techniques in Appendix A.

Beyond Lists

So far we've been discussing operations in the context of the list (array) data structure; it's by far the most common scenario where you'll encounter them. But in a more general sense, these operations can be performed against any collection of values.

Just as we said earlier that array's `map(..)` adapts a single-value operation to all its values, any data structure can provide a `map(..)` operation to do the same. Likewise, it can implement `filter(..)`, `reduce(..)`, or any other operation that makes sense for working with the data structure's values.

The important part to maintain in the spirit of FP is that these operators must behave according to value immutability, meaning that they must return a new data structure rather than mutating the existing one.

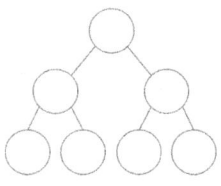

Let's illustrate with a well-known data structure: the binary tree. A binary tree is a node (just an object!) that has at most two references to other nodes (themselves binary trees), typically referred to as *left* and *right* child trees. Each node in the tree holds one value of the overall data structure.

Binary tree

For ease of illustration, we'll make our binary tree a binary search tree (BST). However, the operations we'll identify work the same for any regular non-BST binary tree.

 Note

A binary search tree is a general binary tree with a special constraint on the relationship of values in the tree to each other. Each value of nodes on the left side of a tree is less than the value of the node at the root of that tree, which in turn is less than each value of nodes in the right side of the tree. The notion of "less than" is relative to the kind of data stored; it can be numerical for numbers, lexicographic for strings, and so on. BSTs by definition must remain balanced, which makes searching for a value in the tree more efficient, using a recursive binary search algorithm.

To make a binary tree node object, let's use this factory function:

```
var BinaryTree =
    (value,parent,left,right) => ({ value, parent, left, right });
```

For convenience, we make each node store the `left` and `right` child trees as well as a reference to its own `parent` node.

Let's now define a BST of names of common produce (fruits, vegetables):

```
var banana = BinaryTree( "banana" );
var apple = banana.left = BinaryTree( "apple", banana );
var cherry = banana.right = BinaryTree( "cherry", banana );
var apricot = apple.right = BinaryTree( "apricot", apple );
var avocado = apricot.right = BinaryTree( "avocado", apricot );
var cantaloupe = cherry.left = BinaryTree( "cantaloupe", cherry );
var cucumber = cherry.right = BinaryTree( "cucumber", cherry );
var grape = cucumber.right = BinaryTree( "grape", cucumber );
```

In this particular tree structure, banana is the root node; this tree could have been set up with nodes in different locations, but still had a BST with the same traversal.

Our tree looks like:

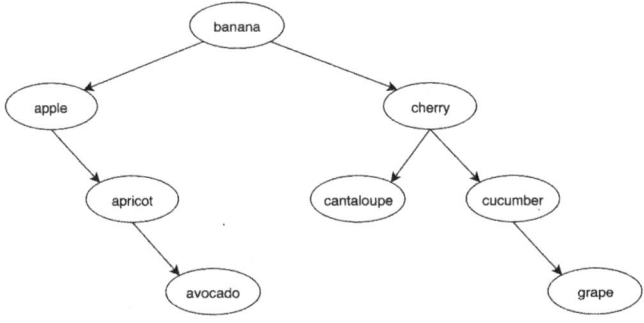

Produce tree

There are multiple ways to traverse a binary tree to process its values. If it's a BST (ours is!) and we do an *in-order* traversal – always visit the left child tree first, then the node itself, then the right child tree – we'll visit the values in ascending (sorted) order.

Because you can't just easily `console.log(..)` a binary tree like you can with an array, let's first define a convenience method, mostly to use for printing. `forEach(..)` will visit the nodes of a binary tree in the same manner as an array:

```
// in-order traversal
BinaryTree.forEach = function forEach(visitFn,node){
    if (node) {
        if (node.left) {
            forEach( visitFn, node.left );
        }

        visitFn( node );

        if (node.right) {
            forEach( visitFn, node.right );
        }
    }
};
```

Note

Working with binary trees lends itself most naturally to recursive processing. Our forEach(..) utility recursively calls itself to process both the left and right child trees. We already discussed recursion in Chapter 8, where we covered recursion in the chapter on recursion.

Recall forEach(..) was described at the beginning of this chapter as only being useful for side effects, which is not very typically desired in FP. In this case, we'll use forEach(..) only for the side effect of I/O, so it's perfectly reasonable as a helper.

Use forEach(..) to print out values from the tree:

```
BinaryTree.forEach( node => console.log( node.value ), banana );
// apple apricot avocado banana cantaloupe cherry cucumber grape

// visit only the `cherry`-rooted subtree
BinaryTree.forEach( node => console.log( node.value ), cherry );
// cantaloupe cherry cucumber grape
```

To operate on our binary tree data structure using FP patterns, let's start by defining a map(..):

```js
BinaryTree.map = function map(mapperFn,node){
    if (node) {
        let newNode = mapperFn( node );
        newNode.parent = node.parent;
        newNode.left = node.left ?
            map( mapperFn, node.left ) : undefined;
        newNode.right = node.right ?
            map( mapperFn, node.right ): undefined;

        if (newNode.left) {
            newNode.left.parent = newNode;
        }
        if (newNode.right) {
            newNode.right.parent = newNode;
        }

        return newNode;
    }
};
```

You might have assumed we'd `map(..)` only the node `value` properties, but in general we might actually want to map the tree nodes themselves. So, the `mapperFn(..)` is passed the whole node being visited, and it expects to receive a new `BinaryTree(..)` node back, with the transformation applied. If you just return the same node, this operation will mutate your tree and quite possibly cause unexpected results!

Let's map our tree to a list of produce with all uppercase names:

```js
var BANANA = BinaryTree.map(
    node => BinaryTree( node.value.toUpperCase() ),
    banana
);

BinaryTree.forEach( node => console.log( node.value ), BANANA );
// APPLE APRICOT AVOCADO BANANA CANTALOUPE CHERRY CUCUMBER GRAPE
```

BANANA is a different tree (with all different nodes) than banana, just like calling map(..) on an array returns a new array. Just like arrays of other objects/arrays, if node.value itself references some object/array, you'll also need to handle manually copying it in the mapper function if you want deeper immutability.

How about reduce(..)? Same basic process: do an in-order traversal of the tree nodes. One usage would be to reduce(..) our tree to an array of its values, which would be useful in further adapting other typical list operations. Or we can reduce(..) our tree to a string concatenation of all its produce names.

We'll mimic the behavior of the array reduce(..), which makes passing the initialValue argument optional. This algorithm is a little trickier, but still manageable:

```
BinaryTree.reduce = function reduce(reducerFn,initialValue,node){
    if (arguments.length < 3) {
        // shift the parameters since `initialValue` was omitted
        node = initialValue;
    }

    if (node) {
        let result;

        if (arguments.length < 3) {
            if (node.left) {
                result = reduce( reducerFn, node.left );
            }
            else {
                return node.right ?
                    reduce( reducerFn, node, node.right ) :
                    node;
            }
        }
        else {
            result = node.left ?
                reduce( reducerFn, initialValue, node.left ) :
                initialValue;
        }
```

```
            result = reducerFn( result, node );
            result = node.right ?
                reduce( reducerFn, result, node.right ) : result;
            return result;
        }

        return initialValue;
    };
```

Let's use `reduce(..)` to make our shopping list (an array):

```
BinaryTree.reduce(
    (result,node) => [ ...result, node.value ],
    [],
    banana
);
// ["apple","apricot","avocado","banana","cantaloupe"
//  "cherry","cucumber","grape"]
```

Finally, let's consider `filter(..)` for our tree. This algorithm is trickiest so far because it effectively (not actually) involves removing nodes from the tree, which requires handling several corner cases. Don't get intimidated by the implementation, though. Just skip over it for now, if you prefer, and focus on how we use it instead.

```
BinaryTree.filter = function filter(predicateFn,node){
    if (node) {
        let newNode;
        let newLeft = node.left ?
            filter( predicateFn, node.left ) : undefined;
        let newRight = node.right ?
            filter( predicateFn, node.right ) : undefined;

        if (predicateFn( node )) {
            newNode = BinaryTree(
                node.value,
                node.parent,
```

```
                newLeft,
                newRight
            );
            if (newLeft) {
                newLeft.parent = newNode;
            }
            if (newRight) {
                newRight.parent = newNode;
            }
        }
        else {
            if (newLeft) {
                if (newRight) {
                    newNode = BinaryTree(
                        undefined,
                        node.parent,
                        newLeft,
                        newRight
                    );
                    newLeft.parent = newRight.parent = newNode;

                    if (newRight.left) {
                        let minRightNode = newRight;
                        while (minRightNode.left) {
                            minRightNode = minRightNode.left;
                        }

                        newNode.value = minRightNode.value;

                        if (minRightNode.right) {
                            minRightNode.parent.left =
                                minRightNode.right;
                            minRightNode.right.parent =
                                minRightNode.parent;
                        }
                        else {
                            minRightNode.parent.left = undefined;
                        }
```

```
                    minRightNode.right =
                        minRightNode.parent = undefined;
                }
                else {
                    newNode.value = newRight.value;
                    newNode.right = newRight.right;
                    if (newRight.right) {
                        newRight.right.parent = newNode;
                    }
                }
            }
            else {
                return newLeft;
            }
        }
        else {
            return newRight;
        }
    }

    return newNode;
    }
};
```

The majority of this code listing is dedicated to handling the shifting of a node's parent/child references if it's "removed" (filtered out) of the duplicated tree structure.

As an example to illustrate using `filter(..)`, let's narrow our produce tree down to only vegetables:

```
var vegetables = [ "asparagus", "avocado", "broccoli", "carrot",
    "celery", "corn", "cucumber", "lettuce", "potato", "squash",
    "zucchini" ];

var whatToBuy = BinaryTree.filter(
    // filter the produce list only for vegetables
    node => vegetables.indexOf( node.value ) != -1,
    banana
);

// shopping list
BinaryTree.reduce(
    (result,node) => [ ...result, node.value ],
    [],
    whatToBuy
);
// ["avocado","cucumber"]
```

> **Note**
>
> We aren't making any effort to rebalance a tree after any of the map/reduce/filter operations on BSTs. Technically, this means the results are not themselves binary *search* trees. Most JS values have a reasonable less-than comparison operation (<) by which we could rebalance such a tree, but some values (like promises) wouldn't have any such definition. For the sake of keeping this chapter practical in length, we'll punt on handling this complication.

You will likely use most of the list operations from this chapter in the context of simple arrays. But now we've seen that the concepts apply to whatever data structures and operations you might need. That's a powerful expression of how FP can be widely applied to many different application scenarios!

Summary

Three common and powerful list operations we looked at:

- `map(..)`: Transforms values as it projects them to a new list.
- `filter(..)`: Selects or excludes values as it projects them to a new list.
- `reduce(..)`: Combines values in a list to produce some other (usually but not always non-list) value.

Other more advanced operations that are useful in processing lists: `unique(..)`, `flatten(..)`, and `merge(..)`.

Fusion uses function composition to consolidate multiple adjacent `map(..)` calls. This is mostly a performance optimization, but it also improves the declarative nature of your list operations.

Lists are typically visualized as arrays, but can be generalized as any data structure that represents/produces an ordered collection of values. As such, all these "list operations" are actually "data structure operations".

Chapter 10: Functional Async

At this point of the book, you now have all the raw concepts in place for the foundations of FP that I call "Functional-Light Programming". In this chapter, we're going to apply these concepts to a different context, but we won't really present particularly new ideas.

So far, almost everything we've done is synchronous, meaning that we call functions with immediate inputs and immediately get back output values. A lot of work can be done this way, but it's not nearly sufficient for the entirety of a modern JS application. To be truly ready for FP in the real world of JS, we need to understand async FP.

Our goal in this chapter is to expand our thinking about managing values with FP, to spread out such operations over time. We'll see that Observables (and Promises!) are one great way to do that.

Time as State

The most complicated state in your entire application is time. That is, it's far easier to manage state when the transition from one state to another is immediate and affirmatively in your control. When the state of your application changes implicitly in response to events spread out over time, management becomes exponentially more difficult.

Every part of how we've presented FP in this text has been about making code easier to read by making it more trustable and more predictable. When you introduce asynchrony to your program, those efforts take a big hit.

But let's be more explicit: it's not the mere fact that some operations don't finish synchronously that is concerning; firing off asynchronous behavior is easy. It's the coordination of the responses to these actions, each of which has the potential to change the state of your application, that requires so much extra effort.

So, is it better for you the author to take that effort, or should you just leave it to the reader of your code to figure out what the state of the program will be if A finishes before B, or vice versa? That's a rhetorical question but one with a pretty concrete answer from my perspective: to have any hope of making such complex code more readable, the author has to take a lot more care than they normally would.

Reducing Time

One of the most important outcomes of async programming patterns is simplifying state change management by abstracting out time from our sphere of concern. To illustrate, let's first look at a scenario where a race condition (aka, time complexity) exists, and must be manually managed:

```
var customerId = 42;
var customer;

lookupCustomer( customerId, function onCustomer(customerRecord){
    var orders = customer ? customer.orders : null;
    customer = customerRecord;
    if (orders) {
        customer.orders = orders;
    }
} );

lookupOrders( customerId, function onOrders(customerOrders){
    if (!customer) {
        customer = {};
    }
    customer.orders = customerOrders;
} );
```

The onCustomer(..) and onOrders(..) callbacks are in a binary race condition. Assuming they both run, it's possible that either might run first, and it's impossible to predict which will happen.

If we could embed the call to lookupOrders(..) inside of onCustomer(..), we'd be sure that onOrders(..) was running after onCustomer(..). But we can't do that, because we need the two lookups to occur concurrently.

So to normalize this time-based state complexity, we use a pairing of if-statement checks in the respective callbacks, along with an outer lexically closed over variable customer. When each callback runs, it checks the state of customer, and thus determines its own relative ordering; if customer is unset for a callback, it's the first to run, otherwise it's the second.

This code works, but it's far from ideal in terms of readability. The time complexity makes this code harder to read. Let's instead use a JS Promise to factor time out of the picture:

```
var customerId = 42;

var customerPromise = lookupCustomer( customerId );
var ordersPromise = lookupOrders( customerId );

customerPromise.then( function onCustomer(customer){
    ordersPromise.then( function onOrders(orders){
        customer.orders = orders;
    } );
} );
```

The onOrders(..) callback is now inside of the onCustomer(..) callback, so their relative ordering is guaranteed. The concurrency of the lookups is accomplished by making the lookupCustomer(..) and lookupOrders(..) calls separately before specifying the then(..) response handling.

It may not be obvious, but there would otherwise inherently be a race condition in this snippet, were it not for how Promises are defined to behave. If the lookup of the orders finishes before the ordersPromise.then(..) is called to provide an onOrders(..) callback, *something* needs to be smart enough to keep that orders list around until onOrders(..) can be called. In fact, the same concern could apply to customer being present before onCustomer(..) is specified to receive it.

That *something* is the same kind of time complexity logic we discussed with the previous snippet. But we don't have to worry about any of that complexity, either in the writing of this code or – more importantly – in the reading of it, because the promises take care of that time normalization for us.

A Promise represents a single (future) value in a time-independent manner. Moreover, extracting the value from a promise is the asynchronous form of the synchronous assignment (via =) of an immediate value. In other words, a promise spreads an = assignment operation out over time, but in a trustable (time-independent) fashion.

We'll now explore how we similarly can spread various synchronous FP operations from earlier in this book asynchronously over time.

Eager vs. Lazy

Eager and lazy in the realm of computer science aren't compliments or insults, but rather ways to describe whether an operation will finish right away or progress over time.

The FP operations that we've seen in this text can be characterized as eager because they operate synchronously (right now) on a discrete immediate value or list/structure of values.

Recall:

```
var a = [1,2,3]

var b = a.map( v => v * 2 );

b;          // [2,4,6]
```

This mapping from a to b is eager because it operates on all the values in the a array at that moment, and produces a new b array. If you later modify a (for example, by adding a new value to the end of it) nothing will change about the contents of b. That's eager FP.

But what would it look like to have a lazy FP operation? Consider something like this:

```
var a = [];

var b = mapLazy( a, v => v * 2 );

a.push( 1 );

a[0];           // 1
b[0];           // 2

a.push( 2 );

a[1];           // 2
b[1];           // 4
```

The mapLazy(..) we've imagined here essentially "listens" to the a array, and every time a new value is added to the end of it (with push(..)), it runs the v => v * 2 mapping function and pushes the transformed value to the b array.

 Note

The implementation of mapLazy(..) has not been shown because this is a fictional illustration, not a real operation. To accomplish this kind of lazy operation pairing between a and b, we'll need something smarter than basic arrays.

Consider the benefits of being able to pair an a and b together, where any time (even asynchronously!) you put a value into a, it's transformed and projected to b. That's the same kind of declarative FP power from of a map(..) operation, but now it can be stretched over time; you don't have to know all the values of a *right now* to set up the mapping from a to b.

Reactive FP

To understand how we could create and use a lazy mapping between two sets of values, we need to abstract our idea of list (array) a bit. Let's imagine a smarter kind of array, not one which simply holds values but one which lazily receives and responds (aka "reacts") to values. Consider:

```
var a = new LazyArray();

var b = a.map( function double(v){
    return v * 2;
} );

setInterval( function everySecond(){
    a.push( Math.random() );
}, 1000 );
```

So far, this snippet doesn't look any different than a normal array. The only unusual thing is that we're used to the map(..) running eagerly and immediately producing a b array with all the currently mapped values from a. The timer pushing random values into a is strange, since all those values are coming *after* the map(..) call.

But this fictional LazyArray is different; it assumes that values will come one at a time, over time; just push(..) values in whenever you want. b will be a lazy mapping of whatever values eventually end up in a.

Also, we don't really need to keep values in a or b once they've been handled; this special kind of array only holds a value as long as it's needed. So these arrays don't strictly grow in memory usage over time, an important characteristic of lazy data structures and operations. In fact, it's less like an array and more like a buffer.

A normal array is eager in that it holds all of its values right now. A "lazy array" is an array where the values will come in over time.

Since we won't necessarily know when a new value has arrived in a, another key thing we need is to be able to listen to b to be notified when new values are made available. We could imagine a listener like this:

```
b.listen( function onValue(v){
    console.log( v );
} );
```

b is *reactive* in that it's set up to *react* to values as they come into a. There's an FP
operation map(..) that describes how each value transfers from the origin a to the
target b. Each discrete mapping operation is exactly how we modeled single-value
operations with normal synchronous FP, but here we're spreading out the sourcing
of values over time.

Note

The term most commonly applied to these concepts is Functional Reactive
Programming (FRP). I'm deliberately avoiding that term because there's
some debate as to whether FP + Reactive genuinely constitutes FRP. We're
not going to fully dive into all the implications of FRP here, so I'll just
keep calling it reactive FP. Alternatively, you could call it evented-FP if
that feels less confusing.

We can think of a as producing values and b as consuming them. So for readability,
let's reorganize this snippet to separate the concerns into *producer* and *consumer*
roles:

```
// producer:

var a = new LazyArray();

setInterval( function everySecond(){
    a.push( Math.random() );
}, 1000 );



// ************************
// consumer:

var b = a.map( function double(v){
    return v * 2;
} );

b.listen( function onValue(v){
```

```
    console.log( v );
} );
```

a is the producer, which acts essentially like a stream of values. We can think of each value arriving in a as an *event*. The `map(..)` operation then triggers a corresponding event on b, which we `listen(..)` to so we can consume the new value.

The reason we separate the *producer* and *consumer* concerns is so that different parts of our application can be responsible for each concern. This code organization can drastically improve both code readability and maintenance.

Declarative Time

We're being very careful about how we introduce time into the discussion. Specifically, just as promises abstract time away from our concern for a single asynchronous operation, reactive FP abstracts (separates) time away from a series of values/operations.

From the perspective of a (the producer), the only evident time concern is our manual `setInterval(..)` loop. But that's only for demonstration purposes.

Imagine a could actually be attached to some other event source, like the user's mouse clicks or keystrokes, websocket messages from a server, etc. In that scenario, a doesn't actually have to concern itself with time. It's merely a time-independent conduit for values, whenever they are ready.

From the perspective of b (the consumer), we do not know or care when/where the values in a come from. As a matter of fact, all the values could already be present. All we care about is that we want those values, whenever they are ready. Again, this is a time-independent (aka lazy) modeling of the `map(..)` transformation operation.

The *time* relationship between a and b is declarative (and implicit!), not imperative (or explicit).

The value of organizing such operations-over-time this way may not feel particularly effective yet. Let's compare to how this same sort of functionality could have been expressed imperatively:

```
// producer:

var a = {
    onValue(v){
        b.onValue( v );
    }
};

setInterval( function everySecond(){
    a.onValue( Math.random() );
}, 1000 );


// **************************
// consumer:

var b = {
    map(v){
        return v * 2;
    },
    onValue(v){
        v = this.map( v );
        console.log( v );
    }
};
```

It may seem rather subtle, but there's an important difference between this more-imperative version of the code and the previous more-declarative version, aside from just b.onValue(..) needing to call this.map(..) itself. In the former snippet, b pulls from a, but in the latter snippet, a pushes to b. In other words, compare b = a.map(..) to b.onValue(v).

In the latter imperative snippet, it's not clear (readability wise) from the consumer's perspective where the v values are coming from. Moreover, the imperative hard coding of b.onValue(..) in the middle of producer a's logic is a violation of separation-of-concerns. That can make it harder to reason about producer and consumer independently.

By contrast, in the former snippet, b = a.map(..) declares that b's values are sourced from a, and treats a as an abstract event stream data source that we don't have to concern ourselves with at that moment. We *declare* that any value that comes from a into b will go through the map(..) operation as specified.

More Than Map

For convenience, we've illustrated this notion of pairing a and b together over time via a one-to-one map(..)ing. But many of our other FP operations could be modeled over time as well.

Consider:

```
var b = a.filter( function isOdd(v) {
    return v % 2 == 1;
} );

b.listen( function onlyOdds(v){
    console.log( "Odd:", v );
} );
```

Here, a value from a only comes into b if it passes the isOdd(..) predicate.

Even reduce(..) can be modeled over time:

```
var b = a.reduce( function sum(total,v){
    return total + v;
} );

b.listen( function runningTotal(v){
    console.log( "New current total:", v );
} );
```

Since we don't specify an initialValue to the reduce(..) call, neither the sum(..) reducer nor the runningTotal(..) event callback will be invoked until at least two values have come through from a.

This snippet implies that the reduction has a *memory* of sorts, in that each time a future value comes in, the `sum(..)` reducer will be invoked with whatever the previous `total` was as well as the new next value `v`.

Other FP operations extended over time could even involve an internal buffer, like for example `unique(..)` keeping track of every value it's seen so far.

Observables

Hopefully by now you can see the importance of a reactive, evented, array-like data structure like the fictional `LazyArray` we've conjured. The good news is, this kind of data structure already exists, and it's called an Observable.

 Note

Just to set some expectation: the following discussion is only a brief intro to the world of Observables. This is a far more in-depth topic than we have space to fully explore. But if you've understood Functional-Light Programming in this text, and now grasped how asynchronous-time can be modeled via FP principles, Observables should follow very naturally for your continued learning.

Observables have been implemented by a variety of userland libraries, most notably RxJS[26] and Most[27]. At the time of this writing, there's an in-progress proposal to add Observables natively to JS, just like Promises were added in ES6. For the sake of demonstration, we'll use RxJS-flavored Observables for these next examples.

Here's our earlier reactive example, expressed with observables instead of `LazyArray`:

---

[26] https://github.com/Reactive-Extensions/RxJS
[27] https://github.com/cujojs/most

```
// producer:

var a = new Rx.Subject();

setInterval( function everySecond(){
    a.next( Math.random() );
}, 1000 );


// **************************
// consumer:

var b = a.map( function double(v){
    return v * 2;
} );

b.subscribe( function onValue(v){
    console.log( v );
} );
```

In the RxJS universe, an Observer subscribes to an Observable. If you combine the functionality of an Observer and an Observable, you get a Subject. So, to keep our snippet simpler, we construct a as a Subject, so that we can call `next(..)` on it to push values (events) into its stream.

If we want to keep the Observer and Observable separate:

```
// producer:

var a = Rx.Observable.create( function onObserve(observer){
    setInterval( function everySecond(){
        observer.next( Math.random() );
    }, 1000 );
} );
```

In this snippet, a is the observable, and unsurprisingly, the separate observer is called `observer`; it's able to "observe" some events (like our `setInterval(..)` loop); we use its `next(..)` method to feed events into the a observable stream.

In addition to `map(..)`, RxJS defines well over a hundred operators that are invoked lazily as each new value comes in. Just like with arrays, each operator on an Observable returns a new Observable, meaning they are chainable. If an invocation of operator function determines a value should be passed along from the input Observable, it will be fired on the output Observable; otherwise it's discarded.

Example of a declarative observable chain:

```
var b =
    a
    .filter( v => v % 2 == 1 )      // only odd numbers
    .distinctUntilChanged()         // only consecutive-distinct
    .throttle( 100 )                // slow it down a bit
    .map( v = v * 2 );              // double them

b.subscribe( function onValue(v){
    console.log( "Next:", v );
} );
```

Note

It's not necessary to assign the observable to `b` and then call `b.subscribe(..)` separately from the chain; that's done here to reinforce that each operator returns a new observable from the previous one. In many coding examples you'll find, the `subscribe(..)` call is just the final method in the chain. Because `subscribe(..)` is technically mutating the internal state of the observable, FPers generally prefer these two steps separated, to mark the side effect more obviously.

Summary

This book has detailed a wide variety of FP operations that take a single value (or an immediate list of values) and transform them into another value/values.

For operations that will be proceed over time, all of these foundational FP principles can be applied time-independently. Exactly like promises model single future values, we can model eager lists of values instead as lazy Observable (event) streams of values that may come in one-at-a-time.

A map(..) on an array runs its mapping function once for each value currently in the array, putting all the mapped values in the outcome array. A map(..) on an Observable runs its mapping function once for each value, whenever it comes in, and pushes all the mapped values to the output Observable.

In other words, if an array is an eager data structure for FP operations, an Observable is its lazy-over-time counterpart.

 Tip
For a different twist on asynchronous FP, check out a library called **fasy**, which is discussed in Appendix C.

Chapter 11: Putting It All Together

By now, you have everything you need to understand Functional-Light JavaScript. There's no more new concepts to introduce.

In this final chapter, our main goal is conceptual cohesiveness. We'll look at code that brings many of the major themes from this book together – application of what we've learned. Above all, this example code is intended to illustrate the "Functional Light" approach to JavaScript – that is, balance and pragmatism over dogma.

You'll want to practice these techniques yourself, extensively. Digesting this chapter is critical to helping you apply FP principles to your real-world code.

Setup

Let's build a simple stock ticker widget.

> **Note**
>
> For reference, the entirety of the code for this example resides in the `ch11-code/` sub-directory – see the GitHub repository for this book[28]. Also, selected FP helpers we've discussed throughout this book that we need for this example are included in `ch11-code/fp-helpers.js`. In this chapter we will only focus on the relevant parts of the code for our discussion.

First, let's talk about the markup for this widget, so we have somewhere to display our information. We start out with an empty `<ul ..>` element in our `ch11-code/index.html` file, but while running, the DOM will be populated to look like:

---

[28]https://github.com/getify/Functional-Light-JS

```
<ul id="stock-ticker">
    <li class="stock" data-stock-id="AAPL">
        <span class="stock-name">AAPL</span>
        <span class="stock-price">$121.95</span>
        <span class="stock-change">+0.01</span>
    </li>
    <li class="stock" data-stock-id="MSFT">
        <span class="stock-name">MSFT</span>
        <span class="stock-price">$65.78</span>
        <span class="stock-change">+1.51</span>
    </li>
    <li class="stock" data-stock-id="GOOG">
        <span class="stock-name">GOOG</span>
        <span class="stock-price">$821.31</span>
        <span class="stock-change">-8.84</span>
    </li>
</ul>
```

Before we go any further, let me remind you: interacting with the DOM is I/O, and that means side effects. We can't eliminate these side effects, but we can limit and control them. We'll want to be really intentional about minimizing the surface area of our application that deals with the DOM. We learned all about these techniques in Chapter 5.

Summarizing our widget's functionality: the code will add the `<li ..>` elements each time a new-stock event is "received", and will update the price and change as stock-update events come through.

In the Chapter 11 example code, in `ch11-code/mock-server.js`, we set up some timers to push out randomly generated fake stock data to a simple event emitter, to simulate as if we were getting messages of stock information from a server. We expose a `connectToServer()` function which pretends to do so, but really just returns the faked event emitter instance.

Note

This file is all fake/mock behavior, so I didn't spend much effort trying to make it very FP-adherent. I wouldn't suggest spending too much time concerned with the code in this file. If you wrote a real server – a very interesting extra credit exercise for the ambitious reader! – you'd clearly want to give that code the FP attention it deserves.

In `ch11-code/stock-ticker-events.js`, we create some observables (via RxJS) hooked up to an event emitter object. We call the `connectToServer()` to get this event emitter, then listen to the event names `"stock"` (adding a new stock to our ticker) and `"stock-update"` (updating the stock's listed price and change amount). Finally, we define transformations on the incoming data of these observables, formatting the data as needed.

In `ch11-code/stock-ticker.js`, we define our UI (DOM side effect) behavior as methods on the `stockTickerUI` object. We also define a variety of helpers, including `getElemAttr(..)`, `stripPrefix(..)`, and others. Finally, we `subscribe(..)` to the two observables that provide us formatted data to render to the DOM.

Stock Events

Let's look at the code in `ch11-code/stock-ticker-events.js`. We'll start with some basic helpers:

```
function addStockName(stock) {
    return setProp( "name", stock, stock.id );
}
function formatSign(val) {
    if (Number(val) > 0) {
        return `+${val}`;
    }
    return val;
}
function formatCurrency(val) {
    return `$${val}`;
}
```

These pure functions should be pretty straightforward to interpret. Recall set-Prop(..) from Chapter 4 actually clones the object before setting the new property. That exercises the principle we saw in Chapter 6: avoiding side effects by treating values as immutable even if they're not.

addStockName(..) is used to add a name property to a stock message object that's equal to its id. The name value is later used as the visible stock name in the widget.

When a stock message is received from the "server", it'll look like:

```
{ id: "AAPL", price: 121.7, change: 0.01 }
```

Prior to display in the DOM, the price needs to be formatted with formatCurrency(..) (to look like "$121.70"), and the change needs to be formatted with formatChange(..) (to look like "+0.01"). But we don't want to mutate the message object, so we need a helper that formats both the numbers and gives us a new stock object:

```
function formatStockNumbers(stock) {
    var stockDataUpdates = [
        [ "price", formatPrice( stock.price ) ],
        [ "change", formatChange( stock.change ) ]
    ];

    return reduce( function formatter(stock,[propName,val]){
        return setProp( propName, stock, val );
    } )
    ( stock )
    ( stockDataUpdates );
}
```

We create the stockDataUpdates array to hold tuples (just arrays) of the property name and the new formatted value, for price and change respectively. We reduce(..) (see Chapter 9) over that array, with the stock object as the initialValue. We destructure the tuple into propName and val, and then return the setProp(..) call, which returns a new cloned object with the property having been set.

Now let's define some more helpers:

```
var formatDecimal = unboundMethod( "toFixed" )( 2 );
var formatPrice = pipe( formatDecimal, formatCurrency );
var formatChange = pipe( formatDecimal, formatSign );
var processNewStock = pipe( addStockName, formatStockNumbers );
```

The `formatDecimal(..)` function takes a number (like `2.1`) and calls its `toFixed( 2 )` method call. We use Chapter 9's `unboundMethod(..)` to create a standalone late-bound method.

`formatPrice(..)`, `formatChange(..)`, and `processNewStock(..)` are all compositions with `pipe(..)`, each composing a couple of operations left-to-right (see Chapter 4).

For creating our observables (see Chapter 10, "Observables") from our event emitter, we're going to want a helper that's a curried (see Chapter 3) standalone of RxJS's `Rx.Observable.fromEvent(..)`:

```
var makeObservableFromEvent =
    curry( Rx.Observable.fromEvent, 2 )( server );
```

This function is specified to listen to the `server` (event emitter), and is just waiting for an event name string to produce its observable. We have all the pieces in place now to create observers for our two events, and to map-transform those observers to format the incoming data:

```
var observableMapperFns = [ processNewStock, formatStockNumbers ];

var stockEventNames = [ "stock", "stock-update" ];

var [ newStocks, stockUpdates ] = pipe(
    map( makeObservableFromEvent ),
    curry( zip )( observableMapperFns ),
    map( spreadArgs( mapObservable ) )
)
( stockEventNames );
```

We start with stockEventNames, an array of event names (["stock","stock-update"]), then map(..) (see Chapter 9) that to a list of two observables, and zip(..) (see Chapter 9) that to a list of observable-mapper functions, producing a list of tuples like [observable, mapperFn]. Finally, we map(..) those tuples with mapObservable(..), spreading out each tuple as individual arguments using spreadArgs(..) (see Chapter 3).

The final result is a list of two mapped observables, which we array-destructure into the assignments for newStocks and stockUpdates, respectively.

That's it; that's our FP-Light approach to setting up our stock ticker event observables! We'll subscribe to these two observables in ch11-code/stock-ticker.js.

Take a step back and reflect on our usage of FP principles here. Did it make sense? Can you see how we applied various concepts covered across the previous chapters from this book? Can you think of other ways to accomplish these tasks?

More importantly, how would you have done it imperatively, and how do you think those two approaches would have compared, broadly? Try that exercise. Write the equivalent using well-established imperative approaches. If you're like me, the imperative form will still feel more natural.

What you need to *get* before moving on is that you can *also* understand and reason about the FP-style we just presented. Think about the shape (the inputs and output) of each function and piece. Do you see how they fit together?

Keep practicing until this stuff clicks for you.

Stock Ticker UI

If you felt pretty comfortable with the FP of the last section, you're ready to dig into ch11-code/stock-ticker.js. It's considerably more involved, so we'll take our time to look at each piece in its entirety.

Let's start by defining some helpers that will assist in our DOM tasks:

```js
function isTextNode(node) {
    return node && node.nodeType == 3;
}
function getElemAttr(prop,elem) {
    return elem.getAttribute( prop );
}
function setElemAttr(elem,prop,val) {
    // !!SIDE EFFECTS!!
    return elem.setAttribute( prop, val );
}
function matchingStockId(id,node){
    return getStockId( node ) == id;
}
function isStockInfoChildElem(elem) {
    return /\bstock-/i.test( getClassName( elem ) );
}
function appendDOMChild(parentNode,childNode) {
    // !!SIDE EFFECTS!!
    parentNode.appendChild( childNode );
    return parentNode;
}
function setDOMContent(elem,html) {
    // !!SIDE EFFECTS!!
    elem.innerHTML = html;
    return elem;
}

var createElement = document.createElement.bind( document );

var getElemAttrByName = curry( getElemAttr, 2 );
var getStockId = getElemAttrByName( "data-stock-id" );
var getClassName = getElemAttrByName( "class" );
var isMatchingStock = curry( matchingStockId, 2 );
```

These should be mostly self-explanatory.

Notice that I called out the side effects of mutating a DOM element's state. We can't as easily clone a DOM object and replace it, so we settle here for a side effect of changing an existing one. At least if we have a bug in our DOM rendering, we can easily search for those code comments to narrow in on likely suspects.

Here are some other miscellaneous helpers:

```
function stripPrefix(prefixRegex,val) {
    return val.replace( prefixRegex, "" );
}

function listify(listOrItem) {
    if (!Array.isArray( listOrItem )) {
        return [ listOrItem ];
    }
    return listOrItem;
}
```

Let's define a helper to get the child nodes of a DOM element:

```
var getDOMChildren = pipe(
    listify,
    flatMap(
        pipe(
            curry( prop )( "childNodes" ),
            Array.from
        )
    )
);
```

First, we use `listify(..)` to ensure we have a list of elements (even if it's only a single item in length). Recall `flatMap(..)` from Chapter 9, which maps a list and then flattens a list-of-lists into a shallower list.

Our mapping function here maps from an element to its `childNodes` list, which we make into a real array (instead of a live NodeList) with `Array.from(..)`. These two functions are composed (via `pipe(..)`) into a single mapper function, which is fusion (see Chapter 9).

Now, let's use this `getDOMChildren(..)` helper to define utilities for retrieving specific DOM elements in our widget:

```
function getStockElem(tickerElem,stockId) {
    return pipe(
        getDOMChildren,
        filterOut( isTextNode ),
        filterIn( isMatchingStock( stockId ) )
    )
    ( tickerElem );
}
function getStockInfoChildElems(stockElem) {
    return pipe(
        getDOMChildren,
        filterOut( isTextNode ),
        filterIn( isStockInfoChildElem )
    )
    ( stockElem );
}
```

`getStockElem(..)` starts with the `tickerElem` DOM element for our widget, retrieves its child elements, then filters to make sure we have the element matching the specified stock identifier. `getStockInfoChildElems(..)` does almost the same thing, except it starts with a stock element, and narrows with different filters.

Both utilities filter out text nodes (since they don't work the same as real DOM nodes), and both utilities return an array of DOM elements, even if it's just a single element.

Main API

We'll use a `stockTickerUI` object to organize our three main UI manipulation methods, like this:

```
var stockTickerUI = {

    updateStockElems(stockInfoChildElemList,data) {
        // ..
    },

    updateStock(tickerElem,data) {
        // ..
    },

    addStock(tickerElem,data) {
        // ..
    }
};
```

Let's first examine updateStock(..), as it's the simplest of the three:

```
updateStock(tickerElem,data) {
    var getStockElemFromId = curry( getStockElem )( tickerElem );
    var stockInfoChildElemList = pipe(
        getStockElemFromId,
        getStockInfoChildElems
    )
    ( data.id );

    return stockTickerUI.updateStockElems(
        stockInfoChildElemList,
        data
    );
},
```

Currying the earlier helper getStockElem(..) with tickerElem gives us get-StockElemFromId(..), which will receive data.id.

Via pipe(..), the return value getStockElemFromId(data.id) is an <li> element (actually, a list containing only that element), which is passed to getStockInfoChildElems(..).

The result is a list (`stockInfoChildElemList`) with the three child `<span>` elements for the stock display info. We pass that list and the stock's `data` message object along to `stockTickerUI.updateStockElems(..)` for actually updating those three `<span>` elements with the new data.

Now let's look at how `stockTickerUI.updateStockElems(..)` is defined:

```
updateStockElems(stockInfoChildElemList,data) {
    var getDataVal = curry( reverseArgs( prop ), 2 )( data );
    var extractInfoChildElemVal = pipe(
        getClassName,
        curry( stripPrefix )( /\bstock-/i ),
        getDataVal
    );
    var orderedDataVals =
        map( extractInfoChildElemVal )( stockInfoChildElemList );
    var elemsValsTuples =
        filterOut( function updateValueMissing([infoChildElem,val]){
            return val === undefined;
        } )
        ( zip( stockInfoChildElemList, orderedDataVals ) );

    // !!SIDE EFFECTS!!
    compose( each, spreadArgs )
    ( setDOMContent )
    ( elemsValsTuples );
},
```

That's a fair bit to take in, I know. But we'll break it down statement by statement.

`getDataVal(..)` is bound to the `data` message object, having been curried after argument-reversing, so it's now waiting for a property name to extract from `data`.

Next, let's look at how `extractInfoChildElemVal(..)` is defined:

```
var extractInfoChildElemVal = pipe(
    getClassName,
    curry( stripPrefix )( /\bstock-/i ),
    getDataVal
);
```

This function takes a DOM element, retrieves it DOM class, strips the `"stock-"` prefix from that value, then uses that resulting value (`"name"`, `"price"`, or `"change"`) as a property name to extract from the `data` object via `getDataVal(..)`.

This may seem like a convoluted way to retrieve values from the `data` object. But the purpose is to be able to extract those values from `data` in the same order as the `<span>` elements appear in the `stockInfoChildElemList` list; we accomplish this by using `extractInfoChildElem(..)` as the mapping function over that list of DOM elements, calling the resulting list `orderedDataVals`.

Next, we're going to zip the list of `<span>`s back with the ordered data values, producing tuples where the DOM element and the value to update it with are paired up:

```
zip( stockInfoChildElemList, orderedDataVals )
```

An interesting wrinkle that wasn't at all obvious up to this point is that because of how we defined the observable's transforms, new-stock message objects will have a `name` property in `data` to match up with the `<span class="stock-name">` element, but `name` will be absent on stock-update message objects.

If the data message object doesn't have a property, we shouldn't update that corresponding DOM element. So, we need to `filterOut(..)` any tuples where the second position (the data value, in this case) is `undefined`:

```
var elemsValsTuples =
    filterOut( function updateValueMissing([infoChildElem,val]){
        return val === undefined;
    } )
    ( zip( stockInfoChildElemList, orderedDataVals ) );
```

The result after this filtering is a list of tuples (like [<span>, ".."]) ready for DOM content updating, which we assign to elemsValsTuples.

Note

Since the updateValueMissing(..) predicate is specified inline here, we're in control of its signature. Instead of using spreadArgs(..) to adapt it to spread out a single array argument as two individual named parameters, we use parameter array-destructuring in the function declaration (function updateValueMissing([infoChildElem,val]){ ..}); see Chapter 2.

Finally, we need to update the DOM content of our <span> elements:

```
// !!SIDE EFFECTS!!
compose( each, spreadArgs )( setDOMContent )
( elemsValsTuples );
```

We iterate this elemsValsTuples list with each(..) (see forEach(..) discussion in Chapter 9).

Instead of using pipe(..) as elsewhere, this composition uses compose(..) (see Chapter 4) to pass setDomContent(..) into spreadArgs(..), and then that is passed as the iterator-function to each(..). Each tuple is spread out as the arguments to setDOMContent(..), which then updates the DOM element accordingly.

That's two of the main UI methods down, one to go: addStock(..). Let's define it in its entirety, then we'll examine it step by step as before:

```
addStock(tickerElem,data) {
    var [stockElem, ...infoChildElems] = map(
        createElement
    )
    ( [ "li", "span", "span", "span" ] );
    var attrValTuples = [
        [ ["class","stock"], ["data-stock-id",data.id] ],
        [ ["class","stock-name"] ],
        [ ["class","stock-price"] ],
        [ ["class","stock-change"] ]
    ];
    var elemsAttrsTuples =
        zip( [stockElem, ...infoChildElems], attrValTuples );

    // !!SIDE EFFECTS!!
    each( function setElemAttrs([elem,attrValTupleList]){
        each(
            spreadArgs( partial( setElemAttr, elem ) )
        )
        ( attrValTupleList );
    } )
    ( elemsAttrsTuples );

    // !!SIDE EFFECTS!!
    stockTickerUI.updateStockElems( infoChildElems, data );
    reduce( appendDOMChild )( stockElem )( infoChildElems );
    appendDOMChild( tickerElem, stockElem );
}
```

This UI method needs to create the bare DOM structure for a new stock element, and then use `stockTickerUI.updateStockElems(..)` to update its content. First:

```
var [stockElem, ...infoChildElems] = map(
    createElement
)
( [ "li", "span", "span", "span" ] );
```

We create the parent <li> and the three children <span> elements, assigning them respectively to stockElem and the infoChildElems list.

To initialize these elements with the appropriate DOM attributes, we create a list of lists-of-tuples. Each item in the main list corresponds to the four DOM elements, in order. Each sub-list contains tuples that represent attribute-value pairs to be set on each corresponding DOM element, respectively:

```
var attrValTuples = [
    [ ["class","stock"], ["data-stock-id",data.id] ],
    [ ["class","stock-name"] ],
    [ ["class","stock-price"] ],
    [ ["class","stock-change"] ]
];
```

We now want to zip(..) a list of the four DOM elements with this attrValTuples list:

```
var elemsAttrsTuples =
    zip( [stockElem, ...infoChildElems], attrValTuples );
```

The structure of this list would now look like:

```
[
    [ <li>, [ ["class","stock"], ["data-stock-id",data.id] ] ],
    [ <span>, [ ["class","stock-name"] ] ],
    ..
]
```

If we wanted to imperatively process this kind of data structure to assign the attribute-value tuples into each DOM element, we'd probably use nested for-loops. Our FP approach will be similar, but with nested each(..) iterations:

```
// !!SIDE EFFECTS!!
each( function setElemAttrs([elem,attrValTupleList]){
    each(
        spreadArgs( partial( setElemAttr, elem ) )
    )
    ( attrValTupleList );
} )
( elemsAttrsTuples );
```

The outer `each(..)` iterates the list of tuples, with each `elem` and its associated `attrValTupleList` spread out as named parameters to `setElemAttrs(..)` via parameter array-destructuring as explained earlier.

Inside this outer iteration "loop", the sub-list of attribute-value tuples is iterated with an inner `each(..)`. The inner iterator-function is an arguments-spread (of each attribute-value tuple) for the partial-application of `setElemAttr(..)` with `elem` as its first argument.

At this point, we have a list of `<span>` elements, each filled out with attributes, but no `innerHTML` content. We set the `data` in the `<span>` elements with `stockTickerUI.updateStockElems(..)`, the same as for a stock-update event.

Now, we need to append these `<span>`s to the parent `<li>`, and we do that with a `reduce(..)` (see Chapter 9):

```
reduce( appendDOMChild )( stockElem )( infoChildElems );
```

Finally, a plain ol' DOM mutation side effect to append the new stock element to the widget's DOM:

```
appendDOMChild( tickerElem, stockElem );
```

Phew! Did you follow all that? I recommend re-reading that discussion a few times, and practicing with the code, before you move on.

Subscribing to Observables

Our last major task is to subscribe to the observables defined in `ch11-code/stock-ticker-events.js`, attaching these subscriptions to the appropriate main UI methods (`addStock(..)` and `updateStock(..)`).

First, we notice that those methods each expect `tickerElem` as first parameter. Let's make a list (`stockTickerUIMethodsWithDOMContext`) that encapsulates the ticker widget's DOM element with each of these two methods, via partial application (aka, closure; see Chapter 2):

```
var ticker = document.getElementById( "stock-ticker" );

var stockTickerUIMethodsWithDOMContext = map(
    pipe( partialRight, unary )( partial, ticker )
)
( [ stockTickerUI.addStock, stockTickerUI.updateStock ] );
```

First, we use `partialRight(..)` (right-partial application) on the `partial(..)` utility, presetting its right-most argument to be `ticker`. Then we pass this right-partially-applied `partial(..)` function through `unary(..)` to protect it from receiving undesired extra arguments from `map(..)` (see Chapter 3), via `pipe(..)`. The result is a mapper function which is expecting a function to partially-apply (with one argument: `ticker`). We use that mapper function to `map(..)` the `stockTickerUI.addStock(..)` and `stockTickerUI.updateStock(..)` functions, respectively.

The result of `map(..)` is the array `stockTickerUIMethodsWithDOMContext`, which holds the two partially applied functions; these two functions are now suitable as observable-subscription handlers.

Though we're using closure to preserve the `ticker` state with these two functions, in Chapter 7 we saw that we could have "kept" this `ticker` value as a property on an object, perhaps via `this`-binding each function to `stockTickerUI`. Because `this` is an implicit input (see Chapter 2) and that's generally not as preferable, I chose the closure form over the object form.

To subscribe to the observables, let's make an unbound-method helper:

```
var subscribeToObservable =
    pipe( unboundMethod, uncurry )( "subscribe" );
```

`unboundMethod("subscribe")` is curried so we `uncurry(..)` it (see Chapter 3).

Now, we just need a list of the observables, so we can `zip(..)` that with the list of DOM-bound UI methods; the resulting tuples will then include both the observable and the listener function to subscribe to it. We process each tuple with `each(..)` and use `spreadArgs(..)` (see Chapter 3) to spread the tuple's contents out as the two arguments to `subscribeToObservable(..)`:

```
var stockTickerObservables = [ newStocks, stockUpdates ];

// !!SIDE EFFECTS!!
each( spreadArgs( subscribeToObservable ) )
( zip( stockTickerUIMethodsWithDOMContext, stockTickerObservables ) );
```

We're technically mutating the state of those observables to subscribe to them, and moreover, we're using `each(..)` – pretty much always associated with side effects! – so we call that out with our code comment.

That's it! Spend the same time reviewing and comparing this code to its imperative alternatives as we did with the stock ticker events discussion earlier. Really, take your time. I know it's been a lot to read, but your whole journey through this book comes down to being able to digest and understand this kind of code.

How do you feel now about using FP in a balanced way in your JavaScript? Keep practicing just like we did here!

Summary

The example code we discussed in this chapter should be viewed in its entirety, not just in the broken-out snippets as presented in this chapter. Stop right now and go read through the full files. Make sure you understand them in full context.

This example code is not meant to be prescriptive of exactly how you should write your code. It's meant to be more descriptive of how to think about and begin approaching such tasks with FP-Light techniques. It's meant to draw as many correlations between the different concepts of this book as possible. It's meant to explore FP in the context of more "real" code than we typically afford for a single snippet.

I am quite sure that as I learn FP better on my own journey, I will continue to improve how I would write this example code. What you see now is just a snapshot on my curve. I hope it will just be such for you, as well.

As we draw the main text of this book to a close, I want to remind you of that readability curve that I shared back in Chapter 1:

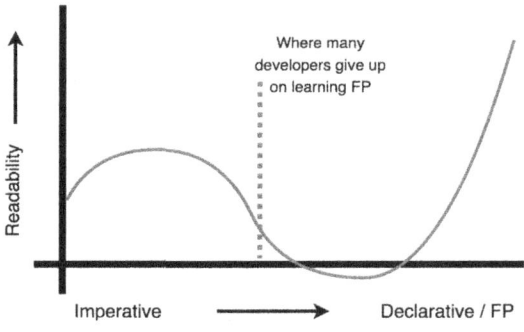

Readability of Declarative FP

It's so important that you internalize the truth of that graph and set realistic expectations for yourself on this journey to learn and apply FP principles to your JavaScript. You've made it this far, and that's quite an accomplishment.

But don't stop when you dip toward that trough of despair and disenchantment. What's waiting on the other side is a way of thinking about and communicating with your code that's more readable, understandable, verifiable, and ultimately, more reliable.

I can't think of any more noble goal for us as developers to strive toward. Thanks for sharing in my journey to learn FP principles in JavaScript. I hope your experience is as rich and hopeful as mine!

Appendix A: Transducing

Transducing is a more advanced technique than we've covered in this book. It extends many of the concepts from Chapter 9 on list operations.

I wouldn't necessarily call this topic strictly "Functional-Light", but more like a bonus on top. I've presented this as an appendix because you might very well need to skip the discussion for now and come back to it once you feel fairly comfortable with – and make sure you've practiced! – the main book concepts.

To be honest, even after teaching transducing many times, and writing this chapter, I am still trying to fully wrap my brain around this technique. So don't feel bad if it twists you up. Bookmark this appendix and come back when you're ready.

Transducing means transforming with reduction.

I know that may sound like a jumble of words that confuses more than it clarifies. But let's take a look at how powerful it can be. I actually think it's one of the best illustrations of what you can do once you grasp the principles of Functional-Light Programming.

As with the rest of this book, my approach is to first explain *why*, then *how*, then finally boil it down to a simplified, repeatable *what*. That's often the reverse of how many teach, but I think you'll learn the topic more deeply this way.

Why, First

Let's start by extending a scenario we covered back in Chapter 3, testing words to see if they're short enough and/or long enough:

```
function isLongEnough(str) {
    return str.length >= 5;
}

function isShortEnough(str) {
    return str.length <= 10;
}
```

In Chapter 3, we used these predicate functions to test a single word. Then in Chapter 9, we learned how to repeat such tests using list operations like `filter(..)`. For example:

```
var words = [ "You", "have", "written", "something", "very",
    "interesting" ];

words
.filter( isLongEnough )
.filter( isShortEnough );
// ["written","something"]
```

It may not be obvious, but this pattern of separate adjacent list operations has some non-ideal characteristics. When we're dealing with only a single array of a small number of values, everything is fine. But if there were lots of values in the array, each `filter(..)` processing the list separately can slow down a bit more than we'd like.

A similar performance problem arises when our arrays are async/lazy (aka Observables), processing values over time in response to events (see Chapter 10). In this scenario, only a single value comes down the event stream at a time, so processing that discrete value with two separate `filter(..)`s function calls isn't really such a big deal.

But what's not obvious is that each `filter(..)` method produces a separate observable. The overhead of pumping a value out of one observable into another can really add up. That's especially true since in these cases, it's not uncommon for thousands or millions of values to be processed; even such small overhead costs add up quickly.

The other downside is readability, especially when we need to repeat the same series of operations against multiple lists (or Observables). For example:

```
zip(
    list1.filter( isLongEnough ).filter( isShortEnough ),
    list2.filter( isLongEnough ).filter( isShortEnough ),
    list3.filter( isLongEnough ).filter( isShortEnough )
)
```

Repetitive, right?

Wouldn't it be better (both for readability and performance) if we could combine the `isLongEnough(..)` predicate with the `isShortEnough(..)` predicate? You could do so manually:

```
function isCorrectLength(str) {
    return isLongEnough( str ) && isShortEnough( str );
}
```

But that's not the FP way!

In Chapter 9, we talked about fusion – composing adjacent mapping functions. Recall:

```
words
.map(
    pipe( removeInvalidChars, upper, elide )
);
```

Unfortunately, combining adjacent predicate functions doesn't work as easily as combining adjacent mapping functions. To understand why, think about the "shape" of the predicate function – a sort of academic way of describing the signature of inputs and output. It takes a single value in, and it returns a `true` or a `false`.

If you tried `isShortEnough(isLongEnough(str))`, it wouldn't work properly. `isLongEnough(..)` will return true/false, not the string value that `isShortEnough(..)` is expecting. Bummer.

A similar frustration exists trying to compose two adjacent reducer functions. The "shape" of a reducer is a function that receives two values as input, and returns a single combined value. The output of a reducer as a single value is not suitable for input to another reducer expecting two inputs.

Moreover, the `reduce(..)` helper takes an optional `initialValue` input. Sometimes this can be omitted, but sometimes it has to be passed in. That even further complicates composition, since one reduction might need one `initialValue` and the other reduction might seem like it needs a different `initialValue`. How can we possibly do that if we only make one `reduce(..)` call with some sort of composed reducer?

Consider a chain like this:

```
words
.map( strUppercase )
.filter( isLongEnough )
.filter( isShortEnough )
.reduce( strConcat, "" );
// "WRITTENSOMETHING"
```

Can you envision a composition that includes all of these steps: `map(strUppercase)`, `filter(isLongEnough)`, `filter(isShortEnough)`, `reduce(strConcat)`? The shape of each operator is different, so they won't directly compose together. We need to bend their shapes a little bit to fit them together.

Hopefully these observations have illustrated why simple fusion-style composition isn't up to the task. We need a more powerful technique, and transducing is that tool.

How, Next

Let's talk about how we might derive a composition of mappers, predicates, and/or reducers.

Don't get too overwhelmed: you won't have to go through all these mental steps we're about to explore in your own programming. Once you understand and can recognize the problem transducing solves, you'll be able to just jump straight to using a `transduce(..)` utility from a FP library and move on with the rest of your application!

Let's jump in.

Expressing Map/Filter as Reduce

The first trick we need to perform is expressing our `filter(..)` and `map(..)` calls as `reduce(..)` calls. Recall how we did that in Chapter 9:

```
function strUppercase(str) { return str.toUpperCase(); }
function strConcat(str1,str2) { return str1 + str2; }

function strUppercaseReducer(list,str) {
    list.push( strUppercase( str ) );
    return list;
}

function isLongEnoughReducer(list,str) {
    if (isLongEnough( str )) list.push( str );
    return list;
}

function isShortEnoughReducer(list,str) {
    if (isShortEnough( str )) list.push( str );
    return list;
}

words
.reduce( strUppercaseReducer, [] )
.reduce( isLongEnoughReducer, [] )
.reduce( isShortEnoughReducer, [] )
.reduce( strConcat, "" );
// "WRITTENSOMETHING"
```

That's a decent improvement. We now have four adjacent `reduce(..)` calls instead of a mixture of three different methods all with different shapes. We still can't just `compose(..)` those four reducers, however, because they accept two arguments instead of one.

In Chapter 9, we sort of cheated and used `list.push(..)` to mutate as a side effect rather than creating a whole new array to concatenate onto. Let's step back and be a bit more formal for now:

```
function strUppercaseReducer(list,str) {
    return [ ...list, strUppercase( str ) ];
}

function isLongEnoughReducer(list,str) {
    if (isLongEnough( str )) return [ ...list, str ];
    return list;
}

function isShortEnoughReducer(list,str) {
    if (isShortEnough( str )) return [ ...list, str ];
    return list;
}
```

Later, we'll revisit whether creating a new array (e.g., `[...list,str]`) to concatenate onto is necessary here or not.

Parameterizing the Reducers

Both filter reducers are almost identical, except they use a different predicate function. Let's parameterize that so we get one utility that can define any filter-reducer:

```
function filterReducer(predicateFn) {
    return function reducer(list,val){
        if (predicateFn( val )) return [ ...list, val ];
        return list;
    };
}

var isLongEnoughReducer = filterReducer( isLongEnough );
var isShortEnoughReducer = filterReducer( isShortEnough );
```

Let's do the same parameterization of the `mapperFn(..)` for a utility to produce any map-reducer:

```
function mapReducer(mapperFn) {
    return function reducer(list,val){
        return [ ...list, mapperFn( val ) ];
    };
}

var strToUppercaseReducer = mapReducer( strUppercase );
```

Our chain still looks the same:

```
words
.reduce( strUppercaseReducer, [] )
.reduce( isLongEnoughReducer, [] )
.reduce( isShortEnoughReducer, [] )
.reduce( strConcat, "" );
```

Extracting Common Combination Logic

Look very closely at the preceding `mapReducer(..)` and `filterReducer(..)` functions. Do you spot the common functionality shared in each?

This part:

```
return [ ...list, .. ];

// or
return list;
```

Let's define a helper for that common logic. But what shall we call it?

```
function WHATSITCALLED(list,val) {
    return [ ...list, val ];
}
```

If you examine what that `WHATSITCALLED(..)` function does, it takes two values (an array and another value) and it "combines" them by creating a new array and concatenating the value onto the end of it. Very uncreatively, we could name this `listCombine(..)`:

```
function listCombine(list,val) {
    return [ ...list, val ];
}
```

Let's now re-define our reducer helpers to use `listCombine(..)`:

```
function mapReducer(mapperFn) {
    return function reducer(list,val){
        return listCombine( list, mapperFn( val ) );
    };
}

function filterReducer(predicateFn) {
    return function reducer(list,val){
        if (predicateFn( val )) return listCombine( list, val );
        return list;
    };
}
```

Our chain still looks the same (so we won't repeat it).

Parameterizing the Combination

Our simple `listCombine(..)` utility is only one possible way that we might combine two values. Let's parameterize the use of it to make our reducers more generalized:

```
function mapReducer(mapperFn,combinerFn) {
    return function reducer(list,val){
        return combinerFn( list, mapperFn( val ) );
    };
}

function filterReducer(predicateFn,combinerFn) {
    return function reducer(list,val){
        if (predicateFn( val )) return combinerFn( list, val );
        return list;
    };
}
```

To use this form of our helpers:

```
var strToUppercaseReducer = mapReducer( strUppercase, listCombine );
var isLongEnoughReducer = filterReducer( isLongEnough, listCombine );
var isShortEnoughReducer = filterReducer( isShortEnough, listCombine );
```

Defining these utilities to take two arguments instead of one is less convenient for composition, so let's use our `curry(..)` approach:

```
var curriedMapReducer =
    curry( function mapReducer(mapperFn,combinerFn){
        return function reducer(list,val){
            return combinerFn( list, mapperFn( val ) );
        };
    } );

var curriedFilterReducer =
    curry( function filterReducer(predicateFn,combinerFn){
        return function reducer(list,val){
            if (predicateFn( val )) return combinerFn( list, val );
            return list;
        };
    } );

var strToUppercaseReducer =
    curriedMapReducer( strUppercase )( listCombine );
var isLongEnoughReducer =
    curriedFilterReducer( isLongEnough )( listCombine );
var isShortEnoughReducer =
    curriedFilterReducer( isShortEnough )( listCombine );
```

That looks a bit more verbose, and probably doesn't seem very useful.

But this is actually necessary to get to the next step of our derivation. Remember, our ultimate goal here is to be able to `compose(..)` these reducers. We're almost there.

Composing Curried

This step is the trickiest of all to visualize. So read slowly and pay close attention here.

Let's consider the curried functions from earlier, but without the listCombine(..) function having been passed in to each:

```
var x = curriedMapReducer( strUppercase );
var y = curriedFilterReducer( isLongEnough );
var z = curriedFilterReducer( isShortEnough );
```

Think about the shape of all three of these intermediate functions, x(..), y(..), and z(..). Each one expects a single combination function, and produces a reducer function with it.

Remember, if we wanted the independent reducers from all these, we could do:

```
var upperReducer = x( listCombine );
var longEnoughReducer = y( listCombine );
var shortEnoughReducer = z( listCombine );
```

But what would you get back if you called y(z), instead of y(listCombine)? Basically, what happens when passing z in as the combinerFn(..) for the y(..) call? That returned reducer function internally looks kinda like this:

```
function reducer(list,val) {
    if (isLongEnough( val )) return z( list, val );
    return list;
}
```

See the z(..) call inside? That should look wrong to you, because the z(..) function is supposed to receive only a single argument (a combinerFn(..)), not two arguments (list and val). The shapes don't match. That won't work.

Let's instead look at the composition y(z(listCombine)). We'll break that down into two separate steps:

```
var shortEnoughReducer = z( listCombine );
var longAndShortEnoughReducer = y( shortEnoughReducer );
```

We create `shortEnoughReducer(..)`, then we pass *it* in as the `combinerFn(..)` to `y(..)` instead of calling `y(listCombine)`; this new call produces `longAndShortEnoughReducer(..)`. Re-read that a few times until it clicks.

Now consider: what do `shortEnoughReducer(..)` and `longAndShortEnoughReducer(..)` look like internally? Can you see them in your mind?

```
// shortEnoughReducer, from calling z(..):
function reducer(list,val) {
    if (isShortEnough( val )) return listCombine( list, val );
    return list;
}

// longAndShortEnoughReducer, from calling y(..):
function reducer(list,val) {
    if (isLongEnough( val )) return shortEnoughReducer( list, val );
    return list;
}
```

Do you see how `shortEnoughReducer(..)` has taken the place of `listCombine(..)` inside `longAndShortEnoughReducer(..)`? Why does that work?

Because **the shape of a `reducer(..)` and the shape of `listCombine(..)` are the same**. In other words, a reducer can be used as a combination function for another reducer; that's how they compose! The `listCombine(..)` function makes the first reducer, then *that reducer* can be used as the combination function to make the next reducer, and so on.

Let's test out our `longAndShortEnoughReducer(..)` with a few different values:

```
longAndShortEnoughReducer( [], "nope" );
// []

longAndShortEnoughReducer( [], "hello" );
// ["hello"]

longAndShortEnoughReducer( [], "hello world" );
// []
```

The `longAndShortEnoughReducer(..)` utility is filtering out both values that are not long enough and values that are not short enough, and it's doing both these filterings in the same step. It's a composed reducer!

Take another moment to let that sink in. It still kinda blows my mind.

Now, to bring `x(..)` (the uppercase reducer producer) into the composition:

```
var longAndShortEnoughReducer = y( z( listCombine ) );
var upperLongAndShortEnoughReducer = x( longAndShortEnoughReducer );
```

As the name `upperLongAndShortEnoughReducer(..)` implies, it does all three steps at once – a mapping and two filters! What it kinda look likes internally:

```
// upperLongAndShortEnoughReducer:
function reducer(list,val) {
    return longAndShortEnoughReducer( list, strUppercase( val ) );
}
```

A string `val` is passed in, uppercased by `strUppercase(..)` and then passed along to `longAndShortEnoughReducer(..)`. *That* function only conditionally adds this uppercased string to the `list` if it's both long enough and short enough. Otherwise, `list` will remain unchanged.

It took my brain weeks to fully understand the implications of that juggling. So don't worry if you need to stop here and re-read a few (dozen!) times to get it. Take your time.

Now let's verify:

```
upperLongAndShortEnoughReducer( [], "nope" );
// []

upperLongAndShortEnoughReducer( [], "hello" );
// ["HELLO"]

upperLongAndShortEnoughReducer( [], "hello world" );
// []
```

This reducer is the composition of the map and both filters! That's amazing! Let's recap where we're at so far:

```
var x = curriedMapReducer( strUppercase );
var y = curriedFilterReducer( isLongEnough );
var z = curriedFilterReducer( isShortEnough );

var upperLongAndShortEnoughReducer = x( y( z( listCombine ) ) );

words.reduce( upperLongAndShortEnoughReducer, [] );
// ["WRITTEN","SOMETHING"]
```

That's pretty cool. But let's make it even better.

`x(y(z( .. )))` is a composition. Let's skip the intermediate x / y / z variable names, and just express that composition directly:

```
var composition = compose(
    curriedMapReducer( strUppercase ),
    curriedFilterReducer( isLongEnough ),
    curriedFilterReducer( isShortEnough )
);

var upperLongAndShortEnoughReducer = composition( listCombine );

words.reduce( upperLongAndShortEnoughReducer, [] );
// ["WRITTEN","SOMETHING"]
```

Think about the flow of "data" in that composed function:

1. `listCombine(..)` flows in as the combination function to make the filter-reducer for `isShortEnough(..)`.
2. *That* resulting reducer function then flows in as the combination function to make the filter-reducer for `isLongEnough(..)`.
3. Finally, *that* resulting reducer function flows in as the combination function to make the map-reducer for `strUppercase(..)`.

In the previous snippet, `composition(..)` is a composed function expecting a combination function to make a reducer; `composition(..)` here has a special name: transducer. Providing the combination function to a transducer produces the composed reducer:

```
var transducer = compose(
    curriedMapReducer( strUppercase ),
    curriedFilterReducer( isLongEnough ),
    curriedFilterReducer( isShortEnough )
);

words
.reduce( transducer( listCombine ), [] );
// ["WRITTEN","SOMETHING"]
```

Note

We should make an observation about the `compose(..)` order in the previous two snippets, which may be confusing. Recall that in our original example chain, we `map(strUppercase)` and then `filter(isLongEnough)` and finally `filter(isShortEnough)`; those operations indeed happen in that order. But in Chapter 4, we learned that `compose(..)` typically has the effect of running its functions in reverse order of listing. So why don't we need to reverse the order *here* to get the same desired outcome? The abstraction of the `combinerFn(..)` from each reducer reverses the effective applied order of operations under the hood. So counter-intuitively, when composing a transducer, you actually want to list them in desired order of execution!

List Combination: Pure vs. Impure

As a quick aside, let's revisit our `listCombine(..)` combination function implementation:

```
function listCombine(list,val) {
    return [ ...list, val ];
}
```

While this approach is pure, it has negative consequences for performance: for each step in the reduction, we're creating a whole new array to append the value onto, effectively throwing away the previous array. That's a lot of arrays being created and thrown away, which is not only bad for CPU but also GC memory churn.

By contrast, look again at the better-performing but impure version:

```
function listCombine(list,val) {
    list.push( val );
    return list;
}
```

Thinking about `listCombine(..)` in isolation, there's no question it's impure and that's usually something we'd want to avoid. However, there's a bigger context we should consider.

`listCombine(..)` is not a function we interact with at all. We don't directly use it anywhere in the program; instead, we let the transducing process use it.

Back in Chapter 5, we asserted that our goal with reducing side effects and defining pure functions was only that we expose pure functions to the API level of functions we'll use throughout our program. We observed that under the covers, inside a pure function, it can cheat for performance sake all it wants, as long as it doesn't violate the external contract of purity.

`listCombine(..)` is more an internal implementation detail of the transducing – in fact, it'll often be provided by the transducing library for you! – rather than a top-level method you'd interact with on a normal basis throughout your program.

Bottom line: I think it's perfectly acceptable, and advisable even, to use the performance-optimal impure version of `listCombine(..)`. Just make sure you document that it's impure with a code comment!

Alternative Combination

So far, this is what we've derived with transducing:

```
words
.reduce( transducer( listCombine ), [] )
.reduce( strConcat, "" );
// WRITTENSOMETHING
```

That's pretty good, but we have one final trick up our sleeve with transducing. And frankly, I think this part is what makes all this mental effort you've expended thus far, actually worth it.

Can we somehow "compose" these two `reduce(..)` calls to get it down to just one `reduce(..)`? Unfortunately, we can't just add `strConcat(..)` into the compose(..) call; because it's a reducer and not a combination-expecting function, its shape is not correct for the composition.

But let's look at these two functions side by side:

```
function strConcat(str1,str2) { return str1 + str2; }

function listCombine(list,val) { list.push( val ); return list; }
```

If you squint your eyes, you can almost see how these two functions are interchangeable. They operate with different data types, but conceptually they do the same thing: combine two values into one.

In other words, `strConcat(..)` is a combination function!

That means we can use *it* instead of `listCombine(..)` if our end goal is to get a string concatenation rather than a list:

```
words.reduce( transducer( strConcat ), "" );
// WRITTENSOMETHING
```

Boom! That's transducing for you. I won't actually drop the mic here, but just gently set it down...

What, Finally

Take a deep breath. That was a lot to digest.

Clearing our brains for a minute, let's turn our attention back to just using transducing in our applications without jumping through all those mental hoops to derive how it works.

Recall the helpers we defined earlier; let's rename them for clarity:

```
var transduceMap =
    curry( function mapReducer(mapperFn,combinerFn){
        return function reducer(list,v){
            return combinerFn( list, mapperFn( v ) );
        };
    } );

var transduceFilter =
    curry( function filterReducer(predicateFn,combinerFn){
        return function reducer(list,v){
            if (predicateFn( v )) return combinerFn( list, v );
            return list;
        };
    } );
```

Also recall that we use them like this:

```
var transducer = compose(
    transduceMap( strUppercase ),
    transduceFilter( isLongEnough ),
    transduceFilter( isShortEnough )
);
```

`transducer(..)` still needs a combination function (like `listCombine(..)` or `strConcat(..)`) passed to it to produce a transduce-reducer function, which can then be used (along with an initial value) in `reduce(..)`.

But to express all these transducing steps more declaratively, let's make a `transduce(..)` utility that does these steps for us:

```
function transduce(transducer,combinerFn,initialValue,list) {
    var reducer = transducer( combinerFn );
    return list.reduce( reducer, initialValue );
}
```

Here's our running example, cleaned up:

```
var transducer = compose(
    transduceMap( strUppercase ),
    transduceFilter( isLongEnough ),
    transduceFilter( isShortEnough )
);

transduce( transducer, listCombine, [], words );
// ["WRITTEN","SOMETHING"]

transduce( transducer, strConcat, "", words );
// WRITTENSOMETHING
```

Not bad, huh!? See the `listCombine(..)` and `strConcat(..)` functions used interchangeably as combination functions?

Transducers.js

Finally, let's illustrate our running example using the `transducers-js` library[29]:

---

[29] https://github.com/cognitect-labs/transducers-js

```
var transformer = transducers.comp(
    transducers.map( strUppercase ),
    transducers.filter( isLongEnough ),
    transducers.filter( isShortEnough )
);

transducers.transduce( transformer, listCombine, [], words );
// ["WRITTEN","SOMETHING"]

transducers.transduce( transformer, strConcat, "", words );
// WRITTENSOMETHING
```

Looks almost identical to above.

Note

The preceding snippet uses `transformers.comp(..)` because the library provides it, but in this case our `compose(..)` from Chapter 4 would produce the same outcome. In other words, composition itself isn't a transducing-sensitive operation.

The composed function in this snippet is named `transformer` instead of `transducer`. That's because if we call `transformer( listCombine )` (or `transformer( strConcat )`), we won't get a straight-up transduce-reducer function as earlier.

`transducers.map(..)` and `transducers.filter(..)` are special helpers that adapt regular predicate or mapper functions into functions that produce a special transform object (with the transducer function wrapped underneath); the library uses these transform objects for transducing. The extra capabilities of this transform object abstraction are beyond what we'll explore, so consult the library's documentation for more information.

Because calling `transformer(..)` produces a transform object and not a typical binary transduce-reducer function, the library also provides `toFn(..)` to adapt the transform object to be useable by native array `reduce(..)`:

```
words.reduce(
    transducers.toFn( transformer, strConcat ),
    ""
);
// WRITTENSOMETHING
```

`into(..)` is another provided helper that automatically selects a default combination function based on the type of empty/initial value specified:

```
transducers.into( [], transformer, words );
// ["WRITTEN","SOMETHING"]

transducers.into( "", transformer, words );
// WRITTENSOMETHING
```

When specifying an empty `[]` array, the `transduce(..)` called under the covers uses a default implementation of a function like our `listCombine(..)` helper. But when specifying an empty `""` string, something like our `strConcat(..)` is used. Cool!

As you can see, the `transducers-js` library makes transducing pretty straightforward. We can very effectively leverage the power of this technique without getting into the weeds of defining all those intermediate transducer-producing utilities ourselves.

Summary

To transduce means to transform with a reduce. More specifically, a transducer is a composable reducer.

We use transducing to compose adjacent `map(..)`, `filter(..)`, and `reduce(..)` operations together. We accomplish this by first expressing `map(..)`s and `filter(..)`s as `reduce(..)`s, and then abstracting out the common combination operation to create unary reducer-producing functions that are easily composed.

Transducing primarily improves performance, which is especially obvious if used on an observable.

But more broadly, transducing is how we express a more declarative composition of functions that would otherwise not be directly composable. The result, if used appropriately as with all other techniques in this book, is clearer, more readable code! A single `reduce(..)` call with a transducer is easier to reason about than tracing through multiple `reduce(..)` calls.

Appendix B: The Humble Monad

Let me just start off this appendix by admitting: I did not know much about what a monad was before starting to write this appendix. And it took a lot of mistakes to get something sensible. If you don't believe me, go look at the commit history of this appendix in the Github repository for this book[30]!

I am including the topic of monads in the book because it's part of the journey that every developer will encounter while learning FP, just as I have in this book writing.

We're basically ending this book with a brief glimpse at monads, whereas most other FP literature kinda almost starts with monads! I do not encounter in my "Functional-Light" programming much of a need to think explicitly in terms of monads, so that's why this material is more bonus than main core. But that's not to say monads aren't useful or prevalent – they very much are.

There's a bit of a joke around the JavaScript FP world that pretty much everybody has to write their own tutorial or blog post on what a monad is, like the writing of it alone is some rite of passage. Over the years, monads have variously been depicted as burritos, onions, and all sorts of other wacky conceptual abstractions. I hope there's none of that silly business going on here!

> *A monad is just a monoid in the category of endofunctors.*

We started the preface with this quote, so it seems fitting we come back to it here. But no, we won't be talking about monoids, endofunctors, or category theory. That quote is not only condescending, but totally unhelpful.

My only hope for what you get out of this discussion is to not be scared of the term monad or the concept anymore – I have been, for years! – and to be able to recognize them when you see them. You might, just maybe, even use them on occasion.

---

[30]https://github.com/getify/Functional-Light-JS

Type

There's a huge area of interest in FP that we've basically stayed entirely away from throughout this book: type theory. I'm not going to get very deep into type theory, because quite frankly I'm not qualified to do so. And you wouldn't appreciate it even if I did.

But what I will say is that a monad is basically a value type.

The number 42 has a value type (number!) that brings with it certain characteristics and capabilities that we rely on. The string `"42"` may look very similar, but it has a different purpose in our program.

In object-oriented programming, when you have a set of data (even a single discrete value) and you have some behavior you want to bundle with it, you create an object/class to represent that "type". Instances are then members of that type. This practice generally goes by the name "data structures".

I'm going to use the notion of data structures very loosely here, and assert that we may find it useful in a program to define a set of behaviors and constraints for a certain value, and bundle them together with that value into a single abstraction. That way, as we work with one or more of those kinds of values in our program, their behaviors come along for free and will make working with them more convenient. And by convenient, I mean more declarative and approachable for the reader of your code!

A monad is a data structure. It's a type. It's a set of behaviors that are specifically designed to make working with a value predictable.

Recall in Chapter 9 that we talked about functors: a value along with a map-like utility to perform an operation on all its constitute data members. A monad is a functor that includes some additional behavior.

Loose Interface

Actually, a monad isn't a single data type, it's really more like a related collection of data types. It's kind of an interface that's implemented differently depending on the needs of different values. Each implementation is a different type of monad.

For example, you may read about the "Identity Monad", the "IO Monad", the "Maybe Monad", the "Either Monad", or a variety of others. Each of these has the basic monad behavior defined, but it extends or overrides the interactions according to the use cases for each different type of monad.

It's a little more than an interface though, because it's not just the presence of certain API methods that makes an object a monad. There's a certain set of guarantees about the interactions of these methods that is necessary, to be monadic. These well-known invariants are critical to usage of monads improving readability by familiarity; otherwise, it's just an ad hoc data structure that must be fully read to be understood by the reader.

As a matter of fact, there's not even just one single unified agreement on the names of these monadic methods, the way a true interface would mandate; a monad is more like a loose interface. Some people call a certain method `bind(..)`, some call it `chain(..)`, some call it `flatMap(..)`, and so on.

So a monad is an object data structure with sufficient methods (of practically any name or sort) that at a minimum satisfy the main behavioral requirements of the monad definition. Each kind of monad has a different kind of extension above the minimum. But, because they all have an overlap in behavior, using two different kinds of monads together is still straightforward and predictable.

It's in that sense that monads are sort of like an interface.

Just a Monad

A basic primitive monad underlying many other monads you will run across is called Just. It's *just* a simple monadic wrapper for any regular (aka, non-empty) value.

Since a monad is a type, you might think we'd define `Just` as a class to be instantiated. That's a valid way of doing it, but it introduces `this`-binding issues in the methods that I don't want to juggle; instead, I'm going to stick with just a simple function approach.

Here's a basic implementation:

```
function Just(val) {
    return { map, chain, ap, inspect };

    // *********************

    function map(fn) { return Just( fn( val ) ); }

    // aka: bind, flatMap
    function chain(fn) { return fn( val ); }

    function ap(anotherMonad) { return anotherMonad.map( val ); }

    function inspect() {
        return `Just(${ val })`;
    }
}
```

Note

The `inspect(..)` method is included here only for our demonstration purposes. It serves no direct role in the monadic sense.

You'll notice that whatever `val` value a `Just(..)` instance holds, it's never changed. All monad methods create new monad instances instead of mutating the monad's value itself.

Don't worry if most of this doesn't make sense right now. We're not gonna obsess too much over the details or the math/theory behind the design of the monad. Instead, we'll focus more on illustrating what we can do with them.

Working with Monad Methods

All monad instances will have `map(..)`, `chain(..)` (also called `bind(..)` or `flatMap(..)`), and `ap(..)` methods. The purpose of these methods and their behavior is to provide a standardized way of multiple monad instances interacting with each other.

Let's look first at the monadic map(..) function. Like map(..) on an array (see Chapter 9) that calls a mapper function with its value(s) and produces a new array, a monad's map(..) calls a mapper function with the monad's value, and whatever is returned is wrapped in a new Just monad instance:

```
var A = Just( 10 );
var B = A.map( v => v * 2 );

B.inspect();                    // Just(20)
```

Monadic chain(..) kinda does the same thing as map(..), but then it sort of unwraps the resulting value from its new monad. However, instead of thinking informally about "unwrapping" a monad, the more formal explanation would be that chain(..) flattens the monad. Consider:

```
var A = Just( 10 );
var eleven = A.chain( v => v + 1 );

eleven;                         // 11
typeof eleven;                  // "number"
```

eleven is the actual primitive number 11, not a monad holding that value.

To connect this chain(..) method conceptually to stuff we've already learned, we'll point out that many monad implementations name this method flatMap(..). Now, recall from Chapter 9 what flatMap(..) does (as compared to map(..)) with an array:

```
var x = [3];

map( v => [v,v+1], x );         // [[3,4]]
flatMap( v => [v,v+1], x );     // [3,4]
```

See the difference? The mapper function `v => [v,v+1]` results in a `[3,4]` array, which ends up in the single first position of the outer array, so we get `[[3,4]]`. But `flatMap(..)` flattens out the inner array into the outer array, so we get just `[3,4]` instead.

That's the same kind of thing going on with a monad's `chain(..)` (often referred to as `flatMap(..)`). Instead of getting a monad holding the value as `map(..)` does, `chain(..)` additionally flattens the monad into the underlying value. Actually, instead of creating that intermediate monad only to immediately flatten it, `chain(..)` is generally implemented more performantly to just take a shortcut and not create the monad in the first place. Either way, the end result is the same.

One way to illustrate `chain(..)` in this manner is in combination with the `identity(..)` utility (see Chapter 3), to effectively extract a value from a monad:

```
var identity = v => v;

A.chain( identity );          // 10
```

`A.chain(..)` calls `identity(..)` with the value in `A`, and whatever value `identity(..)` returns (`10` in this case) just comes right out without any intervening monad. In other words, from that earlier `Just(..)` code listing, we wouldn't actually need to include that optional `inspect(..)` helper, as `chain(identity)` accomplishes the same goal; it's purely for ease of debugging as we learn monads.

At this point, hopefully both `map(..)` and `chain(..)` feel fairly reasonable to you.

By contrast, a monad's `ap(..)` method will likely be much less intuitive at first glance. It will seem like a strange contortion of interaction, but there's deep and important reasoning behind the design. Let's take a moment to break it down.

`ap(..)` takes the value wrapped in a monad and "applies" it to another monad using that other monad's `map(..)`. OK, fine so far.

However, `map(..)` always expects a function. So that means the monad you call `ap(..)` on has to actually contain a function as its value, to pass to that other monad's `map(..)`.

Confused? Yeah, not what you might have expected. We'll try to briefly illuminate, but just expect that these things will be fuzzy for a while until you've had a lot more exposure and practice with monads.

We'll define A as a monad that contains a value 10, and B as a monad that contains the value 3:

```
var A = Just( 10 );
var B = Just( 3 );

A.inspect();                    // Just(10)
B.inspect();                    // Just(3)
```

Now, how could we make a new monad where the values 10 and 3 had been added together, say via a sum(..) function? Turns out ap(..) can help.

To use ap(..), we said we first need to construct a monad that holds a function. Specifically, we need one that holds a function that itself holds (remembers via closure) the value in A. Let that sink in for a moment.

To make a monad from A that holds a value-containing function, we call A.map(..), giving it a curried function that "remembers" that extracted value (see Chapter 3) as its first argument. We'll call this new function-containing monad C:

```
function sum(x,y) { return x + y; }

var C = A.map( curry( sum ) );

C.inspect();
// Just(function curried...)
```

Think about how that works. The curried sum(..) function is expecting two values to do its work, and we give it the first of those values by having A.map(..) extract 10 and pass it in. C now holds the function that remembers 10 via closure.

Now, to get the second value (3 inside B) passed to the waiting curried function in C:

```
var D = C.ap( B );

D.inspect();                    // Just(13)
```

The value 10 came out of C, and 3 came out of B, and sum(..) added them together to 13 and wrapped that in the monad D. Let's put the two steps together so you can see their connection more clearly:

```
var D = A.map( curry( sum ) ).ap( B );

D.inspect();                    // Just(13)
```

To illustrate what ap(..) is helping us with, we could have achieved the same result this way:

```
var D = B.map( A.chain( curry( sum ) ) );

D.inspect();                    // Just(13);
```

And that of course is just a composition (see Chapter 4):

```
var D = compose( B.map, A.chain, curry )( sum );

D.inspect();                    // Just(13)
```

Cool, huh!?

If the *how* of this discussion on monad methods is unclear so far, go back and re-read. If the *why* is elusive, just hang in there. Monads so easily confound developers, that's *just* how it is!

Maybe

It's very common in FP material to cover well-known monads like Maybe. Actually, the Maybe monad is a particular pairing of two other simpler monads: Just and Nothing.

We've already seen Just; Nothing is a monad that holds an empty value. Maybe is a monad that either holds a Just or a Nothing.

Here's a minimal implementation of Maybe:

```
var Maybe = { Just, Nothing, of/* aka: unit, pure */: Just };

function Just(val) { /* .. */ }

function Nothing() {
    return { map: Nothing, chain: Nothing, ap: Nothing, inspect };

    // *********************

    function inspect() {
        return "Nothing";
    }
}
```

Note

Maybe.of(..) (sometimes referred to as unit(..) or pure(..)) is a convenience alias for Just(..).

In contrast to Just() instances, Nothing() instances have no-op definitions for all monadic methods. So if such a monad instance shows up in any monadic operations, it has the effect of basically short-circuiting to have no behavior happen. Notice there's no imposition here of what "empty" means – your code gets to decide that. More on that later.

In Maybe, if a value is non-empty, it's represented by an instance of Just(..); if it's empty, it's represented by an instance of Nothing().

But the importance of this kind of monad representation is that whether we have a Just(..) instance or a Nothing() instance, we'll use the API methods the same.

The power of the Maybe abstraction is to encapsulate that behavior/no-op duality implicitly.

Different Maybes

Many implementations of a JavaScript Maybe monad include a check (usually in `map(..)`) to see if the value is `null/undefined`, and skipping the behavior if so. In fact, Maybe is trumpeted as being valuable precisely because it sort of automatically short-circuits its behavior with the encapsulated empty-value check.

Here's how Maybe is usually illustrated:

```
// instead of unsafe `console.log( someObj.something.else.entirely )`:

Maybe.of( someObj )
.map( prop( "something" ) )
.map( prop( "else" ) )
.map( prop( "entirely" ) )
.map( console.log );
```

In other words, if at any point in the chain we get a `null/undefined` value, the Maybe magically switches into no-op mode -- it's now a `Nothing()` monad instance! -- and stops doing anything for the rest of the chain. That makes the nested-property access safe against throwing JS exceptions if some property is missing/empty. That's cool, and a nice helpful abstraction for sure!

But... *that approach to Maybe is not a pure monad.*

The core spirit of a Monad says that it must be valid for all values and cannot do any inspection of the value, at all -- not even a null check. So those other implementations are cutting corners for the sake of convenience. It's not a huge deal, but when it comes to learning something, you should probably learn it in its purest form first before you go bending the rules.

The earlier implementation of the Maybe monad I provided differs from other Maybes primarily in that it does not have the empty-check in it. Also, we present `Maybe` merely as a loose pairing of `Just(..)/Nothing()`.

So wait. If we don't get the automatic short-circuiting, why is Maybe useful at all?!? That seems like its whole point.

Never fear! We can simply provide the empty-check externally, and the rest of the short-circuiting behavior of the Maybe monad will work just fine. Here's how you could do the nested-property access (someObj.something.else.entirely) from before, but more "correctly":

```
function isEmpty(val) {
    return val === null || val === undefined;
}

var safeProp = curry( function safeProp(prop,obj){
    if (isEmpty( obj[prop] )) return Maybe.Nothing();
    return Maybe.of( obj[prop] );
} );

Maybe.of( someObj )
.chain( safeProp( "something" ) )
.chain( safeProp( "else" ) )
.chain( safeProp( "entirely" ) )
.map( console.log );
```

We made a safeProp(..) that does the empty-check, and selects either a Nothing() monad instance if so, or wraps the value in a Just(..) instance (via Maybe.of(..)). Then instead of map(..), we use chain(..) which knows how to "unwrap" the monad that safeProp(..) returns.

We get the same chain short-circuiting upon encountering an empty value. We just don't embed that logic into the Maybe.

The benefit of the monad, and Maybe specifically, is that our map(..) and chain(..) methods have a consistent and predictable interaction regardless of which kind of monad comes back. That's pretty cool!

Humble

Now that we have a little more understanding of Maybe and what it does, I'm going to put a little twist on it – and add some self-deferential humor to our discussion – by inventing the Maybe+Humble monad. Technically, MaybeHumble(..) is not a monad itself, but a factory function that produces a Maybe monad instance.

Humble is an admittedly contrived data structure wrapper that uses Maybe to track the status of an `egoLevel` number. Specifically, `MaybeHumble(..)`-produced monad instances only operate affirmatively if their ego-level value is low enough (less than 42!) to be considered humble; otherwise it's a `Nothing()` no-op. That should sound a lot like Maybe; it's pretty similar!

Here's the factory function for our Maybe+Humble monad:

```
function MaybeHumble(egoLevel) {
    // accept anything other than a number that's 42 or higher
    return !(Number( egoLevel ) >= 42) ?
        Maybe.of( egoLevel ) :
        Maybe.Nothing();
}
```

You'll notice that this factory function is kinda like `safeProp(..)`, in that it uses a condition to decide if it should pick the `Just(..)` or the `Nothing()` part of the Maybe.

Let's illustrate some basic usage:

```
var bob = MaybeHumble( 45 );
var alice = MaybeHumble( 39 );

bob.inspect();              // Nothing
alice.inspect();            // Just(39)
```

What if Alice wins a big award and is now a bit more proud of herself?

```
function winAward(ego) {
    return MaybeHumble( ego + 3 );
}

alice = alice.chain( winAward );
alice.inspect();            // Nothing
```

The `MaybeHumble( 39 + 3 )` call creates a `Nothing()` monad instance to return back from the `chain(..)` call, so now Alice doesn't qualify as humble anymore.

Now, let's use a few monads together:

```
var bob = MaybeHumble( 41 );
var alice = MaybeHumble( 39 );

var teamMembers = curry( function teamMembers(ego1,ego2){
    console.log( `Our humble team's egos: ${ego1} ${ego2}` );
} );

bob.map( teamMembers ).ap( alice );
// Our humble team's egos: 41 39
```

Recalling the usage of `ap(..)` from earlier, we can now explain how this code works.

Because `teamMembers(..)` is curried, the `bob.map(..)` call passes in the bob ego level (41), and creates a monad instance with the remaining function wrapped up. Calling `ap(alice)` on *that* monad calls `alice.map(..)` and passes to it the function from the monad. The effect is that both the bob and alice monad's numeric values have been provided to `teamMembers(..)` function, printing out the message as shown.

However, if either or both monads are actually `Nothing()` instances (because their ego level was too high):

```
var frank = MaybeHumble( 45 );

bob.map( teamMembers ).ap( frank );
// ..no output..

frank.map( teamMembers ).ap( bob );
// ..no output..
```

`teamMembers(..)` never gets called (and no message is printed), because frank is a `Nothing()` instance. That's the power of the Maybe monad, and our `MaybeHumble(..)` factory allows us to select based on the ego level. Cool!

Humility

One more example to illustrate the behaviors of our Maybe+Humble data structure:

```
function introduction() {
    console.log( "I'm just a learner like you! :)" );
}

var egoChange = curry( function egoChange(amount,concept,egoLevel) {
    console.log( `${amount > 0 ? "Learned" : "Shared"} ${concept}.` );
    return MaybeHumble( egoLevel + amount );
} );

var learn = egoChange( 3 );

var learner = MaybeHumble( 35 );

learner
.chain( learn( "closures" ) )
.chain( learn( "side effects" ) )
.chain( learn( "recursion" ) )
.chain( learn( "map/reduce" ) )
.map( introduction );
// Learned closures.
// Learned side effects.
// Learned recursion.
// ..nothing else..
```

Unfortunately, the learning process seems to have been cut short. You see, I've found that learning a bunch of stuff without sharing with others inflates your ego too much and is not good for your skills.

Let's try a better approach to learning:

```
var share = egoChange( -2 );

learner
.chain( learn( "closures" ) )
.chain( share( "closures" ) )
.chain( learn( "side effects" ) )
.chain( share( "side effects" ) )
.chain( learn( "recursion" ) )
.chain( share( "recursion" ) )
.chain( learn( "map/reduce" ) )
.chain( share( "map/reduce" ) )
.map( introduction );
// Learned closures.
// Shared closures.
// Learned side effects.
// Shared side effects.
// Learned recursion.
// Shared recursion.
// Learned map/reduce.
// Shared map/reduce.
// I'm just a learner like you! :)
```

Sharing while you learn. That's the best way to learn more and learn better.

Summary

What is a monad, anyway? A monad is a value type, an interface, an object data structure with encapsulated behaviors.

But none of those definitions are particularly useful. Here's an attempt at something better: **a monad is how you organize behavior around a value in a more declarative way.**

As with everything else in this book, use monads where they are helpful but don't use them just because everyone else talks about them in FP. Monads aren't a universal silver bullet, but they do offer some utility when used conservatively.

Appendix C: FP Libraries

If you've been reading this book from start to finish, take a minute to stop and look back how far you've come since Chapter 1. It's been quite a journey. I hope you've learned a lot and gained insight into thinking functionally for your own programs.

I want to close this book leaving you with some quick pointers of working with common/popular FP libraries. This is not an exhaustive documentation on each, but a quick glance at the things you should be aware of as you venture beyond "Functional-Light" into broader FP.

Wherever possible, I recommend you *not* reinvent any wheels. If you find an FP library that suits your needs, use it. Only use the ad hoc helper utilities from this book – or invent ones of your own! – if you can't find a suitable library method for your circumstance.

Stuff to Investigate

Let's expand the list of FP libraries to be aware of, from Chapter 1. We won't cover all of these (as there's a lot of overlap), but here are the ones that should probably be on your radar screen:

- Ramda[31]: General FP Utilities
- Sanctuary[32]: Ramda Companion for FP Types
- lodash/fp[33]: General FP Utilities
- functional.js[34]: General FP Utilities
- Immutable[35]: Immutable Data Structures

---

[31] http://ramdajs.com
[32] https://github.com/sanctuary-js/sanctuary
[33] https://github.com/lodash/lodash/wiki/FP-Guide
[34] http://functionaljs.com/
[35] https://github.com/facebook/immutable-js

- Mori[36]: (ClojureScript Inspired) Immutable Data Structures
- Seamless-Immutable[37]: Immutable Data Helpers
- transducers-js[38]: Transducers
- monet.js[39]: Monadic Types

There are dozens of other fine libraries not on this list. Just because it's not on my list here doesn't mean it's not good, nor is this list a particular endorsement. It's just a quick glance at the landscape of FP-in-JavaScript. A much longer list of FP resources can be found here[40].

One resource that's extremely important to the FP world – it's not a library but more an encyclopedia! – is Fantasy Land[41] (aka FL).

This is definitely not light reading for the faint of heart. It's a complete detailed roadmap of all of FP as it's interpreted in JavaScript. FL has become a de facto standard for JavaScript FP libraries to adhere to, to ensure maximum interoperability.

Fantasy Land is pretty much the exact opposite of "Functional-Light". It's the full-on no-holds-barred approach to FP in JavaScript. That said, as you venture beyond this book, it's likely that FL will be on that road for you. I'd recommend you bookmark it, and go back to it after you've had at least six months of real-world practice with this book's concepts.

Ramda (0.23.0)

From the Ramda documentation[42]:

> Ramda functions are automatically curried.
>
> The parameters to Ramda functions are arranged to make it convenient for currying. The data to be operated on is generally supplied last.

---

[36] https://github.com/swannodette/mori
[37] https://github.com/rtfeldman/seamless-immutable
[38] https://github.com/cognitect-labs/transducers-js
[39] https://github.com/monet/monet.js
[40] https://github.com/stoeffel/awesome-fp-js
[41] https://github.com/fantasyland/fantasy-land
[42] http://ramdajs.com/

I find that design decision to be one of Ramda's strengths. It's also important to note that Ramda's form of currying (as with most libraries, it seems) is the "loose currying" we talked about in Chapter 3.

The final example of Chapter 3 – recall defining a point-free `printIf(..)` utility – can be done with Ramda like this:

```
function output(msg) {
    console.log( msg );
}

function isShortEnough(str) {
    return str.length <= 5;
}

var isLongEnough = R.complement( isShortEnough );

var printIf = R.partial( R.flip( R.when ), [output] );

var msg1 = "Hello";
var msg2 = msg1 + " World";

printIf( isShortEnough, msg1 );          // Hello
printIf( isShortEnough, msg2 );

printIf( isLongEnough, msg1 );
printIf( isLongEnough, msg2 );           // Hello World
```

A few differences to point out compared to Chapter 3's approach:

- We use `R.complement(..)` instead of `not(..)` to create a negating function `isLongEnough(..)` around `isShortEnough(..)`.
- We use `R.flip(..)` instead of `reverseArgs(..)`. It's important to note that `R.flip(..)` only swaps the first two arguments, whereas `reverseArgs(..)` reverses all of them. In this case, `flip(..)` is more convenient for us, so we don't need to do `partialRight(..)` or any of that kind of juggling.

- `R.partial(..)` takes all of its subsequent arguments (beyond the function) as a single array.
- Because Ramda is using loose currying, we don't need to use `R.uncurryN(..)` to get a `printIf(..)` that takes both its arguments. If we did, it would look like `R.uncurryN( 2, .. )` wrapped around the `R.partial(..)` call; but that's not necessary.

Ramda is a very popular and powerful library. It's a really good place to start if you're practicing adding FP to your code base.

Lodash/fp (4.17.4)

Lodash is one of the most popular libraries in the entire JS ecosystem. They publish an "FP-friendly" version of their API as "lodash/fp"[43].

In Chapter 9, we looked at composing standalone list operations (`map(..)`, `filter(..)`, and `reduce(..)`). Here's how we could do it with "lodash/fp":

```
var sum = (x,y) => x + y;
var double = x => x * 2;
var isOdd = x => x % 2 == 1;

fp.compose( [
    fp.reduce( sum )( 0 ),
    fp.map( double ),
    fp.filter( isOdd )
] )
( [1,2,3,4,5] );                     // 18
```

Instead of the more familiar `_.` namespace prefix, "lodash/fp" defines its methods with `fp.` as the namespace prefix. I find that a helpful distinguisher, and also generally more easy on my eyes than `_.` anyway!

Notice that `fp.compose(..)` (also known as `_.flowRight(..)` in lodash proper) takes an array of functions instead of individual arguments.

---
[43]https://github.com/lodash/lodash/wiki/FP-Guide

You cannot beat the stability, widespread community support, and performance of lodash. It's a solid bet for your FP explorations.

Mori (0.3.2)

In Chapter 6, we already briefly glanced at the Immutable.js library, probably the most well-known for immutable data structures.

Let's instead look at another popular library: Mori[44]. Mori is designed with a different (ostensibly more FP-like) take on API: it uses standalone functions instead of methods directly on the values.

```
var state = mori.vector( 1, 2, 3, 4 );

var newState = mori.assoc(
    mori.into( state, Array.from( {length: 39} ) ),
    42,
    "meaning of life"
);

state === newState;                     // false

mori.get( state, 2 );                   // 3
mori.get( state, 42 );                  // undefined

mori.get( newState, 2 );                // 3
mori.get( newState, 42 );               // "meaning of life"

mori.toJs( newState ).slice( 1, 3 );    // [2,3]
```

Some interesting things to point out about Mori for this example:

- We're using a `vector` instead of a `list` (as one might assume), mostly because the documentation says it behaves more like we expect JS arrays to be.

---

[44] https://github.com/swannodette/mori

- We cannot just randomly set a position past the end of the vector like we can with JS arrays; that throws an exception. So we have to first "grow" the vector using `mori.into(..)` with an array of the appropriate size of extra slots we want. Once we have a vector with 43 slots (4 + 39), we can set the final slot (position 42) to the `"meaning of life"` value using the `mori.assoc(..)` method.
- The intermediate step of creating a larger vector with `mori.into(..)` and then creating another from it with `mori.assoc(..)` might sound inefficient. But the beauty of immutable data structures is that no cloning is going on here. Each time a "change" is made, the new data structure is just tracking the difference from the previous state.

Mori is heavily inspired by ClojureScript. Its API will be very familiar if you have experience (or currently work in!) that language. Since I don't have that experience, I find the method names a little strange to get used to.

But I really like the standalone function design instead of methods on values. Mori also has some functions that automatically return regular JS arrays, which is a nice convenience.

Bonus: FPO

In Chapter 2, we introduced a pattern for dealing with arguments called "named arguments", which in JS means using an object at the call-site to map properties to destructured function parameters:

```
function foo( {x,y} = {} ) {
    console.log( x, y );
}

foo( {
    y: 3
} );                       // undefined 3
```

Then in Chapter 3, we talked about extending our ideas of currying and partial application to work with named arguments, like this:

```
function foo({ x, y, z } = {}) {
    console.log( `x:${x} y:${y} z:${z}` );
}

var f1 = curryProps( foo, 3 );

f1( {y: 2} )( {x: 1} )( {z: 3} );
```

One major benefit of this style is being able to pass arguments (even with currying or partial application!) in any order without needing to do `reverseArgs(..)`-style juggling of parameters. Another is being able to omit an optional argument by simply not specifying it, instead of passing an ugly placeholder.

In my journey learning FP, I've regularly been frustrated by both of those irritations of functions with traditional positional arguments; thus I've really appreciated the named arguments style for addressing those concerns.

One day, I was musing about with this style of FP coding, and wondered what it would be like if a whole FP library had all its API methods exposed in this style. I started experimenting, showed those experiments to a few FP folks, and got some positive feedback.

From those experiments, eventually the FPO[45] (pronounced "eff-poh") library was born; FPO stands for FP-with-Objects, in case you were wondering.

From the documentation:

```
// Ramda's `reduce(..)`
R.reduce(
    (acc,v) => acc + v,
    0,
    [3,7,9]
);  // 19

// FPO named-argument method style
FPO.reduce({
    arr: [3,7,9],
```

---

[45] https://github.com/getify/fpo

```
        fn: ({acc,v}) => acc + v
} ); // 19
```

With traditional library implementations of `reduce(..)` (like Ramda), the initial value parameter is in the middle, and not optional. FPO's `reduce(..)` method can take the arguments in any order, and you can omit the optional initial value if desired.

As with most other FP libraries, FPO's API methods are automatically loose-curried, so you can not only provide arguments in any order, but specialize the function by providing its arguments over multiple calls:

```
var f = FPO.reduce({ arr: [3,7,9] });

// later

f({ fn: ({acc,v}) => acc + v });      // 19
```

Lastly, all of FPO's API methods are also exposed using the traditional positional arguments style – you'll find they're all very similar to Ramda and other libraries – under the `FPO.std.*` namespace:

```
FPO.std.reduce(
    (acc,v) => acc + v,
    undefined,
    [3,7,9]
);  // 19
```

If FPO's named argument form of FP appeals to you, perhaps check out the library and see what you think. It has a full test suite and most of the major FP functionality you'd expect, including everything we covered in this text to get you up and going with Functional-Light JavaScript!

Bonus #2: fasy

FP iterations (`map(..)`, `filter(..)`, etc.) are almost always modeled as synchronous operations, meaning we eagerly run through all the steps of the iteration immediately. As a matter of fact, other FP patterns like composition and even transducing are also iterations, and are also modeled exactly this way.

But what happens if one or more of the steps in an iteration needs to complete asynchronously? You might jump to thinking that Observables (see Chapter 10) is the natural answer, but they're not what we need.

Let me quickly illustrate.

Imagine you have a list of URLs that represent images you want to load into a web page. The fetching of the images is asynchronous, obviously. So, this isn't going to work quite like you'd hope:

```
var imageURLs = [
    "https://some.tld/image1.png",
    "https://other.tld/image2.png",
    "https://various.tld/image3.png"
];

var images = imageURLs.map( fetchImage );
```

The `images` array won't contain the images. Depending on the behavior of `fetchImage(..)`, it probably returns a promise for the image object once it finishes downloading. So `images` would now be a list of promises.

Of course, you could then use `Promise.all(..)` to wait for all those promises to resolve, and then unwrap an array of the image object results at its completion:

```
Promise.all( images )
.then(function allImages(imgObjs){
    // ..
});
```

Unfortunately, this "trick" only works if you're going to do all the asynchronous steps concurrently (rather than serially, one after the other), and only if the operation is a `map(..)` call as shown. If you want serial asynchrony, or you want to, for example, do a `filter(..)` concurrently, this won't quite work; it's possible, but it's messier.

And some operations naturally require serial asynchrony, like for example an asynchronous `reduce(..)`, which clearly needs to work left-to-right one at a time; those steps can't be run concurrently and have that operation make any sense.

As I said, Observables (see Chapter 10) aren't the answer to these kinds of tasks. The reason is, an Observable's coordination of asynchrony is between separate operations, not between steps/iterations at a single level of operation.

Another way to visualize this distinction is that Observables support "vertical asynchrony", whereas what I'm talking about would be "horizontal asynchrony".

Consider:

```
var obsv = Rx.Observable.from( [1,2,3,4,5] );

obsv
.map( x => x * 2 )
.delay( 100 )          // <-- vertical asynchrony
.map( x => x + 1 )
.subscribe( v => console.log );
// {after 100 ms}
// 3
// 5
// 7
// 9
// 11
```

If for some reason I wanted to ensure that there was a delay of 100 ms between when 1 was processed by the first `map(..)` and when 2 was processed, that would be the "horizontal asynchrony" I'm referring to. There's not really a clean way to model that.

And of course, I'm using an arbitrary delay in that description, but in practice that would more likely be serial-asynchrony like an asynchronous reduce, where each step in that reduction iteration could take some time before it completes and lets the next step be processed.

So, how do we support both serial and concurrent iteration across asynchronous operations?

fasy (pronounced like "Tracy" but with an "f") is a little utility library I built for supporting exactly those kinds of tasks. You can find more information about it here[46].

To illustrate **fasy**, let's consider a concurrent `map(..)` versus a serial `map(..)`:

```
FA.concurrent.map( fetchImage, imageURLs )
.then( function allImages(imgObjs){
    // ..
} );

FA.serial.map( fetchImage, imageURLs )
.then( function allImages(imgObjs){
    // ..
} );
```

In both cases, the `then(..)` handler will only be invoked once all the fetches have fully completed. The difference is whether the fetches will all initiate concurrently (aka, "in parallel") or go out one at a time.

Your instinct might be that concurrent would always be preferable, and while that may be common, it's not always the case.

For example, what if `fetchImage(..)` maintains a cache of fetched images, and it checks the cache before making the actual network request? What if, in addition to that, the list of `imageURLs` could have duplicates in it? You'd certainly want the first fetch of an image URL to complete (and populate the cache) before doing the check on the duplicate image URL later in the list.

Again, there will inevitably be cases where concurrent or serial asynchrony will be called for. Asynchronous reductions will always be serial, whereas asynchronous mappings may likely tend to be more concurrent but can also need to be serial in some cases. That's why **fasy** supports all these options.

Along with Observables, **fasy** will help you extend more FP patterns and principles to your asynchronous operations.

---

[46] https://github.com/getify/fasy

Summary

JavaScript is not particularly designed as an FP language. However, it does have enough of the basics (like function values, closures, etc.) for us to make it FP-friendly. And the libraries we've examined here will help you do that.

Armed with the concepts from this book, you're ready to start tackling real-world code. Find a good, comfortable FP library and jump in. Practice, practice, practice!

So... that's it. I've shared what I have for you, for now. I hereby officially certify you as a "Functional-Light JavaScript" programmer! It's time to close out this "chapter" of our story of learning FP together. But my learning journey still continues; I hope yours does, too!

Super Special Thanks To All My Crowd-Funding Backers

Christoph Bastanier, Marc Udoff, Gaston Longhitano, Sibin Kutty, Andres Carreno, Thao Dinh, Tim Saunders, James Butler, Aerox, Craig Rodrigues, Adam Fahy, Sheri Richardson, Florian Eschenbacher, Tyom Semonov, Wouter Appelmans, Marc Grabanski, Raul Costa, Benjamin Weber, Mason Spencer, Bob Woodard, Sam Blacklock, Vedran Blazenka, Austin Thompson, Rodrigo Perez Mendoza, Harishkumar Singh, Sebastian De Deyne, Vyacheslav Istomin, Eric Flamm, ximenean, Mhretab Kidane Tewele, Rodrigo Pimentel, Marcos Felipe Rodrigues, Hernan Onzalo, Derik Badman, byronbuckley, Altrim Beqiri, Luis Ruiz Pavón, Armand Zerilli, Joaquin Bonet Sanchez, Radimir Bitsov, Philipp Spieß, Nejc Zdovc, Jay Greasley, Eric Anderson, jens.anders.bakke, Matthew Bramer, Theodore Keloglou, Stoyan Delev, Gerardo Lisboa, Swee Me Chai, Christopher Lee, Daniel Henning, Brian Collins, Mark Jagger, Debjit Biswas, Federico Fazzeri, Chantal Galvez Omana, Piotr Seefeld, Chris Sanders, Francisco Gileno, Mario Blokland, hello, chris, David Gowrie, Alexander Matveyenko, simonkeary, Paolo Mariotti, VG Venkataraman, Pablo Hernan Codeiro, Tim Stone, virtualandy, Dror Ben-Gai, Garrett Dawson, Rob McMichael, Simon Angell, Raymond Zhou, Kiran Aghor, Ruozhou Fan, Jesse Harlin, Marissa Shaffer, Adam Rackis, Louis Phang, muraligold, liamsoup, Muhamed Delic, Laura, Goutham N Reddy, Christoph Herr, mary, cat2608, Chris Verachtert, Struan King, Christopher moate, Greg Bulmash, Michael Raumer, bondydaa, Scott Mueller, Ramnesh Bansal, Dean Gilewicz, Vassilis Mastorostergios, Richard Kichenama, Tyler Weeres, asgbja, Patrik Jarl, mightyvt, Paul Wilkins, Jason Yamada-Hanff, bfulop, Jonathan Church, Lex Szentmiklosy, girish.tryambake, Timo Laak, Joel McKinnon, Derek Trower, Patrik Niebur, James Spence, James Morgan, Tim Goshinski, Sean Reimer, ratracegrad, Michael Hearn, Kelly Ong, Charlie Hill, Daniel Osborne, James Williams, Rahat Ahmed, theo.fidry, Xinting He, Greg Marr, Todd Bernhardt, Saad Koubeissi, Will Hogan, Marko Lorentz, edhellon, Kai Schröder, Cy Iurinic, Andreas Windt, Salva MA, Nikita Sobyanin, Kieran Hoban, Werner Krauß, Dario De Bastiani, Matteo Hertel, Roland Jansen, Rolf Langenhuijzen, Heinrich Henning, Yurii Bodarev, Vickie Comrie, Chase Hagwood, philip.a.murphy, Christopher Stewart, Ernest Weems, Suhail Idrees, ashley wharton, Oscar Funes, Eduardo Rabelo, kajalchatterjee, Danko Dolinar, Brookes Stephens, Jeff Trimble, shoto miki, Rob Huelga, Jeroen Engels, Jay Buchta, Kristen Dyrr, kajalchatterjee, Barney Scott, Lluis Arévalo Salom, Jim Laughton, Kieran Hoban, Melissa Gore, Benjamin Diuguid, Romell Ian B. De La Cruz, Thanh Dung TRUONG, Newton Kitonga, Dan Talpau, Arthur Kashaev, David Pastor,

Trey Aughenbaugh, melonique, Alexander Mays, Jacob Venable, Ricardo Valdivia Pinto, Niklas Lindgren, Paul Anguiano, Riyadh Al Nur, diogoantunes.pt, Courtney Myers, Stephanie Barnes, frank edwards, lukas.weber, dimitar.trifonov, nils, Scott Hardman, marco.scarpa, Nicholas Baldwin, Jan Hjørdie, Peter Morcinek, Ronald Sim, paul, Terry J Godes, Tommy Koswara, Christian Buysschaert, Raziel Gershoni, Trevor Weaver, jeremymabbott, Richard A Gonzales, Michael Staub, Žan Kočevar, Zachary Schultz, Regenwurm, robert jorgenson, Justin Hinerman, salgado_75, Refael Ackermann, Bruno Belotti, Eric Lezotte, Juan Aramis, John Harding, viktor.bartusek, caneris, Mike Farrow, Peter Balkus, Joostc Schermers, Mr Miron Machnicki, Tomasz Kawik, Andrew Zen, Wil Pannell, Peter kellner, Ryan Zimmerman, daniel stenger, Mauro Gestoso, Tyler Wendlandt, Tim Evko, Aleksandar Benic, David Bachmann, Pavel Kovalyov, Richard Yu, Andy Gaskell, Daniele Morosinotto, Denislav Ganchev, Steve Pick, Alex Liang, Mozammel Haque, Matthew Hinton, Nick Cox, Emīls Kraucis, Jason Yamada-Hanff, NEVZAT AKKAYA, jowoos, Laszlo Vadasz, Danko Dolinar, Benjamin Gandhi-Shepard, Josh Magness, Oleksii Doroshenko, Hendrik Neumann, Richard Kalehoff, Greg Munker, Chase Hagwood, Nicholas Paldino, Massimiliano Giroldi, John Doe, Arnar Birgisson, John Mercer, Dave Marks, anthony_falez, Bernat Martinez Vidal, Andrés Roberto Rojas, David Beermann, Evan Johnson, Phill Price, Sean Reed, Uberto Rapizzi, Robert Dudley, Martin Flodin, Daniel Ehrlich, Christopher Schmitt, Michelle Janosi, Yurii Bodarev, Luis G Silva, Darko Kukovec, Ernest Weems, Matt Langston, Tim Pinoy, Ron Male, Luis Silva, Magnus Vaughan, James Hattox, Scott Arnold, Nick Cernis, Sundar Joshi, Linus Gubenis, Cai Lu, Sergey Samokhov, Javier Santa, Gabin Aureche, Nader Dabit, Misha Reyzlin, Tuija Latva, Ardian Haxha, Andrew Robbins, Jeff Bridgforth, Dallen Richard Loder, Stephan B, Grzegorz Ziolkowski, Andreas Gebhardt, Sergey Samokhov, Minh Nguyen, Dougal Campbell, Paul Thaden, Ravi Varanasi, Spandan Chatterjee, Andrew Leonard, Cindy Wong, Jerry Hampton, Marlon Huber-Smith, Dan Denney, Orhan Kupusoglu, Eric Masiello, David Litmark, Skip McBride, Benji Kay, Diego La Manno, Nick Cernis, web, Alexis Villegas Torres, Jon Samp, Galen Weber, Simone Lusenti, Corinna Cohn, shino.sk, Jaycee Cheong, Nathan Finch, Debjit Biswas, Robert Wilde, Marcelo Lazaroni de Rezende Junior, Stephen Price, Iurii Kucherov, Jedidiah Broadbent, Daniel Carral, Zach Wentz, Ivan Saveliev, Alex Tsai, Roland Tanglao, Brookes Stephens, Nick Perkins, Jinsy A Oommen, Simon de turck, Mihai Paun, Alexandar Anguelov, Gabin Aureche, herve giraud, Brad, eduplessis, Chetan Shenoy, Mark Lozano, Johannes Jaeger, paganio, Tony Brown, Mario Luevanos, Randy Ferrer, ncubica,

Travis Nelson, ShangYo Chen, mko, Leo van Hengel, swr, Nick Freeman, Maarten Tibau, Matt Reich, DJ Adams, Nikola Malich, François Freelo, Sharon DiOrio, Mads Jensen, Colyn Brown, Brandon Newton, ajmchambers, jmrussell22, Justin Lowery, Nathan Schlehlein, Felipe Andrés Sepulveda, Conlin Durbin, Fer To, Mick Schouten - Bravebox, Dan Perrera, Benjamin Gandhi-Shepard, Sorin Gitlan, Loïc Laudet, Yu Wu, Juan Pablo Lomeli Diaz, Dirk Peters, Fernando Agüero, Robbie Delfs, Alistair McDonald, Robin Valins, Vickie Comrie, Iago Sanjurjo, Jonathan Ng, Steven Nguyen, Cai Lu, Gunar Cassiano Gessner, Nick Klunder, Eduardo Rabelo, Zhera Paaverud, Marcin Szyszko, Michael Green, Kaleb G Berry, Sarah Federman, Mark Keith, Marty Engleen, Chris Burke, Nick Plekhanov, Jason Bergquist, pyjter, Rob Staenke, Howard Fiorella, francescodip, Mauricio Nagaoka, Javier Santa, Robert Vane, Rodrigo Perez Mendoza, Victor Paolo Reyes, Derick Rodriguez, Iaroslav Miniailo, Austin Wood, Yoko Dev, Andoni Zubimendi, Humza Bhakhrani, Xavier Gil, Sara Canfield, mail, danyadsmith, Nick Walt, Blake Johnston, annoyingmouse, Sergio Minutoli, Dan Sumption, Viet Truong, Francisco Ramini, Sean Matheson, Vedran Zakanj, Craig Riviere, Mike Behnke, Todd Spatafore, Bogdan Ungureanu, Vladyslava Tykhomyrova, Linus Gubenis, Jem Bezooyen, Matthew Cooley, Jesper Zachariassen, Eric Lawrence, Jaime García, juniormcbride, Marcus Nielsen, Marcus Nielsen, David Demaree, francis.auyeung, Ivan Saveliev, Brooke Mitchell, Marcus Nielsen, Kimmo Saari, jacobboomer, Michael Iglesias, Kees van Ginkel, Charlie Hardt, Mike Doran, Marcel Barros Aparici, Kristoffer Östlund, Girish Nayak, Emmanuel Baidoo, walterplus, Sheikh Hassan, alexreardon, Virginia Older, Michael Porter, Nathan Gibbons, Jakub Synowiec, eonilsson, jones.r.joshua, Salva MA, Michael Anderson, Terrance Peppers, Mark Trostler, Doron Brikman, Daniel Auger, Amila Welihinda, gaya.kessler, Thomas Hopkins, Florian Goße, Michael Scherr, Josh Adam, montogeek, Teodora Nikolaeva, Wayne Montague, Wes Bos, Brian Whitton, Moises Sacal, John Robinson, emiliehester, Jonathan Boiser, Danny Arnold, Ivan Pintado, Jerzy Redlarski, Acie Slade, Callie O'Brien, Pablo Villoslada Puigcerber, Martin Pitt, Aiden Montgomery, Kieran Russell, Abraham Alcaina, Doris Y Riggs, Yasin Yaqoobi, Suhail Idrees, Ayush Mathur, dlteron.green, Dusan Radojevic, Michael Iglesias, Paulo Elias, Carles Andres, Dave Nugent, Jelle Kralt, VATSAL PANDE, Vladimir Jelincic, Kasper Filstrup, Jeffrey Denton, Ken Farrell, Anderson LM, Alex Lindgren, Mark Holmes, Mark Kramer, Thomas North Gamble, Mike Schall, ashley wharton, Daniel Bolívar, Pietari Heino, John Derr, Adrian Suciu, Marcel Michelfelder, Roberto Modica, Nicolas Quiroz, Marcin L, Benjamin Seber, bc, Deepak Vadithala, Daniel Legare, Anthony Maldarelli,

Laura Little, palarose, Francisco Silva, Olivier Camon, Bohdan Ganický, Kishore Shiraguppi, paul.sebborn, Kanagaraj Mayilsamy, Arijit Bhattacharya, joshua.travis, René Schapka, Robert Bak, Pavlo Kovalov, pp.koch, Geert Plaisier, Stef Käser, Martin Lekvall, Erwin Mombay, Roger Saladrigas Sitja, Patrick Metzdorf, Brian Johnson, Lucas Everett, auremoser, J David Eisenberg, Jason Shoreman, Yuya Saito, Brian Ashenfelter, Minoru TODA, Andrew O'Neill, Denise Nepraunig, Eric J, Cristina Solana, bob, Scott Warren, Ryan Collins, John Meyer, Mohamed Chiadmi, Doug Shamoo, paulo vieira, Tim Gaudette, Trent Stromkins, fogeltine, dhtrinh02, Facundo De La Diaz, Kostas Minaidis, Peter Surma, Tara Manicsic, Luis Del Aguila, Eric Kinsella, Lukasz Pietraszek, Kamran Yahya, Scott Walter, John Cole, Leonardo Lewandowski, Rolf Langenhuijzen, Carlos López, Eric Alas, Victor Longon, marko, Adam Spooner, michael, Olivier Tille, Jose Luis Piedrahita, Simon St.Laurent, Adam Stocks, Richard Yoesting, Rik Watson, Ajaypal Cheema, Wayne Patterson, Ian Littman, Nick Cantelmi, Dennis Sänger, jcreighton08, Stefan Trost, Aaron Olson, Shreyas Anand, Philippe leger, Sindre Seppola, wil.moore, Roman Zolotarev, carlos.araya, Fredric Hawk, Fred Ostrander, Veli-Matti Hietala, soundslikework, Cam McVey, Marco Zapata, Erik Reyna, Jurmarcus Allen, Hugo Cruz, Christophe Pouliot, Vladimir Simonov, Nicholas Taylor, Jeff Trimble, Cássio Martins Antonio, Eric Alas, Peter deHaan, Paul Grock, Ivan Votti, Per Fröjd, Dennis Palmer, Tom Randolph, Ryan Ewing, Shaheer Ahmed Mir, Jarkko Tuunanen, Stefan Bruvik, Chris C, Gustavo Morales, Matteo Hertel, cthos, David Neal, Craig Patchett, Dan Rocha, derhaug, mike3ike, Nicolantonio Vignola, Francisco Javier Lopez Gonzalez, Cody Lindley, Ian jones, jack pallot, Thomas Greenhalgh, smukkekim, Mattias Johansson, Justin Harrison, Gajus Kuizinas, Norbert Sienkiewicz, Serge Lachapelle, jay.paige, Charles W Neill, Michael Pelikan, Joseph Cortese, brian.r.hough, John Hoover, Seth Messer, Jesse Tomchak, philip.a.murphy, Stuart Robson, adam cavan, Rey Bango, Andres Mijares, ali, Shawn Searcy, Konstantin Pschera, Richard Hinkamp, Simeon Vincent, Geoffrey Wiseman, Nick Dunn, r3dDoX, nsteiner, fcojonathan, baldur.bjarnason, Artem Sapegin, Jeremy Tymes, James Simpson, jostylr, Horváth László Gábor, Tom Martineau, Mike Stapp, G P, M. Filacchioni, Simon MacDonald, Devin Clark, David Vujic, Henry Andre, Django Janny, Dorian Camilleri, Kenneth Christiansen, Denis Wolf, A. Bottazini, Zouhir Chahoud, Marcello Romanelli, Dale Fukami, Miguel de la Cruz, Jason Finch, Lucy Barker, Vijay Pardeshi, Geoffrey Dhuyvetters, Chris Deck, Richard Japenga, waldron.rick, John Gibbon, dciccale, Jeff Adams, juanfran, erwin.heiser, Martin Sachse, Conor Cussell, S. Wijesinghe, P. Mierzejewski

Made in the USA
Coppell, TX
24 November 2020